More Praise for *Replc*
The Unconscious Script . . .

Replacement Children: The Unconscious Script is valuable reading, not just for all who have lived some form of replacement experience, but surely instructive for mental health professionals and ought become familiar to obstetricians, pediatricians and family physicians.

Albert Cain, Ph.D.
Professor of Psychology and Director,
Child Bereavement Project,
University of Michigan

. . . informative and heartfelt book that sheds light on a phenomenon often as neglected as the plight of its subjects—an experience often overlooked because it is hidden in plain sight.

Jack Schwartz
Veteran journalist and author of
The Fine Print: My Life as a Deskman

One of the major strengths of the book is that the authors have extended the classic definition beyond its original meaning to include children who have to "live for two" when a surviving sibling is incapacitated by illness or infirmity or children who have been adopted after a couple is unable to conceive. This book is a superb contribution.

Sylvia R. Karasu, M.D.
Clinical Professor of Psychiatry, Weill Cornell Medicine

A profoundly moving and insightful journey into the dynamics of losing a child, grieving a sibling and most of all, finding one's place in a home that has been bereft of joy. This is a book that will bring you to tears, but also, stir within you a deep gratitude for the life you do live and for each moment that you taste joy.

Dr. Shefali
NYT bestselling author, *The Conscious Parent,*
Clinical psychologist and international speaker

Replacement Children: The Unconscious Script deals thoughtfully with a family dynamic that is all too common, the psychological substitution of one child for another who has died or is absent. As the authors note, the consequences for the replacement child can vary widely, from impacts that are barely perceptible, or are even positive, to those that are debilitating or devastating.

Foreword Review

To Lindy,
With all my love!
Enjoy, Rita

Replacement Children

The Unconscious Script

Rita Battat Silverman

Abigail Brenner, M.D.

Published by Sand Hill Review Press, LLC
www.sandhillreviewpress.com
P.O. Box 1275, San Mateo, CA 94401 (415) 297-3571

Library of Congress Control Number: 2015935928

ISBN: 978-1-937818-34-0 Kindle edition, October 15, 2015
ISBN: 978-1-937818-29-6 Paperback edition, December 15, 2015
ISBN: 978-1-937818-35-7 Case laminate edition, April 15, 2016
Paperback available from Ingram or directly through the publisher.
Case laminate available from Ingram.

Cover painting, Awkward Age, by Jim Warren
www.JimWarren.com
Cover graphics by Backspace Ink with thanks to Jen T. Johnson

Table of Contents

◆ Denotes sections written by authors with factual information on RC

◆ Denotes sections written by authors with factual information on RC

Foreword

The poet Elizabeth Bishop wrote that, "The art of losing isn't hard to master." When it comes to the loss of a loved one to death, I respectfully disagree. There is nothing as searing and shattering, especially if it is the death of someone who has so much life to be lived. This is something I've learned from experience.

My husband Jay used to say I was born on a sunny day. I think my endlessly cheery outlook on life was, in many ways, informed by a life devoid of sorrow and hardship. But when I turned forty, little did I know that the decade that stretched before me, one full of so many possibilities, would hit a dead end, shockingly and unexpectedly.

Jay was just 41 when he was diagnosed with stage four colon cancer. His prognosis was bleak, but we soldiered on. Jay didn't want to know the odds. I spent every waking hour desperately trying to keep him from becoming just another sad statistic.

Meanwhile, my response to every piece of bad news—that the cancer had spread to his liver, then to his lungs and ultimately his brain—was a ridiculously unrealistic and emphatic, "We will figure it out!" Of course, I knew that wasn't true, but facing the harsh realities of Jay's situation somehow meant giving up hope, something I just refused to do.

I tried to be slightly more realistic with Ellie, who was five at the time when she asked if Daddy would get better. "Well, honey," I would tell her, "The doctors are doing everything they possibly can, and Daddy is trying really hard to get better." The doctors DID use every available weapon in their arsenal, but no one figured it out. Cancer can be the most ruthless, heartless and intrepid disease dwarfing modern medicine and even the strongest will to live.

Following Jay's death I tried to help Ellie and Carrie, who were just six and two when their father died, as best I could. Our apartment was full of photographs of Jay at various stages of his life and of our once perfect nuclear family. When Carrie would cover her hamburger with ketchup, I would remark that her Dad loved his hamburger the same way. If a song came on the radio that flooded me with memories, I would tell the girls that their Dad loved that song too... and that he was an incredible dancer. The memories would cascade out of me, one leading to another to another. I knew talking about him wouldn't bring him back, but talking about him would at least keep his memory alive.

Just two years after my sister Emily read the eulogy I had written for my husband at his funeral, she was diagnosed with pancreatic cancer. Like Jay, she handled her impending death with courage, dignity and extraordinary grace. And once again, my family was left with an inescapable emptiness that accompanies loss. We still had not mastered it. But as all those who have been on this journey learn (and at some point, we all will walk this walk) death is a part of life, something we have to learn how to master, no matter how difficult it is. Ironically, dealing with death teaches us life skills like resiliency that will serve us well when we are faced with other challenges, disappointments, setbacks, and inevitably, other losses. I hope this is a gift I have given my daughters, while knowing full well it is the byproduct of an experience no one wanted them to have.

Because there were few resources for our grieving family and for my children at the time of my husband's death, and because death makes people so uncomfortable, I jumped at the chance to host a Sesame Street video called "When Families Grieve." This program was designed to help children and adults talk openly and honestly about this confusing and difficult topic and summon the strength to heal following such a traumatic life experience.

But as difficult as any significant loss may be, the death of a child at any age, so unnatural in the order of life, is unimaginable and deserves special attention. Many parents do find their way through tragedy, successfully moving on in their life, often having subsequent children who are welcomed and loved. But if parents are unable to effectively work through their grief they may not let their deceased child go. Beyond the death of a child, unresolved parental grief may even include grief over the loss of an ideal, or of unfulfilled hopes and dreams.

Enter the replacement child—one born to take a deceased sibling's place, or an older child whose life is "redirected" to fill the shoes of a dead sibling, or a child who is made to feel responsible for a sibling who is handicapped, challenged, or has suffered an incapacitating illness or accident, or even an adopted child who may come to fill the place of a biological child the parents were unable to have. The huge price these children pay in the process of replacing another is the loss of their own identity and the inability to find and establish who they are as individuals in their own right. The truth is you simply cannot replace another child. Or take away grief that is not being talked about or dealt with and resolved. But like death in general, this phenomenon is rarely discussed and often misunderstood.

In *Replacement Children: The Unconscious Script*, the authors bring together the best of the research, clinical studies, and personal stories to give a comprehensive overview of the replacement child syndrome. This book will give parents, therapists and replacement children a better understanding of how to navigate this complicated set of circumstances and provide much-needed information, guidance, and support to adult replacement children as they try to come to terms with who they are and how their lives have been shaped by loss, a concept that while hard—is absolutely essential—to master.

Katie Couric

Introduction

The birth of a child is one of life's greatest miracles. The death or incapacitation of a child is one of its greatest tragedies.

It may not come as a surprise that sometimes a parent or parents might be driven, either consciously or not, to have another child to compensate for their devastating loss. There is no "right" time to expand a family. That depends on personal preference and circumstances. In a healthy case scenario, when parents are able to grieve and process their loss, and then move forward in their lives, a child born or adopted after the loss of another can be welcomed into the family with no responsibilities and/or conditions other than to become who they are in their own right.

This child, a subsequent child, can bring a sense of normalcy, balance, joy, and hope back into the family. The lost child is always remembered and their memory honored, but the parents are able to accept and celebrate the new child as his/her unique individual self.

Parents who have lost a child are survivors; they're trying to do the best they can while attempting to find various ways to cope. But, surviving without being able to process the grief of loss, getting to a place of fully accepting the reality of the loss so a path can be open to another depth of experience, is the factor that may precipitate heavy consequences for everyone. Parents are looking to return their lives to normal, but are often overwhelmed, making it difficult to think and act as rationally as they had before the loss.

There may be expectations, often unconscious, that place an undue burden on another child in the family. Parents in turmoil may be so consumed by their own grief that they may not be aware of how their children are feeling and of the patterns that are being established within the family. Certainly, there are no manuals or guidelines to consult.

Psychologist Albert Cain and Barbara Cain, M.S.W. originated the term "replacement child" in the 1960s in reference to a child who is conceived to take the place of a child who has died. Over the years, the term has been expanded to include a child who is already a member of the family but takes on the role of a dead or impaired sibling, as well as a child who is adopted to replace an idealized child his/her parents were unable to conceive.

Many people, especially parents, without understanding the phenomenon in its entirety, are initially upset by the term "replacement child." Of course, no one can ever be replaced, and not every child born or adopted after the loss of another will have the experience of a replacement child. However, there is, indeed, a huge difference between a subsequent child, one who comes into life without conditions compared to one who is burdened with a responsibility, the unconscious script, of having to carry on for another. *We have come to understand that the term "replacement child" is about experience and not blame.*

Unlike their parents, adult replacement children generally do not find the term offensive, but instead, believe that it helps them to define their feelings and describe their experience. It affords many of them a sense of comfort to finally be able to understand the reasons behind the complicated issues surrounding their own identity—the result of having grown up in this very unique set of circumstances.

There are similarities and patterns of thoughts, feelings, and emotional issues shared by those who find themselves under the umbrella of the syndrome that is the "replacement child." While exploring feelings and behaviors in this context, adult replacement children can obtain an understanding of themselves in a whole new light, gaining clarity about why they react in specific ways and the reasons they have been lead to make certain choices.

Replacement is a consequence of denial. If a parent cannot integrate the reality and fully accept a loss, they may never be able to fully connect to the child who "replaces" the lost "other." This pushes the child into a different path in life, often one not of their own choosing.

As an adult, co-author Rita Battat Silverman came to recognize that she, herself, is a "replacement child."

"My light bulb moment occurred many years ago during a conversation with a mother of a ten-year-old, who I'll call Susan. I had noticed that Susan's mother seemed to have difficulty setting limits on her daughter's behavior, but was highly critical of everything she did. This was a far cry from the way Susan's younger siblings were treated. It almost seemed as though Susan had been raised by a different set of parents.

Susan's mother confided that Susan was actually her second child. Her first daughter had died of leukemia while an infant. Doctors, knowing the infant would die, had suggested the couple become pregnant again as soon as possible. Consequently, Susan was born just a few months after the death of her sister.

Susan's mother went on to say that although this daughter was much loved and wanted, her birth did not take away the feelings of emptiness; overwhelming grief left her parents feeling emotionally and physically depleted. They were unable to connect to her in the same joyful way they greeted their first daughter and, later, their two younger children. Frozen emotions rocked their parenting style from overindulgent to hypercritical. From her very first breath, Susan had been living in the shadow of her lost sister.

As I listened to Susan's story, I had a moment of powerful recognition as pieces from my past began to fit together—our stories were woven from the same fabric. It was the first time I realized that I, too, was a replacement child—for a brother who had died when he was 14, eighteen months before I was born. This was the beginning of my quest to reconstruct the missing pieces of my own life. Further exploration led me to understand how this uncharted territory held the key to so many unanswered questions with their far-reaching effects—and was the inspiration for writing this book.

This realization—in addition to co-author Dr. Abigail Brenner's concerns about the lack of information provided to adult replacement children, parents, and therapists—became our impetus.

On the other hand, the challenges that replacement children face may serve as the catalyst for unlocking their own rich creative potential; developing the skills, talents, resourcefulness, self-reliance and the capacity to think outside the box, that so often serves these children well later on. If you have ever been influenced by Elvis Presley, Katharine Hepburn, Vincent Van Gogh, or Carl Jung, to name but a few, you have been touched by the life of a replacement child.

As researcher Andrea Sabbadini noted, replacement children "may be treated more as the embodiment of a memory than a person in their own right." This means the adult replacement child may actually have to learn to live his life all over again. He must find the missing pieces of himself, examine years of uncertainty, ask questions that have never been asked, no less answered, and ultimately try to connect with himself apart from the shadow of the "other" whom he has replaced.[1]

In writing this book, the authors' goal is to bring awareness, guidance, and support to the experience of the replacement child to those who recognize themselves as RCs, as well as to their parents, families, friends, teachers, doctors, therapists, and all others who are so much a part of their lives.

We are extremely grateful to the many people who, with great courage and commitment to a larger process, so generously shared these experiences, as well as their knowledge and insights, so that others could benefit. Often it is what we observe in others that best illuminates what we need to understand about ourselves.

Rita Battat Silverman
Abigail Brenner, M.D.

PART ONE

The Broad Spectrum of the Replacement Child

YOU ARE A CHILD OF THE UNIVERSE,

NO LESS THAN THE TREES OR STARS

YOU HAVE A RIGHT TO BE HERE.

AND, WHETHER OR NOT IT IS CLEAR TO YOU,

NO DOUBT THE UNIVERSE IS

UNFOLDING AS IT SHOULD.

DESIDERATA

I. The Replacement Child Experience

Until you make the unconscious conscious it will direct your life and you will call it fate.

—Carl Jung

The Girl Who Never Grew Up

"Although I never saw her, the image of my sister is burned into my brain," says Shelly, a 37-year-old woman with dark eyes, pale, slightly freckled skin, and a slender build.

My sister stands against a doorway frame, olive skinned and skinny; her large kneecaps peeking out from a black dress with neon 1970's style flowers and a white Peter Pan collar. Her coal-colored eyes match her dark black hair, parted on the left hand side, tumbling past her shoulders and onto her waist. An adult tooth sticks out of a sideways smile and the twinkle in her eye is personified by the tilt in her head.

That photo sat on an old wooden dresser in the foyer of my childhood home. The same photo is on my other sister's mantle in her living room, on the wooden bookshelf on the left hand side of my father's study, and over the baker's rack in the untouched blue room in my mother's musty pristine home. I am the only one who doesn't need to own the image. For more than eight years I thought that photo was of me.

My sister Jennifer died a few days before her eighth birthday on a warm summer's day outside my family's first home. She was running through the sprinklers in the front yard when my father returned from his afternoon classes. He paused, wondering if he should tell Jennifer to go inside and change out of her bathing suit before it got too cold, but decided to let her play for just a bit longer and headed in to the house. Jennifer crossed our small street, which connected two highways, to visit the neighbor girl and was struck by a speeding car. The young woman never saw Jennifer coming. My other sister Joanne, who was six at the time, watched from the window and could do nothing but cry for help. Five minutes after my father had stepped inside the house Jennifer was dead. Three years later I was born.

I know every detail of this story; the color of the bathing suit Jennifer was wearing, the look on my sister's face as she saw the crash, the height of the neighbor girl, the make and model of the young woman's car. I used to tell myself that this knowledge was proof that deep inside I was Jennifer. She had been unfairly taken from the world and God had decided to return her to earth through me. I believed I knew the story so well, because to me, it wasn't a story, it was memory.

I grew up believing I was Jennifer and my father confirmed it. He told me every single day I was just like her. I looked like her, sounded like her, and had the same likes and dislikes, the same talents. It was a comfort. I believed I was put on this earth for a glorious purpose. I carried an invisible twin that I could talk to whenever I wanted and I was never alone. I felt like I had no pressing decisions to make about what I was supposed to do or say. My only goal was to be like her. I never thought of it as a burden. The conscious me never thought of it much at all. It was only fact. It was a tragedy, but it was my life. I had a sister. She was perfect. She died. I was born. She haunted me. I talked to her every night before bed. I thought everyone lived with ghosts.

Yet, as much as I tried, I could never be as perfect as a photo on a shelf.

I was her twin, but with none of her talent. The first failure came at four when I couldn't recite an opera by heart. At age six, I decided I hated classical music. I couldn't come close to writing the poetry Jennifer had written in the second grade, and, at age seven, the biggest disappointment of all, the look on my father's face as I was pulled out of Jennifer's favorite activity, ballet, for being disruptive.

Jennifer followed me around. I planted peonies in the yard with my father every year, not because they were beautiful, but because they were Jennifer's favorite. The white birch tree in our front yard was also special because it had been Jennifer's favorite tree. It looked exactly like the one planted in her memory at the front of my elementary school, which I passed by twice a day, five days a week, for five years.

On the first day of second grade, a teacher pulled me out of class and took me into the hallway. I stood, uncomfortably, with my back against the tile wall, as she told me how sorry she was for me. She explained that Jennifer had been in her class and how much she loved her. The teacher cried. I looked at her and pretended to be sad, because the truth was I had no feelings about my dead sister at all. I didn't know her. I only knew the idea of her.

I buried the shame of not being who my father wanted, and went about my life. I sat through the lectures, memorized Jennifer's writings, stared and stared and stared at the photo on the shelf that I could never be. Every year we would go to Jennifer's grave and my sister, mother, and father would hug and cry while my older brother, who was only two at the time of the accident, would play hide and seek with me on the gravestones. I felt left out. I couldn't grieve for someone I never knew, and at the same time, I was expected to. I felt like screaming "I'M RIGHT HERE!" but that wouldn't be something that Jennifer would do, so I didn't.

I was a failure at being someone else. I was shown her trophies and triumphs daily, but could create none of my own. I sought approval, but could never receive it. I played with the ballerina on the small charm bracelet tucked inside a glass bottle in my father's study, but was never allowed to try it on. I felt like I was looking in a store window for something I could never afford to buy. I fought hard to please everyone, but was never really heard. I was never seen as me. I lived as the joy of my father's life, but also as a failure to be what he wanted. I knew no matter what he said, all he really wanted was Jennifer. As a child, I never understood why.

I asked my mother why I was born and she told me, "I always wanted to have three children." So I understood that I came into this world as part of a numbers game. My father told me why I was alive when I was eight, as we were driving in the car. "You know," he said, "If Jennifer hadn't died, you would have never been born." The damage of the statement was done before he added, "And I'm so glad you were." It would take me twenty-eight years, when he announced over beers and dumplings in a small Viennese café, "I like spending time with you," that the second part of that statement finally sunk in.

As I finally passed the age that Jennifer died, so did the comparisons.

Jennifer began to fade away from my everyday life, as did the constant need to try to be like her. My father spoke less of her, and that gave way for me to begin to make decisions of my own, but the effects of having to live up to someone who never grew up still took its toll on me.

I became an overachiever. I never broke the rules. I did what was expected. I am terrified to fail at anything and terrified to be better than that image I had of perfection. Even today, the need for me to become a success is overwhelming. For the most part, I have been. I did well in school, got the leads in plays, got in to my first choice college. I am warm and loving, in a great marriage, and I have great friends.

However, small setbacks will still put me into an hysterical state. In high school when I didn't get into the elite summer Pennsylvania Governor's School for the Arts I went into a deep depression that lasted almost a year. I constantly think of myself as a failure if I don't get somewhere on time or can't fit into a piece of clothing. I can't see myself as good, only as not good enough. I take everything entirely too seriously and I find myself saying out loud that I am a failure if the littlest thing doesn't go my way.

Until I was contacted for this book, I never understood that I had been telling myself I am a failure because I am not perfect. I'm not like Jennifer. And I have convinced myself that being perfect is the price I must pay for being born. I have been through years of therapy with a very good therapist, but not once have we talked about Jennifer except as one of the many tragedies in my life. We have talked about my fear and obsession with death, but in the context of me being afraid of failure. We've talked about how I was never listened to as a child, but not because I was always being looked at as someone else. I have gone over how my parents were well-meaning but unable to help me because they were dealing with their own grief after the loss of their child, but not how the loss of their child kept me from finding my identity.

I blame myself for a lot of this. I never wanted to think about Jennifer after age eight. I shoved her aside and refused to examine my feelings about her. I had spent too much time with her, but even as I write this I realize that I can never leave her. I am thirty-seven. She is still the child I will never be. A ghost.

◆ Defining the RC Syndrome

When parents cannot accept the loss of a child they may carry over their expectations, fears, and guilt to subsequent children. Sometimes these parents are overly protective, restrictive, and controlling. For them, the world may be viewed as an unsafe place and subsequent children are kept close by so that nothing will happen to them.[2] Because of this heightened overprotective stance, many subsequent or "substitute" children are anxious and fearful, lacking self-esteem and confidence. [3] Others forge ahead and become reckless and take undue risks. We hope that this sampling of causes and effects will give you a better perspective of the broad consequences of unresolved grief in the replacement child syndrome.

To clarify, the term replacement child is conceptual rather than literal. It is not meant to describe one child taking another's place (or suggest that anyone is ever "replaceable"), but rather describes an actual psychological/ emotional syndrome. Children born or adopted after a loss are not automatically replacement children and should not be referred to as such. The term, replacement child, describes the experience of an individual caught up in a complex family dynamic when trauma from a loss keeps parents (or a parent), from moving forward. The results can manifest in the lives of subsequent children or in an older child whose life is redirected because of the loss. It is the experience of a child living in the shadow of a loss, including an emotional loss or loss of a pregnancy.

With the loss or incapacitation of a child, parenthood can feel like a long walk in the dark. Parents overwhelmed by unprocessed grief may not be able to integrate the reality and fully accept their loss. Shelly is a classic example of a replacement child enmeshed in an unconscious script: designated to fill in for another who has died or become incapacitated. In an unprocessed trauma, time stands still. Shelly's dad was trapped in grief. When trauma is not talked about and processed it can get in the way of moving forward and making new connections. Shelly was constantly being seen, not as who she was, but as who she was not.

The term "replacement child" was coined by psychologist Albert Cain and Barbara Cain, M.S.W. Their 1964 study and subsequent paper "On Replacing a Child" is one of a series that emerged from the broader Mourning and Familial Loss Project which sought to study the impact of the loss of a family member on the surviving family members, especially children. This paper reported on six families in psychiatric treatment after the death of a child or adolescent. The subsequent "substitute" children of these families developed psychiatric problems. Although a very small study, the Cain paper identified certain behaviors common to all of the families observed. These include unresolved parental grief in the replacement child syndrome, guilt, and hyper-idealization. Green and Solnit published findings in their article "Reactions to the Threatened Loss of a Child: A Vulnerable Child Syndrome." They described a constellation of clinical features in a group of twenty-five children who had an illness or were involved in an accident where parents expected the child to die but from which the child recovered. Even after recovery, the parents remained anxious, believing that their children were still vulnerable.

This over-involvement resulted in maladaptive behaviors between parents and children including becoming overly protective of their children and overly concerned about their child's health. The children responded with a number of symptoms, including difficulty separating (separation anxiety), exhibiting out-of-control behavior, underachieving in school, and not being able to accurately assess issues concerning their own health. On the other hand, some parents of replacement children are afraid to attach to the child in light of the loss of another. They may remain distant, aloof, and uninvolved, often leaving the care giving to the other parent.

An even more difficult case scenario for some replacement children is that in being required to assume the identity of the deceased (and often a designated family role), they may experience difficulty in developing their own unique identity. The Cain study found that parents of replacement children experienced the mourning process in a distorted way, more like a *pseudo resolution* of mourning rather than a healthy completion. It may follow that if parents can't accept the loss of their child, then the substitute child, having been put in the deceased's place, may exhibit a *pseudo* or *non-identity*.

Guilt plays a large part in the dynamic of replacement children who may suffer "survivor guilt." As irrational as it may seem, in some families the substitute child is made to feel responsible for the other child's death. For some parents the subsequent child is a constant reminder that the beloved deceased child would be here if not for the subsequent child.

Hyper-idealization of the deceased child is common. The lost child is never far away. The dilemma for some replacement children is that they may never meet the unrealistic expectations of the parents in filling the image of the deceased. They may suffer guilt about anger that cannot be acknowledged, let alone expressed, at the constant comparisons to the deceased and to the notion that they (the replacement child) will never measure up, will never be as good as the deceased child would have been.

In extreme cases, the replacement child is a constant cruel reminder to one or both of the parents of the loss of the much loved child, the "angel," the perfect one. In its most extreme form, the replacement child is not only resented, criticized, judged and found lacking, but may even be ignored and made to feel worthless and unloved. Although the parents may have knowingly and deliberately elected to have a child to expand their family, they may look upon the subsequent child as the problem, the irrational rationalization that somehow the deceased would still be here were it not for the new child.

But it is essential to note that there is a lack of any significant study, and certainly a study designed to include a much larger sampling, that would help to better describe and understand the replacement child experience. So much so, that people still refer back to the initial Cain study when they speak of the replacement child. But this is unfortunate because the study describes the syndrome in its most pathological form and that does not represent the majority of people that might be categorized as replacement children.

It's only recently, and often more anecdotally rather than clinically, that it has become apparent that the RC exists on a much broader spectrum, including those who are barely aware that they are replacement children to the most extreme cases, to those who are "middle of the road" examples of the syndrome.

No research is complete without a balanced perspective. Replacement children are a portion of the population who have not been fully recognized or addressed. Each thinks they're alone in this phenomenon. There is a level of unconsciousness about the issue of being the "other" in the family. This issue is certainly very relevant—though not mainstream and rarely addressed, even during therapy. The truth is replacement children are a whole community with shared traits, feelings and unanswered questions.

While it's true that most replacement children have key issues to deal with apart from their peers, there seems to be little written about those replacement children who are able to navigate through the inherent difficulties and come out on top stronger for their efforts.

"The Girl Who Never Grew Up" is a classic example of the replacement child. Judy Mandel's memoir lays bare her family's tragic history, its devastating impact, and her own path to self-discovery. "Yes, I Am an Replacement Child" explores the results when survivor guilt and identity confusion merge. "The Little Doll" tells the story of an adopted child caught up in the RC dilemma. In "Carolyn and Cary" the severe disability of a twin forces the healthy sibling to overcompensate in an effort to live a life for two. Yet, one does not have to be a subsequent child to become a replacement child. In "The Great White Hope", 17 year old Andrea feels the burden of picking up the pieces for her family after her sister tragically dies. "The Fantasy is Real" poignantly reminds us that a replacement child often feels the presence of a deceased sibling they never knew. All of these various outcomes stem from the same source—unresolved parental grief.

Journey of a Replacement Child

Judy Mandel's memoir *Replacement Child* seeks to shed light on those replacement children who have struggled with issues beyond the normal trials and tribulations of life that we all go through. In her book she tells the story of a freak accident, a plane crash in 1952, that instantly changed the lives of her family. In addition to her older sister, all of the passengers as well as people on the ground were killed, a total of thirty-one lives lost.

I went through a good part of my life oblivious to my replacement child status, although the effects were evident in my life choices and my underlying issues with self worth and identity. I was halfway through writing my memoir, which I later named Replacement Child, when I began to understand the ramifications of being born, I believe, to replace my sister who was killed when a plane crashed into my parents' home.

As I did research to better understand what my parents had gone through after losing their seven-year-old daughter, I read about the different grieving patterns between individuals, and between men and women. I gained a new perspective of my father's aloofness, my mother's clinging, and the underlying reasons for being overprotective of me. Then, I came upon the term "replacement child," coined in 1964 by Albert and Barbara Cain in their article "On Replacing a Child."

Their definition of children who "could barely breathe as individuals with their own characteristics and identity" rang true for me.

The pieces were coming together. It began to make sense that I would look to the men in my life to fill the emotional chasm left by my father. It was counterintuitive, though, that I would be drawn to men who mirrored that same detachment.

In reaction to my parents concern for my safety, I took unwarranted risks, always with the purpose of disproving their outlook of the world. Testing the boundaries of my safe world philosophy, I jumped out of planes, flew gliders, and experimented with drugs. My parents knew none of it, of course, because that would conflict with my other role as the replacement child; to be the easy one, the one they didn't need to worry about.

As a child, the presence of my deceased sister, Donna, was that of a phantom. My parents hardly mentioned her name. I was fifty, and both my parents gone, before I knew her birthday, mentioned inadvertently by my other sister, Linda. But, all those years, my mother and father never marked the day, which must have been a particularly difficult one for them.

A wall of photos of Donna, on the wall next to my father's side of my parents' bed, was the daily reminder of the daughter they lost. As I was writing Replacement Child, and looking at those photos every day on my own bulletin board in my office, I realized for the first time that my mother had given me Donna's same hairstyle for several years. That stopped after I passed the age when Donna had been killed.

Writing Replacement Child was a journey of understanding and forgiveness for me. I am convinced that my parents did the very best they could in the aftermath of a terrible tragedy. I have no doubt of their love for me as an individual. Understanding my father's grief, in particular, helped me to forgive anything he did inadvertently that hurt me or affected me in a negative way.

It's interesting to note that replacement children are often more vulnerable during the period that corresponds to the actual life of their deceased sibling, especially when a child has died after being alive for many years. Parents may try to create a scenario where the replacement child "resembles" the deceased sibling. But this focus on the replacement child seems to diminish once they have passed the age when their deceased sibling died.

Yes, I am a Replacement Child

Born after her sister Lara's death, Aryn struggled with some of the basic issues confronting replacement children—survivor guilt, feeling like second best, and identity confusion—but she never knew what to call it. Now she has a name for it.

So, I have a double whammy; my father gave up a daughter for adoption in 1963 and then my parents' first child Lara, born Sept 27, 1971, died four days after her birth. I was born Sept 21, 1972.

Interestingly enough, I just started examining the impact of those events and the scope of impact on my life about five years ago. I never had a name for it until today. Yes, I am a replacement child. There is no doubt about it.

My childhood was good. However, I always knew that I was second. I could never (and still can't) seem to live up to expectations. I am constantly driving to meet expectations, but never seem to quite make it. My parents never overtly idealized Lara as they did not have time to get to know her, yet in the same regard, she was always there and idealized. It is a conundrum. I was good and loved the best, but never the best. I'm not sure that I can explain it properly.

The guilt?? Oh, yes, I have the guilt that goes along with the environment of a replacement child. So much so that I always felt guilty that my dad always thought my birthday was Lara's date. It isn't my fault that I wasn't born on her birthday, but I certainly felt guilty about it; to the point that I don't really celebrate my birthday to this day. It just doesn't seem that important and I feel guilty for making a big deal out of it.

The disconnectedness from my family is definitely there. I am the only child that does not live close by. I am always off doing something and constantly creating a physical distance between my parents and myself. Yes, this is by purposeful design and I've often wondered why this is.

I think that some of this is because I am trying to create my own identity, yet when I do that, the guilt comes back.

But, I honestly don't think that my parents did anything maliciously. I am quite lucky compared to some of the stories that I have read. It was/is what it is and I have to try and muddle through it. I'm glad that there is a name for it and that I'm not the only one. Sometimes I felt like I was going crazy with all of the questions I had and misunderstanding of my behavior—I just didn't get it. It was to the point a few months ago that I questioned my mother as to whether or not I was biologically my parents' child. I don't look like either of them and the disconnectedness didn't make sense. It was this inner compulsion that I couldn't stop and my mom thought I was crazy for asking.

◆ Expanding the Definition of RC

Although the classic definition of a replacement child is *a child who is conceived to replace a deceased child*, some researchers have sought to expand the definition to include any child born to replace a child who has died, not only a child born immediately after the death of another child, or even a living child who "takes over" for a sibling who dies at an older age, literally "replacing" the deceased. In this latter case, the replacement child may assume the role (and often the interests) of the deceased sibling on their own, or this shift may be pushed by parents who can't let the deceased child go.

Replacement children may include children who are adopted when parents are unable to conceive a child, and can even include those who carry the hopes and dreams of a family when another sibling is incapacitated due to illness, accident, or handicap. The unique experience of twins must be considered, for when a twin dies the remaining twin has the "double" responsibility of carrying on for the "other" and replacing the void left by the deceased twin within the family.

More importantly, the phenomenon of the replacement child needs to be viewed in a broader perspective, along a clinical continuum, from the most extreme cases as observed early on to the "middle of the road" experiences of many adult replacement children.

The Little Doll

When a couple can't have a child of their own they may elect to adopt a child, one "who then has to take the place of the biological child who never was, with all the parents' attendant fantasies."[4] For many, adoption is a "win-win" situation for everyone. A child who is truly welcomed into a family will most certainly grow into a confident individual who is appreciated and cherished for the individual he/she is, regardless of the differences.

Parents who can meet their own emotional needs are able to be fully available to their children and their emerging needs, and are best able to serve as healthy role models. While it's daunting and rewarding for all parents to raise children, it may be especially so for adoptive parents who must be patient, understanding, and flexible enough to be able to meet the challenges they may face raising a child from a different background—socially, ethnically, and racially.

There are fundamental issues that need to be addressed in adoptive families. Perhaps most important of all is a deep sense of loss felt by many adopted children. In *Being Adopted: The Lifelong Search for Self*, the authors note, "The loss inherent in adoption is unlike other losses we have come to expect in a lifetime, such as death and divorce. Adoption is more pervasive, less socially recognized, and more profound." [5] There are the inevitable questions about the biological parents—who they are, what they look like, why they gave the child away. However, sometimes these issues are not acknowledged because a child may be worried about hurting their adoptive parent's feelings and/or because of a fear of rejection.

Adoptive parents too, need to be able to acknowledge their own sense of loss—the loss of their hopes and dreams when a biological child has died, or at their inability to conceive a child of their own. As with biological parents who have suffered the loss of a child, parents need to attend to their own grief before they make the decision to adopt.

Optimally, children should know their adoption story. They should know that the decision to give them up had nothing to do with them personally. Children need to be able to ask all of the questions and fully express their emotions.

Sunny is a sixty-year-old woman born in Washington D.C. She was adopted at three days of age into an upper middle class family, through a private adoption because her parents were too old to adopt through the usual channels. Her mother was forty-five and her father was fifty-five when Sunny was born. There was already an adopted brother from a different family, who was five years older than Sunny.

Sunny believes her mother was mentally ill, suffering from a narcissistic personality. She describes her mother as emotionally destructive, running "hot and cold, back-and-forth." Childhood was not pleasant for either child. Sunny was always the good one while her brother acted out. She remembers anger and drama from her mother while her father, who was a very sweet man, would withdraw. He owned his own business and was away much of the time.

Sunny "divorced" herself from her mother when she was in her late thirties. This was the solution after many years in therapy. She tried to get her mother into therapy but her mother said she was too old to change.

She describes herself as a "people pleaser," always trying to be perfect. Because he was "wild," Sunny's brother took much of the attention away from her. She describes her brother as exuding a "sexual energy; dark and dangerous." When Sunny was ten, her fifteen-year-old brother stole a Porsche from their father. He was drinking at the time, crashed the car, and died instantly in what was reported as an accident. Sunny wonders whether or not he actually "suicided." She believes that when her brother died she masked her grief. She didn't attend his funeral, doesn't remember crying, didn't talk about his death, and never really said goodbye to him.

A friend of her parents took Sunny aside and told her, "Now you've got to be the one to take care of your parents." It was up to her to pull the family together. But after her brother's death, her mother became overprotective, now watching Sunny like a hawk. She felt smothered; now she had to explain everything and take care of her mother's feelings. She felt like her mother's "little doll." Sunny had lived in fear of her mother's harsh words and belittlement but this became more pronounced after her brother's death. She couldn't wait to get out of the house and even tried running away from home.

When the time came, her parents told her she could attend college within a thousand mile radius of their home. Sunny thought she could finally get away, but found that she was still miserable and depressed and this eventually led her into therapy. After college, she moved several times for her jobs—New Orleans, San Antonio, and Chicago. She found herself returning home less and less.

Sunny understood what she needed to do to find her own way through life. She was able to identify and assess what was healthy and what was not for her own growth, and she had the courage to pursue her goals in order to survive and thrive in her own right.

Carolyn and Cary

The siblings of a child who has a severe mental or physical handicap will almost certainly be affected in some way by the special needs of the handicapped/ challenged brother or sister. Parental anxiety may have damaging consequences—the parental preoccupation with the sick sibling may leave the remaining children feeling neglected and left out, which in some situations may lead to self-esteem issues and even depression. Or conversely, the parents may pin all of their hopes and expectations on another child in the family and may consequently push that child to achieve and succeed, even if that aspiration is not in sync with who that child is or what that child wishes to do.

In "Observations of the Reactions of Healthy Children to Their Chronically Ill Sibling," Bergmann and Wolfe suggest that a healthy sibling may suffer survivor guilt (the ill child may wonder why this happened to them and the healthy one may wonder why it didn't happen to them) and may thus, qualify as a replacement child even when a sibling has not actually died.

The following story is not only one that describes and speaks to the effect that a handicapped/challenged child has upon a sibling. It's also the story of the intimacy of twins and the profound effect the illness of one has upon the other.

Carolyn and her twin brother Cary were totally unexpected. Their mother, probably in her mid-forties at the time, didn't know she was expecting until she was about six months pregnant. There were two older brothers in the family, Jerry who was nineteen and David who was fifteen. Also, living with the family in the small four-room apartment were two teenage first cousins.

Their mother worked full-time and also volunteered. At the time, Carolyn's mother told the doctor that she felt like she was having twins but was told she was wrong. Cary was born with the umbilical cord wrapped around his neck but the medical staff never told the parents. However, their mother knew something was very wrong early on.

Cary was never able to crawl or sit up; in fact, he never developed beyond a six month old. Carolyn was told very little about her childhood; few, if any, family stories were shared. The little she knows comes from her teenage cousin, Rozie who lived with the family. Rozie remembers that when the twins were in their individual cribs, Carolyn could hear Cary cry and instinctively knew there was something wrong with him or that he needed something. She would cry and thrash about until she heard that his cries had stopped. Carolyn felt that she was always taking care of her twin from early infancy until his death.

Carolyn didn't have friends when she was very young because the neighborhood children were not allowed to play with her. The ignorant mothers in that neighborhood felt that whatever was wrong with Cary could be contagious and wanted to keep their children away. Carolyn didn't really care since she liked to play and be with Cary. Even though he would not be able to react in any way, she always felt comfortable about being around him and preferred being with him.

When her mother tried to send her to nursery school, it didn't last more than one day because Carolyn cried the whole time—going there, while in the nursery school, and all the way home until she was reunited with her twin. She couldn't comfortably separate from him and, at an early age, she knew that they needed each other.

When the twins were five years old the family moved to a different neighborhood, still staying in Chicago. By this time, Cary was too heavy for their mother to carry around continuously. It was then explained to Carolyn that she would be going to her school and Cary would be going to his school, which turned out to be a state institution called the Lincoln State School, which was a ten hour round-trip drive from where they lived.

Once a month, the family would drive the ten hours to visit Cary. Their father stayed in the car the whole time; he would not go in and wanted nothing to do with Cary. Carolyn and her mother would spend the whole day feeding him, taking him to the park, and just being with him. Carolyn's two older brothers never went to see him and, like the father, wanted nothing to do with Cary. Carolyn and her parents made the trip every month for five years.

When Carolyn was ten, her mother was very bothered by a few extremely disabled people she saw at the institution and never wanted Carolyn to return. It was very painful for Carolyn to not be allowed to visit Cary. She always looked forward to seeing Cary and her love for him exceeded the awful sights they saw the day her mother decided never to allow her to return. No one ever considered Carolyn's feelings or asked her if she wanted to see Cary. She didn't see her brother again until after she graduated from college.

However, the entire time Cary was at Lincoln, Carolyn would come home from school complaining that something hurt—arms, legs, stomach, etc. Without fail, her mother would receive a phone call later in the day only to learn that something had happened to Cary or that he had the same symptoms that Carolyn had complained about. Her mother never explained any of this to Carolyn; she only knew from overhearing the conversations on the phone.

No one was allowed to speak about Cary at home until their father died. He could never acknowledge that he had a son that was not normal. Since they could not discuss Cary at home, Carolyn grew up feeling guilty and blamed herself for Cary's retardation. Since no one had ever spoken to her about the cause, it was natural that she blamed herself. When she learned at twenty-two what had caused Cary's retardation, it was too late for her to undo the damage that had already been done. She lived her life with survivor guilt. At twenty-two, she was also named legal guardian for Cary.

When the state institution closed and the residents were moved to various other places, Carolyn went to see Cary with her older brother, Jerry who had not seen his younger brother since Cary was five. The whole time they were there, Cary kept his eyes on Carolyn. He even lifted his arm and touched her. He never touched or looked at Jerry.

Years later, Carolyn moved to New York with her husband. Cary was still being cared for in Chicago. In 1998, Carolyn suddenly became extremely depressed, crying and feeling like screaming. But she couldn't understand why she was feeling this way since this was far from normal for her. She thought something was wrong with Cary but her mother wouldn't acknowledge this. During this time, Cary was in the hospital and was diagnosed with esophageal cancer. Once Carolyn was told that Cary was very ill, she felt compelled to leave to be with him. Her plan was to go on a Thursday and stay through Tuesday. As ill as Cary was, once Carolyn and her mother entered the hospital room, he never stopped looking at Carolyn and followed her movements with his eyes as he always did. He didn't pay attention to his mother. Carolyn's feelings were correct; Cary died on that Tuesday morning at age forty-seven. She feels his presence all the time.

Since she was very young, Carolyn felt that she shared every achievement and failure with Cary. She took on extra projects and worked harder than most. She became an over-achiever and now works and volunteers, always keeping busy and involved. Carolyn's feeling is that whatever she does she is doing for the two of them; this is the way she's always lived her life.

Carolyn continues to be upset that her father would never acknowledge Cary, that he was never spoken about at home, and that her older brothers didn't seem to care at all about him. She feels that her father could have been man enough to acknowledge that he had a retarded son, but believes that he did the best he could for the person he was. She remains frustrated and disappointed that her own feelings were not only unacknowledged but ignored.

Ironically, their brother, David is the grandfather of a "twinless" twin, now sixteen years old. His daughter, Mickey had twin girls, Lindsey and Michaela. Michaela died shortly before she was born. Interestingly, Lindsey didn't know that there had been another baby who was her twin sister and had never heard the name that they were going to give her. One day when she was about two years old, her mother heard her talking in her room and asked who she was talking to. Lindsey answered that she was talking to her friend, Michaela.

Lindsey and Carolyn are members of "Twinless Twins Support Group International" where all members have lost their twin (or a sibling of a multiple). For Carolyn, this group has been a saving grace, especially since she could never talk about Cary in her home with her family. It doesn't matter when, where or how one "lost" their twin; the fact that everyone feels this loss and emptiness—a broken heart—is what binds this group together. Comfort, support, sharing and learning from one another give people the strength to carry on knowing they are not alone. It's a special club that no one wants to be in, but once in—an immediate unexplained connection to others takes place.

The Great White Hope

A replacement child is not always born to replace a deceased child. Sometimes, a child becomes a replacement to fill the huge void when another child dies. What may have been an ordinary, uncomplicated life before a sibling's death may radically change as a result of parents' dependency and expectations on a remaining child, and/or the child's desire and/or sense of obligation to take care of parents devastated by their unimaginable loss. When tragedy of this magnitude strikes, the burden on an only child may be tremendous.

Allison was killed when she was fourteen years old by a van while riding her bike. Andrea, seventeen at the time, was not a witness to the accident, which made it more difficult for her to comprehend what had happened and left her with a feeling that the whole incident was "unreal."

Because Andrea hadn't seen her sister's body before the funeral, this sense of unreality was reinforced. Since the family didn't belong to a temple, the rabbi officiating at the funeral didn't know Allison. The lack of familiarity and intimacy at the service created an awkward and uncomfortable atmosphere even though many friends and family filled the chapel.

Pictures of Allison were left around the house but talking about her was difficult, especially for her mother. Her parents tried attending a grief group but found that it wasn't helpful. They observed that families that had lost sons were given more attention as if somehow they were more important. Andrea thinks that this may not really have been the case but that her mother was uncomfortable and stopped attending.

The family had been dealing with many issues even before Allison died, and Andrea was "given" the role of picking up the pieces. However, after her sister's death, Andrea felt obligated to "be there" to take care of her parents. Her role as caretaker was never discussed openly in any way. Her mother started calling her "the Great White Hope."

"I felt the burden from my parents of being all they had left." She reacted to this by being rebellious and spent her early teen years hanging out with people who weren't good for her and making some personal choices that she later regretted.

She experienced survivor guilt and "lots of guilt about our rivalry before Allison's death, but also a lot of sadness about having lost my only sibling." Andrea believed that she now had to be perfect and achieve the accomplishments of two daughters. Although she continued to be a good student, the stress and sadness weighed heavily and she began to compensate with comfort food and over-eating, as well as continuous relationships that were, at times, damaging.

Andrea left for college a year after the accident. There she began her quest to seek a deeper understanding and meaning for her life as a result of her experience. She found peace, answers, and a strong identity in Judaism, seeing this too, as something positive that she could pass on to her own children.

The oldest of her daughters is named for Andrea's sister. Her second daughter is proud that she looks just like her Aunt Allison and wears it like a badge of honor. People remark about the similarities all the time. Andrea's three daughters ask about their Aunt Allison often. They're curious to hear all about her, what she was like, and Andrea is open and honest with them.

"I had three children because I wanted to create a different family structure than I had growing up with just two siblings. It's painful for me to see my daughters fight, and it's always tempting to say to them, 'I lost my sister and would give anything to have her here with me right now—you have to love each other every second!' I hold back from saying that kind of thing because I don't want them to feel guilty about normal sibling rivalry."

Andrea leads a full life and her accomplishments are many. The role of replacement child, placed on her shoulders as a young woman, has influenced her adult life in many ways. Her sensitivity to the fragility of life has made her keenly aware of what can happen to children and she's overly cautious about her own. Because she was cast in the role of the family's only remaining hope, she learned to achieve and succeed, not just for herself, but for her parents. There are still remnants of her replacement child role—she is an over-achiever, a workaholic, and a perfectionist. But then too, she's tougher and more resilient than she otherwise might have been.

The Fantasy Is Real

Stephen slowly figured out that there was another child before him. Even though the family kept it a secret, her presence influenced his life.

I am 65, and am a replacement for little girl who died at six months, on Boxing Day 1947. I was born just under 11 months later, in November 1948. It's only now that I'm really forming some real perspective on my situation.

I heard her name—for the first and only time from my parents at any rate—in June 1960, when my parents were driving past the cemetery where her ashes had been scattered. My father remarked in a low voice to my mother that, "Janet would have been 13 today."

I obviously stored this information at a deep level, otherwise I wouldn't have remembered exactly where I was, etc. At the time, though, I can't remember having any particular reaction, even so much as to ask who Janet was. Yet I think that, from the nature of the comment, I would have picked up that he was talking about a child of theirs.

As I say, she was only mentioned the once, when I wasn't supposed to hear. But what's struck me recently is that there wasn't a single sign in the house of her ever having existed. While this was just after the war, where death was so widespread and matter of fact and life had to go on, I find this truly shocking.

Sometime in my life I learnt that my father's father had died in 1910, when he himself would have been 10. He and his two brothers were brought up by my grandmother, whose maxim was: "Of course he/she can do it – he/she is 'a Brice.'"

Thus, all had to be positive—the family had to be an exemplar of achievement etc., etc. Because I was academically clever, winning a scholarship to public (i.e. private!) school and a further minor scholarship to Cambridge University, I—unfortunately for me in that it compounded the confusion about my part in the family—fitted into this model. I fitted so well that, in some ways at least, I grew up thinking that my family—being 'a Brice'—was, in reality, blessed. When I won those awards etc, I felt 'Well, how else would it be?' This was very much a handing over of achievements to enhance the reflected glory. Looking back, there was no self in the way to say, "Actually that is my achievement."

Looking back, what I cannot remember not feeling is anxious incomprehension, that I had some job to do to justify myself, to be 'something', always looking out to see what I had to do or whether what I'd done was the right thing, while, at some level, knowing that I needed to protect myself from what was happening. At 65, I have tried to go back objectively to how my little instinct would have picked up the situation when I was born.

While my existence was obviously vital to them, I can't help feeling that it was mainly—and, insofar as I can be certain, especially when I arrived and first peered out on the world—as a continuation of the life that had been lost. The only time I ever spoke about all this with my mother, when I was in my 30's, she said, "We were told to have another as soon as possible." Whether or not that was the normal advice then, they could have used their own brains and feelings to consider their situation. That they plainly did not is something I find profoundly stupid, but fits in with a pattern of their having nil psychology.

I don't think any mourning whatever had taken place, (as probably it hadn't taken place after my father's father died). How could it possibly have, when I was conceived within a few weeks of Janet's death, and she had been airbrushed out, at any rate, physically?

I had therapy for three years after my first marriage failed (1981). The therapist, a Jungian and Head of the London School of Psychotherapy, didn't really crack the fact of my being a replacement or grasp its centrality to my problems. He did, though, venture the thought that my first marriage was an attempt to bring the lost sister back to life.

The same therapist asked me, "Why can't you just let the fantasy go?" I didn't answer at the time, as the question made me feel generally weak-willed. From this point in my life, I can say that the "fantasy" was as real and integral part of my existence as walking and eating, and as rooted in my subconscious as any sense. The last thing that I felt it was, was a fantasy.

Stephen's story is sure to resonate with many replacement children. Sometimes, parents attempt to close the book on the loss of a child. They may agree to keep forever silent on the matter. Occasionally a name will slip out, or perhaps a specific reference to that child. Sometimes, a family member can't keep silent. But the fact is that many children who come along after a deceased child often sense, just seem to "know" that someone has been there before them, and their life, their very sense of who they are, is informed and influenced by that knowledge.

II. The Essential Issue of Unresolved Parental Grief

♦ Grieving and Mourning

My mother, despondent with bereavement, was not encouraged to hold the child. No lock of hair or tactile object was taken to help with mourning. The child was buried in my grandfather's plot without a stone, without a name on the stone.

But he had a name. My mother and father had named him Claude Bunch Barbre III, the name they would give to me at my birth. Thus began my life as a replacement child, companion to my firstborn, full-term, stillborn brother that shares my name. The double nature of trouble and healing that characterizes the mystery of hope and transformation resonates along my own spiritual path—a troubling that began before my birth as the conundrums of the replacement child was born into my double beginnings. [6]

—Dr. Claude Barbre,
Psychotherapy and Religion:
Many Paths, One Journey

Before we can even begin to address what unresolved parental grief looks like in the families of replacement children, it's important to understand what grief and mourning following any death looks like. You may think this is something most of us know about already, but the reality is that death, although a natural part of life, is a situation most of us have little knowledge about and even less mastery over, unless we've had the experience of personally going through the death of a loved one. Many people are afraid of death and simply don't want to talk about it. But having some basic information beforehand may help when it's really needed. Then, too, understanding death in "normal" circumstances may help to better comprehend what happens to families and individuals when death is unexpected and tragic, such as when a child dies.

Each person's capacity to endure through difficulty, to cope through hardship, and to handle extremely adverse obstacles throughout life is dependent on many things. Some people seem to have a natural ability, whether constitutionally inherent or acquired over time, to effectively meet life's challenges.

Some people heartily embrace and even thrive on situations that require drawing upon inner resources, seeing these as welcomed opportunities for growth. They may even choose to view these difficult situations as vehicles for discovering their inner strength, for learning how tough they are, and for seeing what they're really made of. On the other hand, some individuals simply can't cope with what may even be small changes in their lives.

When a person is able to acknowledge their loss it means that they have a clear understanding about what has happened; they recognize the reality of the situation and accept the meaning of this reality. The death of a loved one must be experienced to be known and only after that can one say how they feel and what they'll need to do for themselves as their life moves forward.

While the external process following death seems to unfold in an almost linear way, the internal process has its own time frame. This is the work of grieving and mourning. In virtually ever culture and religion there are funeral practices and rituals designed to move through the immediate experience, for after all, death is a rite of passage. These rites and rituals organize what could otherwise be a chaotic experience, informing participants how to behave and orchestrating the appropriate actions necessary for the critical, but relatively short period following death.

Although mourning and grieving are often thought of as the same process, there is an important difference. **Grieving** means to sorrow for. It's the normal response to loss on every level—psychological, emotional, physical, and behavioral. But more accurately from the Latin, grieving means to burden, from the word gravis meaning heavy. We carry the burden of a heavy heart, not only for the loss of the loved one, but for ourselves now that we're left without them. Loss is really about how we experience the absence of those we love and how we navigate the void left without them.

Mourning literally means to be anxious, to be careful; to pine away. The work of mourning, from a therapeutic perspective, is to separate from the deceased. In clinical terms, decathect. More than physical separation, this is the process of detaching and withdrawing the mental and emotional energy with which the deceased has been invested.

Once that separation is complete, one is able to attach to another object, someone or something that is equivalently significant. While a deceased child will never be forgotten, the work of mourning is to be able to separate from the child emotionally in a way so that life can go on for parents, siblings, and family members.

When people remain in the mourning process, pining away for the lost "other" and unable to move forward, it's safe to say that they're pathologically stuck. They remain attached to the past, unable or unwilling to close out that chapter of their life. They continue to live in the shadow of what once was, often idealizing it, memorializing it, keeping it "alive" to justify their existence.

Both grieving and mourning require patience and the ability to freely address and express the palette of varying emotions and feelings that will surely emerge. It's essential to recognize that there is no specified time period for grieving a loss. But at some point in the near future, grief must be completed, for to live in a state of prolonged grief and/or incomplete grief prevents movement forward in a healthy way. Mourning, on the other hand, may continue for months or even longer.

Mourning—A Mother's Journey

Gladys describes her difficult and, at times, impossible journey through grief and mourning after the death of her daughter. She poignantly takes us through her process—emotionally, psychologically, and physically —through the hell she was living to a place of peace; and to a place of profound gratitude for the life she had with her daughter, for her daughter's "message," and for the future she was able to build for herself as a consequence of the death.

Claudia, my middle child, died of flu at age thirteen, after a battle with myasthenia gravis. Was it thirty-nine years ago? Or was it yesterday? My body is not able to know. But my head does and takes over immediately. I know... and feel that today I am a very happy person, that I enjoy inner peace most of the time. I am a person who loves and enjoys life.

How was I able to get there? How was I able to turn the hell I was going through around, to overcome the "poison" that inhabited my mind and body ALL OF THE TIME, to be able to feel the way I do today? Let me see... I know there was a huge change in my life when I understood the meaning of the words, "You need to love others and then to love yourself." It was a test for me. I had to ask myself, "How do we love others? By giving them what they need? By giving them what you need? I thought I loved people, but there was something I felt I was not getting.

Back to Claudia. Right after she died I had the urge to go look for some "clue" in her desk; I had no idea what I was looking for. I found some beautiful poems. In one of the poems that I chose to be read at her funeral were these words: "The essential thing in life is love." It seemed amazing to everyone; we wrote it on her gravestone.

Many difficult and harsh years passed by. I continued with my work—I'm a psychoanalyst. During my training in the U.S. to become an Imago couples' therapist the old idea about needing to love others and Claudia's words, "The essential thing in life is love," seemed to come together. I understood, almost like a revelation, what it meant to "love others": to be able to put myself in their shoes, to look at their positive aspects, to consider that what may seem to me to be negative in them may be their best way to express their needs, to validate them, to accept their point of view as legitimate, even if it differs from mine, to be able to recognize in them their inner wounded child. And alas, being able to feel that when I looked at someone standing right in front of me, I understood Claudia's words and I felt a warm sensation in my chest and a sense of expansion.

All of a sudden, the toxicity, the "poison" in my body disappeared, not to return. Claudia always told me that I didn't understand her, and for sure I didn't. At the weekend club our family frequented she had befriended a poet and a psychiatrist with whom she spent most of the time. They understood her, for sure.

By keeping her good qualities within me, I feel I have Claudia with me by continuing what she would have wanted to do, that now, from above she is saying, "Now you are getting me, Mom." I may not be certain about what she would have really wanted, but for sure I am feeling and doing something she would have appreciated a lot. I feel her energy alive in me, eliciting good things in me, and I'm trying to spread this around as much as I can. This makes me very happy. I feel that I'm completing Claudia's mission in life and I'm convinced it's the best mission one could have.

As much as one can completely end the grief around a deceased child, I believe I've done well. For a very long time I couldn't look at her picture without crying; couldn't say her name either. Writing these words down touched me a bit only on the first line. Claudia is around me, so to speak, in a positive and active way, sustaining me to find better ways to get closer to others

◆ When a Child Dies

In the natural order of things, parents are not meant to bury their children, yet due to illness, accident, or tragedy a parent's worst nightmare may occur. The death of a child dashes a parent's hopes and dreams, totally shattering the idea about the way life is supposed to unfold. Parents expect to watch their children grow into adulthood, having given them what they'll need to succeed. And then as life continues, parents expect to relax and enjoy their children's lives, and the lives of their grandchildren. The death of a child cheats parents and siblings of this reward.

Unlike illness, painful as that kind of passage is, which gives some extended, quality time with the child, death by accident, suicide, or catastrophic tragedy as when someone is killed, offers no warning and no time to prepare. There is no time to process what has occurred and no time to say good-bye. The invisible cords that bind us to one another are abruptly and violently ripped apart.

The unimaginable loss of a child is probably the most devastating event, the harshest and cruelest reality that anyone will endure during a lifetime. Many parents are eventually able to make sense of what has happened and to make peace with their loss. They never forget, but they may emerge from the experience more appreciative of their life and of those dear to them. Yet, some parents have never fully resolved the deaths of their children and when that happens it's tough to successfully move on with their own lives. Unresolved grief affects everyone in the immediate family.

For those who have lost a child, the rituals of one's religion may initially help to get them through the funeral and the initial period of grief and mourning. The immediate period after death provides structured actions—things required to be done in and around the ritual of mourning and burial. Thus, profound sorrow and grief are contained within the immediacy of rituals surrounding death. But so much happens once the rituals are done.

It's important for parents to give themselves whatever time they'll need to sort things out since they will not be living in "ordinary" time in the usual sense. The linear and logical will inevitably interweave with memory and reverie, so parents need to give themselves the latitude to find their own rhythm and their own way through this experience.

Grieving parents can expect that all of their inner resources will be fully spent, over a long period of time. It's important for them to limit their responsibilities and obligations to only what's absolutely necessary while grieving and mourning. There should be no pressure to do or be anything other than who they are, where they are. There's no urgency about making immediate changes or decisions until after the grieving process is completed. A better, more realistic perspective is achieved by giving things time to settle themselves and then figuring out what needs to be done.

Both grieving and mourning are essential for healing to occur: to gather back one's sense of self, to let go, and to move on. Therapeutically, healing begins once the perspective has been shifted from asking the *why* questions to asking the *how* questions. Asking *why* keeps one mired in the past, searching for reasons that will not likely give an adequate answer. Asking *why* leaves one in a situation beyond their own control.

How implies action. *How* begins the process of working through loss, eventually finding a way to start life over again. *How* lights the way to other possibilities that will, hopefully, restore meaning and purpose to a future life.

Embracing Grief

Lynn speaks openly about the absolute necessity of grieving for the loss of a child. Often it is the outsider, the stranger who has difficulty with the grief process and the knowledge that a parent is enduring an unimaginable loss. And sadly, the tables are often turned and it is the parent who is the one to comfort another and offer reassurances, although it clearly should be the other way around.

There is no such thing as getting over the death of a child. You will grieve your entire life. It is part of who you are, and affects every aspect of your life and being. I feel very sad when I meet someone who has experienced such a loss and they haven't ever felt they can openly grieve about the child they no longer have. People think that if you don't talk about it then you are okay. They are afraid to bring it up because, if they do, then they cause you to be sad, or make you think about something you are trying to "get over."

Many times when I am the one to initiate a conversation about my daughter who died I make people feel uncomfortable, or sad, or make them think about "what if?" I feel like I have upset them, yet I am the one who lost my child... She existed and still does. I think the biggest fear when you lose a child is that child will be forgotten... Or that they never even existed. There is not a moment that goes by that she is not with me. Many people seem to have such a difficult time with death and grief. What we really need is for people to embrace it... Embrace us.

In my opinion there are many misconceptions about how to deal with death and loss. For example, my niece, who was four years old at the time of my daughter's death, was kept away from the memorial party, or any gatherings. My sister and husband didn't think it was necessary for her to be part of the grieving—she was too young; they didn't want her to see them so upset. While my sister and family talk about Charlotte, see photographs, and acknowledge her existence I feel like my niece missed out on experiencing her feeling over the loss of her cousin (at the level of a four-year-old). I selfishly felt hurt that she was not with us all as many of the children who were friends with Charlotte came to the memorial... She was part of their life... She existed to them.

If I had to give advice on how to interact with someone who has lost a child the first thing I would say is tell them how horribly sad it is and to acknowledge their broken heart. As time goes by, let them grieve, do not be upset for them that they are not "happy" as they will not be happy for a long, long time. I remember one of my co-workers telling another how they were worried about me because I was depressed. I immediately felt like "why can't I just be sad?" I became very angry that people were upset at me being upset... It felt like a huge burden. I began to ask people to please just let me be sad... Because that is what I am right now and I need to feel okay about that.

There is nothing anyone can say that will make us feel worse, or any sadder than we already are, or remind us of our loss as if we have put it out of our mind. I wish that people could get beyond their own fears and have real compassion for those of us who have experienced the loss. There were many times when I felt like I had the plague, or caused someone to be very upset by telling them that I had a child who died. I would feel resentful that I had to worry about their feelings when I was the one whose child died. All I ever wanted was to be free to express myself without making anyone else feel bad.

We are not heroes or pillars of strength. We are transcending through a sea of loss because that is what we need to do. We need to experience every moment of it. We want people to be interested and curious about the person (my child). One of the coolest things someone once said to me was, "You must miss her scent." I missed her scent so much and I was able to tell her that. I was able to tell her that I have articles of clothing with my things and I take a whiff of them to try and capture her scent.

Lynn has stayed with her grief, embraced it, and has been able to move beyond it in order to allow her subsequent children to be who they are in their own right.

◆ Bereavement and Subsequent Pregnancy

With a child's death, parents may feel that a part of themselves has died, too. In addition to the loss of the child is the loss of the parenting role. Without that role, parents may question what the purpose of their life is. When a child dies in the perinatal period, parents often feel the need to fill the void left by the deceased child by having another child. Some professionals suggest that having a subsequent child should not be considered until the parents have resolved their grief over the loss of their child.

In the article, "The Impact of Previous Perinatal Loss on Subsequent Pregnancy and Parenting," Elizabeth Lamb focuses on four issues: the influence of the grieving process on subsequent pregnancy, the coping mechanisms of parents during the subsequent pregnancy, the phenomenon of the replacement child, and parenting the subsequent child. [7]

As already noted, unresolved grief can occur if pregnancy follows too soon after the death of a child and can influence the parenting of a subsequent child. Yet, some parents want to make an informed decision themselves about a subsequent pregnancy rather than being advised by their doctors about the timing of the subsequent pregnancy.

Parents who suffer the loss of a child may struggle with both anxiety and depression, and there is evidence as well of pregnancy-related anxiety and symptoms of depression during subsequent pregnancies. Lamb suggests that much more research is needed. "Parenting children after a previous perinatal loss and the effects of perinatal loss on parenting behaviors are not completely documented or understood." [8]

In "Grief and Its Impact on Prenatal Attachment in the Subsequent Pregnancy," J. O'Leary addresses the issue of "parents [who] struggle to be parents to two babies as they continue to hold parental feelings for the baby who died while they begin the attachment process to the baby in the current pregnancy." [9]

Part of the problem seems to be that the parents' social network of family and friends may not understand the depth of the loss and, therefore, may not validate the loss or the parents' response to it, expecting rather, that the parents should just get on with their life and have another child—as if that solution will simply take care of the problem.

Outsiders, no matter how well intentioned, may not understand that many parents feel an attachment to their deceased baby. Parents who have recently lost a child may be feeling guilty and conflicted, fearful of forgetting and/or abandoning their dead child. O'Leary suggests that parents need to be able to acknowledge the relationship they have with *all of their children*.

Since a subsequent pregnancy may not, in itself, resolve parental grief, a proposed solution may be to facilitate the grief reaction for the loss of one child while allowing for attachment to the new child. In this way, a place is kept for the deceased child within the family; no one takes their place, or is expected to.

Current thinking in obstetric and neonatal practice suggests that parents need to have contact with their dead infant, including naming the child, taking pictures, and "being parents," if only for a little while. This time together creates a bond, *a real experience* with *this* baby and is felt to be beneficial, both in grieving the loss and in enhancing the parenting experience for subsequent children. In this way, the deceased child is always a part of the family, yet separate from the living children, including subsequent children.

But the bottom line is that there is simply no easy answer to fit everyone and every situation. One must consider many factors—the personality styles of the parents, their ability to cope and adapt, a history of pre-existing psychological conditions such as anxiety and depression, and cultural and familial influences—in determining whether grief is unresolved and/or pathological, or normal.

Subsequent or Replacement Child?

Since writing her memoir, *Replacement Child,* Judy Mandel has been called upon to speak and/or write about her experience as a replacement child. Her keen personal observations and advice help others to understand the syndrome of the replacement child from the inside out.

Often, when I have been speaking about my experience as a replacement child, or talking about my memoir, I'll be asked what my parents could have done differently. What can prevent a subsequent child, born after the death of another child, from becoming a replacement child? Some parents have even been upset with my referring to the term replacement child. "We just wanted to add to our family," they say, after the loss of their other child.

First, I explain that I am no psychiatric expert. I have no psychology degree, just my own experience and the benefit of research and consultation with psychiatrists and psychologists. But, I feel that my own experience as a child brought into a family as a path to their healing gives me a unique understanding.

As I have heard several psychiatrists recommend, it's important for parents to get through a grieving process as much as possible before conceiving another child. When I read this, I also understand that the grieving for a lost child will never be completed. For my mother, I know, it never ended. It was a new normal for her, but never overcome. And her fertile years were coming to an end. She knew she had limited time to conceive another child at 37. Nevertheless, it seems important for parents to be able to look forward and embrace life in order to welcome a new baby. Seeking professional counseling makes sense when parents have such a devastating loss. I wish my own parents had more of an opportunity to do that. As it was, they visited a psychiatrist only once when my mother's depression threatened to drown her. His prescription was to have me!

A subsequent child can offer healing, bringing back a normalcy to the family. I like to think my birth did that for my mother and other sister, and my father to an extent. It's when the lost child becomes a ghost in the house that there is a problem. It becomes detrimental when the new baby is named for the dead child, given her clothes, her hairstyle, the expectations for her behaviors and accomplishments.

When a new child is accepted as a unique individual from the start, that's when the word 'replacement' will not apply.

Some of us, who have felt branded as replacements, even if unconsciously, made our uniqueness known in overt ways. For me, I was a tomboy while I knew my sister had been very feminine and dainty. I sought attention through performing as a musician. I took some stupid chances to set myself apart. All, I believe, in forging my own identity.

Talking about the previous child can also lend a normal tone to her existence. My parents never discussed my sister, except in the glossiest terms. The result was that my impression of her was that of an angel child, not a real person with foibles and flaws along with her good qualities. To this day, I don't know if she had any. It's impossible to live up to the expectations of an angel. No child should have to try to do that."

The Turning Point

Clare openly speaks of her feelings and observations about loss and subsequent pregnancy. What is clear is that she and her husband were left to work out many of the essential issues of parental loss and bereavement on their own. Her conclusions run to the heart of the matter—each child is a special and unique being and it is up to the parents to help them become that.

From the moment Clare's son was born, he seemed very different from the other children in the family; bonding with him was difficult. Clare went into therapy to try to understand and to work on this "mother-child disconnect."

Over time, this relationship shifted into a loving, enjoyable one. But still she wondered why things had been more difficult with this child.

Clare and her husband openly communicated about everything, but especially about their children. During one of these discussions, Clare confessed that she just didn't get it, she couldn't understand why this son was so different from the others. It suddenly dawned on her that the idea that all of their children needed to be a certain way was nothing more than a flawed parental expectation that had no place in the reality of their life. This was a turning point, a total shift toward the acceptance of her son just the way he was—and is—in his own right.

Clare knows what can happen to children no matter how hard parents try to protect them. She's "on guard" all of the time about her surviving children's safety, but tries not to impose her anxiety upon them. She got pregnant very soon after her daughter's death, hoping that another child would be able to ease the excruciating pain of loss. In some way, Clare was hoping to "erase" the loss by filling in with another child. She realized almost immediately that she had attempted to bypass the grief process and that she was totally unprepared to parent another child so soon after the death of her daughter.

Perhaps, what was so different about this child were his parents. Grief and loss essentially altered them forever. The parents of this replacement/subsequent child were not the same parents they had been for their other children, pre-tragedy. But to their credit, they were able to recognize the complex issues involved and to work hard to remedy them.

The Good Kind of Replacement Child

Amalia's story emphasizes the enormous difference it makes for replacement/subsequent children when parents, in spite of their grief, are able to embrace each of their children as the unique individual he/she is, including the deceased child who always holds a place within the family. Amalia reminds us, too, that there are valuable lessons to be learned from the dark side of life, and what we choose to do with what we've learned, has the potential to work for the good.

I am the definition of a replacement child. But I believe there is such a thing as a good replacement child and luckily, that describes me perfectly.

I was born not even a year after my parents lost their 5- month-old baby boy to cancer. The first place I visited after I left the hospital, only days old, was the cemetery. My parents wanted to leave my 'welcome to the world' flowers at the grave of my deceased older brother. Although I came at a very hard time for my parents, my mom and dad did an incredible job in raising me. I seriously am amazed everyday as to how they did it, and I cannot thank them enough it for it. They never seemed to compare me to my older brother—maybe it was because he only lived for a few months or maybe it's because I am a girl—but comparing me to what they had lost was just not an option to them.

One of the unfortunate things I was forced to deal with as being a replacement child, was witnessing the raw aftermath of losing a baby to a horrible disease in such a short amount of time. I was born only two days before the one year anniversary of my brother's death. 363 days after he passed, to be exact.

My parents were very young at the time, only 27 years old. They were busy raising a young son (my oldest brother), had just recently lost their new baby boy to cancer, and then brought me into the world not even a year after. So, to say they had a lot on their plates is kind of an understatement.

The depression and anxiety throughout my family was always very apparent to me. My mother is severely depressed and I often witnessed her breaking down and crying at random times. She also suffers from Post Traumatic Stress Disorder (PTSD) and can check out mentally when it comes to medical issues because of the trauma she faced of losing a young son at such a young age. But witnessing all of this depression and anxiety just made me more determined to bring more light into my parents' life, and it gave me a clear reason on why I was born and what my purpose was. Constantly making sure everyone is happy and okay is definitely exhausting at some times, yes, but I felt it was my job on this earth to keep those around me happy, and that has grown me into the young woman I am today.

As a little girl, I remember everyone always used to call me carefree. I was a young girl who was just simply happy all the time with not a care in the world, and that was refreshing for my family to have after such a deep and dark time in their lives. Sometimes, I think to myself what if my brother was never diagnosed with cancer? Wouldn't my life be completely different? The truth is I probably wouldn't even be here if my family didn't lose my brother, but that just goes to show me that everything happens for a reason, and I was put on this Earth for a purpose.

So yes, I am a replacement child. But the good kind. Being a replacement child has taught me the different ways people deal with grief and that it is totally okay to express yourself when you feel the need. I also learned so much from my mother who has always been so eager to give back to the hospital that helped her in the time of her need, and to help other families who are dealing with children with terminal illnesses like my brother.

Yes, I experienced probably some of the darkest times of my family's history as a young girl, but all of this just gave me more of a reason to keep on being that little carefree girl with a constant need to keep smiles on everyone's faces. My parents are some of the strongest and kindest people that I know, and I am not just saying that because they are my parents. I know for a fact that not a lot of people would be able to experience what they have and still go on about life and raise me the way that they have. And like I said, I cannot thank them enough for that because they are truly the reason I am the way I am today.

My mom calls my oldest brother her "Inspiration", my other older brother who left this world too soon her "Hope" and me, her "Joy." I was the light at the end of a dark tunnel, and luckily I brought a huge relief to my family in a very dark time. So, I guess what point I'm trying to get across is being a replacement child is not always a bad thing, sometimes being the band aid to soothe such a deep wound as the loss of a child gives you a very important reason to be alive. Knowing that I held my family together in such a dark time and was able to give them so much joy makes me proud, and I will continue to spread my joy everyday because of that.

A Special Place in the Family

This is Fay's story as told by her daughter Nancy. The continuing grief of Fay's father after his son's death contributed in large part to his remaining aloof from the new baby in the family—the stranger, the girl. She was not supposed to be here—another Frank was.

Having four boys, my grandparents believed they had the perfect family; they were finished having children. Then the unthinkable happened. One night the four boys went to sleep as usual, and the next day only three woke up. For some unknown reason, nine-year-old Frank had died in his sleep.

Of course, both of my grandparents were devastated, but it hit my grandfather especially hard. Frank, his firstborn, had always been his favorite. Moreover, my grandfather was a highly respected and successful doctor; yet he could do nothing to save his beloved son.

With Frank gone, my grandparents decided to have another child, and to name him after Frank. Having had only boys, they absolutely expected to have another one, but their baby turned out to be a girl. Nevertheless, they named her after Frank. They called her Fay. My grandmother and the boys quickly accepted Fay: she was, after all, not only a baby, but their baby. My grandfather, on the other hand, could not get over his disappointment. He wanted to have nothing to do with the girl, and he didn't. He acted as if she didn't exist, completely ignoring her. And that's the way it went for two years.

At two, Fay was an adorable smiling, talking, walking, jumping, playing, demanding little person, as most two year olds are. It was at that point that her father started picking her up and otherwise paying attention to her. From then on, he was smitten. Fay became his favorite, and he couldn't do enough for her. She was even sent to school in a fur coat, which actually embarrassed her because none of the other children were so well-dressed.

Just as my grandfather adored my mother, she adored him. Consequently, his unexpected death, when she was only twelve, was quite a loss to her. Yet the relationship she had had with her father, as well as her continuing relationship with her brothers, had a lasting effect on her life. She grew up to be extremely self-confident. Moreover, she was always completely at ease with men and got along unusually well with them. At the same time, men always seemed to take to her and treat her with the utmost respect. Even when she was in her nineties and there were very few men around in her age group, somehow they seemed to seek my mother out.

My mother never told me how she felt about being a replacement child. However, she did say she felt fortunate to have been born a girl. Being the only girl in a family of boys assured her of having a very special place in her family, growing up feeling special and learning to get along well with men.

This story bridges the gap, demonstrating a change in status from replacement to subsequent child—a healthy change that benefitted not only this father and daughter but the entire family as well. Even though Fay's father had first rejected her because of his disappointment, he was able to let go of the fantasy of keeping his firstborn alive through another child and was able to see and appreciate his young daughter for being herself. Through this transition he regained a joy he had lost with the death of his son, and Fay developed into a confident woman with a strong sense of self.

To Carry on the Family Name

Although a replacement for the deceased male child, Nino is really a subsequent child. By the time he came along, parental grief was completed. All of the subsequent siblings were planned and wanted. According to birth order theory, although Nino is the sixth child by order of birth, the large gap between the birth of the youngest sister and Nino's birth technically qualifies him as a firstborn. Best of all, Nino's father was grateful to have his son as bearer of the family name.

Nino's parents were Sicilian. Soon after they were married their daughter, Pineta was born, followed two years later by their son, Anthony. Pineta died of rheumatic fever when she was seven or eight.

Two years later, while playing, Anthony slid down the banister, fell on the marble floor, hit his head, suffered a concussion and blood clot, and died shortly after.

Within a six-year period after those two children died, three daughters were born—each two years apart. Nino's father went to fight in World War II. When he returned, he told his wife that he wanted a son—it was important for him to carry on the family name. After a romantic weekend in Naples, Nino was conceived and was born when the youngest of his three sisters was eight years old.

He was named Joseph Anthony after his grandfather, but the name Anthony was shortened to Nino because the deceased brother was called Anthony. Pictures of Pineta and Anthony were displayed and these children were openly talked about; nothing was hidden. Nino's father made him feel very special; if a photo was taken his father insisted that Nino be in the picture. Nino knew from a very young age that he had a unique role because he would carry on the family name. He now has a grown son named Anthony.

Nino acknowledges that his parents were very good about making all of the children feel that they were "in addition to and not instead of." His sisters weren't jealous of Nino because they were all much older when he was born. For Nino, there was no downside to replacing the family's firstborn son.

◆ Unresolved Parental Grief

In *Grief Counseling and Grief Therapy,* Dr. J.W. Worden makes the point that grief is not a passive process, a succession of stages that a person must pass through, but rather a dynamic process that requires the bereaved to take action, requiring four tasks:

- **accepting** the loss as a reality
- **acknowledging** the pain of loss and working through it
- **adjusting and adapting** to the loss (for when a child dies the parenting role for that child ceases to exist)
- and establishing a **forever connection** with the deceased child

It is in the last task that parents (and other close relatives) may get stuck, finding themselves unable to live into the future. It's as if time stands still with the child's death and all things are measured in the 'before and after' of the child's life. Some experts believe that it's important for parents to continue the relationship with the deceased child, not by trying to keep him/her alive, but through memories and other creative ways of remembrance, for example, projects and foundations to honor his/her memory.

While it's expected that individuals suffering such a loss will be able to return to life as they were before the loss, that is, to a level of normal functioning and a sense of emotional well-being, those who are unable to do so for whatever reason may remain in a state of incomplete and unresolved grief. The inability to live life into the future and beyond the immediacy of loss disturbs and complicates life for everyone. This is frequently the scenario into which the replacement child is born.

Complicated grief may become pathological if there is failure to successfully accomplish the "tasks" of grieving. For parents of replacement children, the signs of unresolved grief can take many forms:

- **Intense grief** may last beyond what is considered to be the norm. This period may vary according to one's cultural and social background, but beyond one year and certainly longer than that is considered prolonged and pathological.
- **Depression and anxiety** that won't resolve over time may need professional intervention.
- **Withdrawal and social isolation** may be symptoms of depression and/or may indicate a lack of a support system.
- **Guilt and anger** may be exaggerated. Often parents of a deceased child feel that in some way they could have done something to prevent the death.
- **Parents may either memorialize the child** by keeping possessions, by preserving the room of the deceased intact, or by creating a shrine to the deceased. Conversely, they may choose to discard everything associated with the child.

His Mother's Sadness

Zachary, now seventy-three, was born six years after his sister Josie died of pneumonia at seven. There was one other child, a brother a few years older than Josie.

After Josie's death, their father got rid of all of the photos and anything associated with her. There was nothing left in the house that would remind anyone that there had ever been another child, and she was never mentioned.

Their mother went through a deep depression and was never the same. She didn't like to go out and never seemed to be able to enjoy anything. She felt guilty about her daughter's death even though she had done everything she could for her (it was in the days before the discovery of antibiotics).

Zachary didn't understand the reason his mother always seemed sad since no one ever told him about Josie's existence until he was about eighteen and his brother mentioned that they had once had a sister. His brother admonished him not to mention anything about his sister to their mother. However, Zachary did speak to his father about her and was told that after Josie died, he had gotten rid of everything because he felt that it would make their mother too sad to see her clothing and photos of her. He felt it was best for their mother not to bring these memories back. Zachary's father had a very hard life and said that you just have to put depression behind you.

When Zachary's brother told him about his sister, he emphasized that it should not be mentioned again. So there were no further conversations with his brother about her. Since all of Josie's pictures had been destroyed, Zachary never knew what she looked like or had any idea about what she was like as a person. The only descriptive detail Zachary ever got about Josie from his brother was that she was cute and pretty. Seeing a picture of her might have helped make her more real for him.

Zachary was affected by his mother's sadness. She was overly protective of him, for example, rushing him to the doctor for the slightest thing, and she always babied him. He saw that she tried to hide her feelings around other people. His aunt, his mother's sister, used to say that his mother had been a much happier person, but she too never mentioned the reason for the depression. Zachary was upset that he had not been told about his sister earlier in his life. He felt that knowing about her would have helped him to understand his mother's depression and knowing that might have helped him to better understand more about himself.

On the Outside Looking In

Lisa describes what it's like to grow up in a home where denial and addiction are the chief modalities for dealing with unresolved parental grief. Beyond the inability of her parents to deal with the loss of their child, the consequences of that tragedy have profoundly influenced the family as a whole, and Lisa's life in particular.

I am a replacement child. I was told this repeatedly growing up. My parents wanted three children and their third died from congenital heart failure at ten days old. My parents and my brother and sister had this huge hole in their lives—a pregnant mommy, a new baby coming home from the hospital, and then a sick baby who went back to the hospital, never to return home. No one ever spoke of this child then, and we still don't talk about it. I have only heard the story in its entirety once. Unfortunately the parent telling the story was intoxicated.

Then, along comes me... No connection at all to the tragedy, except to plug the hole. I couldn't figure out why I always felt like I was on the outside looking in, why I felt misunderstood, why I was criticized, resented and/or ignored. When I was eighteen months old, I nearly drowned. Dad and I were outside in the backyard—he was doing yard work while the others had gone to church. He wasn't paying attention to me, the usual, and I toddled into the unsecured pool. I nearly drowned. This became a running joke (I never thought it so funny), and I am wearing a life jacket in all pool pics until I join the swim team.

I found this strange since they had lost one child already. How could he so negligently lose track of another... into the backyard pool!

I have always felt like I stand behind a veil—they can see that someone is behind it, but they do not see who I am. I am desperate to be "acceptable," but it seems futile because I am repeatedly told how difficult and challenging that I am. Criticized, resented, ignored. As a result, I have had my struggles. I believe our family uses denial and addiction to hide from the unfinished business of grief.

I was always the problem in the family. I figured it was because I was the clumsiest drunk from a family full of alcoholics. Once I got into recovery at twenty-two, I was just as much the family problem as I was when I was drinking/using. I am still sober, for twenty-three years continuously, and have my own family now. I am overprotective of my youngest—the third child in our family. Maybe because I felt so unsafe. We still do not speak of my deceased brother.

Old Scars Go Deep

Karla read an article by Dr. Brenner and reflects on the consequences of unresolved parental grief on her childhood and adult life. Clearly, her parents were emotionally disconnected from much of life—depressed, alcoholic, and mainly concerned with making up for their own lost youth. Yet, to her credit, Karla has forgiven them, understanding that they probably did the best they could under the circumstances.

It's ironic. I came to your article (The Replacement Child on Dr. Brenner's blog, "In Flux" *for* "Psychology Today"*) via a post about sibling birth order, and they mentioned ghost children. So, then I came upon the term RC, which I—unbeknownst to the psychological term—have used to describe myself for most of my life. I couldn't believe it when I read the article how much those issues apply to me: anxiety, death obsession, feeling worthless. Mind me, I am handling it quite okay, but I have always wondered if and why there was anything wrong with me...*

I was born in Germany in July, 1954 (emigrated to the U.S. in 1994). My brother was born April 1, 1953 and died after just a few hours, from asphyxiation; he weighed ten pounds, while my mother was a petite five-foot person. She was not supposed to get pregnant for a year, and I was unplanned—and told that, too. My brother's name was Karl; I was named Karla. So I didn't even get a name of my own. They always talked about him affectionately as "Karlchen" meaning Little Karl. I never had a pet name. During most of my childhood I was told often that I could never measure up to the angel my brother would have been. Had you asked me if my parents would have preferred me to be dead and him alive, I certainly would have said, of course.

My mother had lost her father at age four, her mother in the middle of the war at age fifteen. She lived in a town that was heavily bombarded and had to carry her ailing mother to the air raid shelter every night. My father was a black ops paratrooper; had been drafted at eighteen, then five years in the war, and six years as a POW— the man was emotionally quite barren.

Both had an alcohol problem. My mom also had psych drug abuse issues and was institutionalized two or three times for "nerves," all allegedly my fault. There was physical abuse by my mom. And as though they had to relive their lost youth, I was regularly left home alone all night starting at about age two when they went out to parties. Nonetheless, they were also very strict and demanding. Good school performance was a must to get a minimum of affection. My mom tried, but she just couldn't. Her health was no good either, with many ulcers that were my fault as well.

Early on, I kind of internally disconnected, even though I really, really wanted to be loved, but somehow I was never good enough. I was lucky to have a neighbor woman who gave me a safe haven when things got too bad. She would really light up when I went there and say, "There is my Karly." I have much to thank her for...

When I was fifteen, I decided I could not take the abuse anymore and when my mom slapped me around again, I kicked her in the shins and told her that I would not take it anymore. Two weeks later I was sent to a Catholic convent boarding school and not allowed to come home except once a month, even though it was only forty miles away.

After that, I got my act together and stopped trying to make them love me. They told me their expectations for me were prostitute or inmate... I knew they wanted me to finish school (thirteen years, equivalent with high school plus Associate's degree in the U.S.), even though that's where it stopped and there were no plans for a university education. So, with three years of school left, I told them I would quit if I couldn't leave the convent, even though I had no intentions not to graduate, and they believed it and I went back to my old school.

I started to smoke weed and experiment with pretty much any kind of drug available in the seventies. Moved out of parents' house at nineteen, and made them pay my rent while I went to school. I told them if they didn't I would make their lives a living hell. I had very little compassion at that point. After I moved out, I still saw them once a month. The relation was quite amicable at that point. I even took care of them for a week when they both came down with the flu.

At twenty-five, I had worked as a radiation specialist in the local university clinic for four years, a two year school I had originally done as a premed. I was still smoking weed, but much less. Then I met my future husband who was a musician at that time. My parents were not happy about "that loser." I went back to school and got a degree in Chinese language and cultural studies, just because I wanted to do it. I got married and had a daughter. We started a company, which was successful and moved it to the States in 1994.

Still, all my life, I have had periods when I was super-anxious; the anxiety is simply that I think I might be dying suddenly within the next few minutes, hours. Always evening or night-time. I'm also very aware that my life will inevitably end in death and I need to have a few hours of therapy every few years.

I did a two-year talk therapy, after my daughter was born because I was so anxious all the time that I would repeat my awful childhood, and I really didn't want that. I should not have worried. She's a wonderful person who would assure you she had a great childhood. The therapy was very painful and exhausting for me though, and for a couple of years after that my parents got to hear it at many occasions. I am glad that I didn't let hatred poison my heart, though. They were getting older, and I decided I really needed to forgive them for my own sake. Because, you know when people are dead you cannot tell them anymore, and I did not want to add this to my heartaches. My dad died a few years later in 1992. I had told him that I loved him nonetheless on several occasions, and he had acknowledged it. So that was as good as it would get and I could accept it.

My mother was very helpless and drinking more than ever after he died. She was much more emotionally available and for the next ten years, until she passed, we had a very loving relationship. Many times she told me how sorry she was for all the bad stuff that had happened, and how proud she was of me and that she loved me so much. After all, they both had been victims of circumstance as well, but personally I think, they made poor choices as well.

I was lucky enough in a way, to physically display my inner turmoil throughout my childhood. I was a very sickly child, probably also because both parents smoked like chimneys. But when I was sick, it also gave me time-out regarding my situation. Mentally, I was quite resilient. My love of books helped me escape as well. A lot of my teachers really liked me and that gave me at least a little self-esteem.

Still, even at my age, I sometimes have problems when I feel like I'm treated as worthless, even if it isn't meant that way. The old scars go deep. Anxiety phases come on and off, and I am worried about getting older, because of the inevitability of death. Don't know yet if I can gracefully handle that. I also still have trust issues and it took literally years until I felt sure my husband would not want to off me if he had a chance because I was annoying him. He always humored me, and would reassure me. I don't have really close friends, but can easily open up and have eighty percent friendships with people I really like. That's enough for me. I need a lot of time for myself. Luckily my husband has hobbies.

Your article has given me hope and a new perspective, that I'm completely normal—or even better than normal—considering the circumstances of my childhood. I am glad we moved here, because Germany was so symbolic of my childhood I had to leave it as well (ha-ha —leaving the motherland is kind of drastic now that I think about it...) Most of the time I am a happy person. I have a strong spiritual side (though not affiliated to any religion), and meditate daily. I find happiness in the small things—a flower, a cloud, birds. We live in an area of great natural beauty.

My husband is very supportive, even though I think I will never stop worrying that I'll be too much/ annoying/a burden at some point. My daughter loves me very much, but she needs to have her own life. I don't want to be needy, but I really love my family. Our twenty employees love me; they're like an extended family that I can go home from in the afternoon. I also have a small cat rescue, mostly unadoptable hospice cats. Those fifteen rescue cats and my three boys at home give me so much unconditional love and happiness as well.

In hindsight, I think the following factors were really what helped me to overcome the issues to a point where I could lead a normal fairly happy life.

1) The forced separation from my parents, when they sent me to the convent, even though it was jarring, was beneficial in the end in that it allowed me to put some emotional distance between me and them, so I was not so vulnerable anymore. Of course, I would have loved to be loved and accepted by them, but it was clear that wouldn't happen, so I learned to be less dependent on them emotionally.

2) Therapy, in my case, analytic talk therapy; I think it's a must. I try to be open with the people closest to me. My husband and daughter know I have issues, but they love me nonetheless. Actually my husband is still mad at my parents, even though I have forgiven them, and we've been married for thirty-one years.

3) Even though my parents were bad parents, when I could find forgiveness, I was the main beneficiary. I know I shouldn't torture myself. Yes, sometimes, I have to go there and dig up the bad stuff in order to heal, but I try not to dwell on it. I'm working to actively find good memories of my childhood even if they're long and far between.

My advice: Accept yourself; you are a good and worthy-to-be loved person. Yes, you have emotional scars; yes you have trust issues, but this is who you are. Love yourself; you're worth it. Your parents were wrong not to see that. There is happiness in the world for you, too.

Karla, like so many replacement children, has met the many challenges that confront the replacement child, emerging stronger and more accomplished from her difficult journey.

III. Famous Replacement Children

◆ Going Beyond Their Special Gifts

The theme of the replacement child is a universal one. The replacement child is represented in every culture, ethnic group, race, class, and social status. Many famous people—artists, actors, musicians, writers, and analysts are replacement children.

While it's inspirational to read about well-known, extraordinarily talented individuals, it's also fascinating and instructive to understand who these people are beyond their special gifts. The human condition plays out for all of us without prejudice; being famous does not shield or protect one from life's triumphs and tragedies.

In days gone by, say a century or two ago, replacement children were common. There were many more unplanned pregnancies and infant mortality was high. So the phenomenon of the replacement child was part of life, but no less tragic for parents when a child died.

In her paper "Life after Death: The Replacement Child's Search for Self" analyst Kristina Schellinski, quoting author Maurice Porot, notes that "there are three ways out for a replacement child: madness, creativity, or becoming a psychologist."[10] That's perhaps a bit of a dramatic pronouncement, but worth looking at. Schellinski adds her own fourth way—*individuation*, discovering a way to one's own self.

Although there's something romantic about the notion of a mad genius, madness as a solution is somewhat overstated—except for Van Gogh, of course, as you'll see when you read the brief bios of several famous people. As for becoming a therapist or analyst, one can say that many people are lead into the field of psychology or psychiatry for various reasons of their own—obviously, not just because they're replacement children. There's no doubt that for many, becoming a therapist is a natural outcropping of working through their own personal issues and dynamics.

Certainly many replacement children will tell you that they have researched whatever they can find on the topic and some have spent a fair amount of time in therapy. It's fortunate if a replacement child happens upon a therapist who is familiar with the phenomenon, since an understanding of the dilemma of the replacement child in general, and its inherent issues and conflicts, may help place the presenting symptoms in a broader therapeutic perspective.

So that leaves creativity. Researchers have tried for a long time to link creativity and madness, but as intriguing as this connection is, there seems to be no clear-cut connection as yet; the research leaves us with a lot of unanswered questions. However, researchers *have* established a definite link between mood disorders such as depression, manic depression and bipolar disorder and creativity.

An article in The New York Times titled "Exploring Artistic Creativity and Its Link to Madness" by Kate Stone Lombardi draws on the expertise of many in the field. Dr. Arnold M. Ludwig, a professor of psychiatry at the University of Kentucky has pointed to higher rates of psychiatric disturbances in artists as a group, and particularly poets as a subgroup.[11] Yet another study proposes that prose writers suffer more depression. Research has even suggested that there may be a genetic link based on a mechanism of action between affective disorders and creativity. Continued research is needed to shed more light on these suggested connections.

That leaves individuation as a way to resolve the replacement child's dilemma. What we do know is that the replacement child, famous or not, struggles with psychological and emotional issues of a unique nature that are thrust upon them, that these are superimposed on developmental and psychological issues that confront all humans, and that these additional issues interface with the essential issue of establishing one's own identity.

What made Van Gogh such a tortured soul? His mental illness complicated by epilepsy interfered with his creativity, rather than enhanced it. In contrast, what allowed Dali to utilize his artistic process to successfully separate from his shared identity with his *double*, his deceased brother? Dali resurrected the myth of the Twins, Castor and Pollux, and creatively molded it in a new way to fit his own needs, which was to *embody* the twins (along with his beloved Gala). Rather than just identify with his twin or double, he was able to create his own individual identity as a *mythic twin*. Dali's art, his creative projects were then able to draw inspiration from his life.

Perhaps, the one advantage a gifted artist has over the general population is that their special talent sets them apart from everyone else. At least in some way, their identity is determined and recognized by the uniqueness of what they do. Just as Dali did, some famous replacement children have been able to use their creativity to help carve out their own identities. In other words, they worked with what they had, creatively morphing their initial conflicts in such a way to help them resolve their dilemma.

George Bernard Shaw said, "Life isn't about finding yourself. Life is about creating yourself." And maybe that, in part, is a way to individuate for any replacement child. By finding that creative source, that sense of our own aliveness, each of us has an opportunity to reconnect with who we are at our core.

From Van Gogh, a tortured soul whose astonishing creativity was only recognized after his death to Dali, an eccentric, prolific genius; from Elizabeth Montgomery, the "Bewitched" actress to Peter Sellers, comedian and film actor who brilliantly mastered the character of everyone but himself, and the legendary Barbara Walters and Katharine Hepburn; from James Barrie, the creator of Peter Pan to Coltrane, a renowned jazz saxophonist, to Carl Jung, founder of analytical psychology and profoundly influential writer and therapist—the lives of famous replacement children reflect the usual "cast of characters"—unresolved parental (often maternal) grief, survivor guilt, the struggle to separate from the idealized double or twin (the deceased sibling), the need to be seen for one's self, and the desire to be 'good enough' in one's own right.

Vincent Van Gogh

Vincent Van Gogh was born on March 30, 1853 to Theodorus Van Gogh and Anna Cornelius Carbentus, a year to the day after the birth of a stillborn son. The deceased brother and Van Gogh carried the identical name—Vincent Willem Van Gogh. They even shared the same number, twenty-nine, in the parish register. The family lived in the rectory of the parish in which Vincent's father was minister and so Vincent passed his brother's grave—same name, same birth date—daily on his way to school. He would always be 'second' and perhaps he meant that fact on many levels, not just birth order.

Due to his family's financial difficulty, Vincent had to leave school and go to work. His first job was in his uncle's art dealership. Fluent in several languages, Vincent moved to London, remaining in the field of art. But he denounced the art world when his marriage proposal to Eugenie Loyer was rejected. Next, he moved to theology, teaching in a Methodist school and preaching. He entertained the idea of studying theology but was denied entrance to school. In 1880, Van Gogh decided to become an artist and was financially supported by his brother, Theo.

Vincent had a penchant for troubled women. His widowed cousin, Kate, rejected him and he eventually took up with Clasina, an alcoholic prostitute. When his family threatened to withdraw financial support, he left Clasina, wandering for a while before he moved to Paris. There he studied with Toulouse-Lautrec and Pissarro.

Van Gogh was hospitalized on a few occasions and given various diagnoses including epilepsy, schizophrenia, and syphilis, although some biographers have suggested that his suffering was largely caused by replacing his deceased brother. In "Van Gogh's Fantasies of Replacement: Being a Double and a Twin," Harold P. Blum theorizes that a replacement child may fantasize that he/she is the "embodiment of the dead child" and suggests that perhaps Van Gogh's fantasies about being a twin/double contributed to his severe pathology, but also to his exquisite creativity as an artist.

In her paper, "Life after Death: The Replacement Child's Search for Self," Kristina Schellinski notes, "The idealized-presence-through-absence of the dead brother made him fall in his own eyes. Vincent, the painter failed, where the other Vincent—dead—would have succeeded... he rivaled against a dead person against whom he could never win. His success was—paradoxically—an attack on the dead brother's "fantasized" record." [12]

The only long-term close emotional connection Van Gogh had was with his brother, Theo who was four years younger. So closely bound was Van Gogh to his beloved brother that he found Theo's marriage to Jo Bonger extremely hard to tolerate. But the straw that may have broken the camel's back was the birth of Theo's first son, Vincent Willem, born on January 31, 1890. Six months later Van Gogh suffered a psychotic break, shot himself on July 27th, and died on July 29th at the age of thirty-seven.

James Barrie

James Matthew Barrie was born in Scotland on May 9, 1860 to working-class parents, the ninth child of ten, two of whom died before he was born. Barrie's brother, David, died in an ice skating accident two days before his fourteenth birthday when Barrie was six years old.

David had always been his mother's favorite and with his death she became deeply depressed. However, she derived some comfort knowing that David would stay a boy forever—he would never grow up, nor would he ever leave her. In his biographical book about his mother, *Margaret Ogilvy,* Barrie describes a night after his brother's death when his older sister urged him to go to their mother and tell her that she still had another boy.

"*...but the room was dark, and when I heard the door shut and no sound come from the bed I was afraid, and I stood still...after a while I heard a listless voice that had never been listless before say, 'Is that you?' I think the tone hurt me, for I made no answer, and then the voice said* *more anxiously, 'Is that you?' again. I thought it was the dead boy she was speaking to, and I said in a little lonely voice, 'No, it's no him, it's just me.' Then I heard a cry, and my mother turned in bed, and though it was dark I knew that she was holding out her arms."* [13]

After that night, Barrie sat with his mother night after night in her bedroom, trying to make her forget his deceased brother. As a result, Barrie was an insomniac for the rest of his life. To take his brother's place and gain his mother's favor, Barry dressed up in David's clothes and learned how to whistle the way he did. When Barrie turned fourteen, (the same age as David when he died), he stopped growing at only about five feet tall! The ties between mother and son strengthened over the years, but there would be a price to pay for their unusual bond.

Although his parents wanted him to go into the ministry (perhaps because this is what they wanted for David) Barrie had other ideas. As a teenager, he developed an interest in literature and the theatre. After university, Barrie pursued a career as a reporter and freelance writer. He had much success as an author of books and plays.

Barrie married actress Mary Ansell although he questioned his attractiveness and masculinity. But purportedly, he was impotent, and declined to have sexual relations with his wife, remarking, "Boys can't love." The couple divorced after Mary had an affair.

Barrie traveled in high literary circles and had many famous friends. He had a long correspondence with Robert Louis Stevenson. He befriended Antarctica explorer Robert Scott and was the godfather to Scott's son, Peter. He was asked by Scott to take care of his wife and son while he was on his expedition to the South Pole. Barrie was so proud of Scott's letter to him that he carried it with him for the rest of his life.

It's said that Barrie's mother read the stories of Robert Lewis Stevenson, stories of adventures and pirates. She inspired the character of Wendy. At eight years of age, Margaret lost her own mother and had to take over the role of mistress of the house and mother to her younger brother—much as Wendy does for the "lost boys."

David was never far from his mind. The last play Barrie wrote was *The Boy David* based on the Biblical story of King Saul and a young David. Barrie also published a novel, *The Little White Bird,* which tells the story of a bachelor who befriends the boy, David. On walks through Kensington Gardens, he tells David about Peter Pan who appears at night in the Gardens. The play *Peter Pan* was produced in 1904 and the book, *Peter and Wendy,* was published a few years later. Apparently, *Peter Pan* took shape through the stories Barrie told to the sons of his dear friend, Sylvia Llewelyn Davies.

Childless himself, Barrie became the guardian of these five boys after both of their parents died of cancer. Eventually, he adopted the boys and they became his family—"the lost boys." Sadly, death befell three of the boys as adults. In 1937, Barrie died at seventy-seven.

Barrie assumed the role of the replacement child for his mother following his brother's death. In his younger years, Barrie's job in life was to make his mother happy—to be her companion, to entertain and to heal her. Having achieved fame and wealth, his mission in later life was to take care of children. Ultimately, he sacrificed a more intimate personal life for others.

Carl Jung

I am not what happened to me. I am what I choose to become.

—C. G. Jung

By the time Jung was born on July 26, 1875, his mother, Emilie, had already lost three children—two daughters, both stillborn, and a son who died five days after birth. While Jung's birth, about two years after his brother's death, was a reason for great joy, it can be assumed that his parents experienced much anxiety and great concern that this child might die as well. Clearly, from this perspective, he was a replacement child for the several deceased children who had preceded him. Jung was to remain the only child of the family until his sister was born nine years later.

Jung's father, Paul, was a pastor in the Swiss Reformed Church. Both of his parents came from very large families. Early on, Jung was aware that his parents had a troubled marriage and that his mother suffered from depression. Emilie was raised in a household where the spirit world was accepted as a reality. It's purported that she developed the powers of a medium early in her life.

His mother was predictable enough by day, but at night seemed to become a different person—a strange creature, said to commune in a trance state with the spirit world. When Jung was three, his mother was hospitalized and he was sent away to be cared for by a spinster aunt who was many years older than his mother. For quite some time, Jung didn't trust the reliability of women, with one exception—the family maid.

Interpersonal relationships were difficult for him; he was much more content when he was alone, in his own inner world. Jung felt that he had two personalities: Personality No.1 was a school boy, the son of his parents who had trouble in school and difficulty with relationships, and Personality No.2, a much older man, more comfortable in nature and in the world of dreams rather than with other people. Jung felt that becoming a psychiatrist was a way to bring these divergent parts of himself together.

In February 1903 Jung married Emma Rauschenbach, a wealthy Swiss heiress. They had five children. It's been suggested that Emma's family wealth enabled Jung to have a certain amount of professional independence. Interestingly, his involvement with such women as Sabina Spielrein, Toni Wolff, Louise Von Franz and others belonging to the Zurich Pelzmantel (wealthy women in Jung's social circle) continued both professionally and personally. Some scrutiny and speculation swirl around these relationships but it's clear that Jung was an attractive figure to women and Jung was fascinated by women.

Jung's correspondence with Freud, beginning in 1906, lasted for several years. Over time, however, their basic disagreement over libido theory lead to the deterioration and ultimate disintegration of their relationship. Clearly, Freud didn't want to be challenged by Jung and Jung didn't want to be seen as the "adopted son" and successor to Freud, but rather as an equal. Jung resigned as president of the International Psychoanalytic Association and as editor of the *Jahrbuch.* He still had his patients and was financially secure enough, but his professional life had radically changed.

Following the break with Freud, Jung entered into a period of personal crisis, a time of "inner uncertainty." His feeling of disorientation led him into a reexamination of his life—an "experiment with the unconscious." Unable to get a handle on what bothered him, he decided to simply go with the flow of the unconscious, to work with whatever came to him.

He remembered that as a boy of ten or eleven, he enjoyed playing with building blocks. Following his instincts, he collected stones from a lake and its surrounding area and began to build a village. From *Confrontation with the Unconscious*, Jung remarks, "Naturally, I thought about the significance of what I was doing, and asked myself, 'Now, really, what are you about? You are building a small town, and doing it as if it were a rite!' I had no answer to my question, only the inner certainty that I was on the way to discovering my own myth." [14]

This child's play allowed Jung to access numerous fantasies, which he was able to utilize to find the answers he was seeking. Whenever uncertainty occurred in future years, Jung utilized this technique to help him find what he needed. This creative game ultimately brought Jung back to himself.

Jung's contribution to the world is enormous. He founded analytical psychology, illuminated the concept of individuation and self, and brought us the collective unconscious, archetypes, anima and animus, and synchronicity. Jung died on June 6, 1961.

Salvador Dali

Every day, I kill the image of my poor brother...I assassinate him regularly, for the 'Divine Dali' cannot have anything in common with this former terrestrial being.

— Salvador Dali

Salvador Dali was born in 1904 in Figueras, Spain. His elder brother, Salvador Galo Dali died when he was twenty-one months and twenty days old, exactly nine months and ten days before the birth of Salvador Dali, the painter. His status of replacement child seems well established and we find recurrent themes relating to being a replacement child in the life and work of the artist.

After the death of her first child, Dali's mother was distraught; totally beside herself. Everything about that son delighted her and his loss was a terrible shock from which she never recovered. Dali's birth relieved his parents' despair, but the painter was always aware of their anguish. He felt his brother's presence on a very deep level, especially since his parents chose to view their second son as the reincarnation of his deceased brother. Dali remarked that his "despairing parents...committed the crime of giving the same first name to the new Dali that their dead son had borne." And the presence of his lost brother stayed with Dali forever.

Dali's dead brother was his "ghostly double" and as such, created tremendous conflict and stress for the painter, resulting in a kind of splitting of the personality. Dali essentially lived the life of two people—himself and his deceased brother. Having one foot in the grave and one foot on the Earth, Dali developed a fascination with the theme of "decay and putrefaction," and images of these found their way into his art.

After his mother's death in 1921, Dali struggled to find and establish an identity as an adult on his own—apart from his family and away from his father, who had remarried his late wife's sister. In 1922 Dali went to study in Madrid at the Academia de San Fernando.

Aside from a personality "shared" with his deceased brother, Dali thought of himself as a part of one (larger) personality called the *four Salvadors* which included himself, his father, his deceased brother, and Jesus Christ (Salvador in Spanish).

The year 1929 was a turning point for Dali. He joined the French Surrealists and he met Gala (Elena Ivanovna Diakonova) who became his muse and the love of his life. But his father disapproved of the relationship and a thirty year estrangement between father and son followed. Eventually, they reconciled.

The deceased Salvador had the middle name, Galo, most probably named after Dali's grandfather, Gal. The artist said, "I name my wife: Gala, Galusha, Gradiva..." In essence, by transmuting his brother's name into the feminine form, Gala, Dali was able to "free" himself. Gala became "Gala the Savior, or Gala the Rescuer" (in Spanish: *Gala Salvadora*). And Surrealism "liberated" Dali from the parental power that inhibited him, helping him to creatively channel his impulses.

Dali identified himself with the Dioscuri (Dioskouroi), the Divine Twins—Castor and Pollux (Polydeuces). As the mythic tale goes, Zeus transforms himself into a swan and mates with Leda. The union produces two eggs. In one telling of the myth, one egg produces the twins, Castor and Pollux, and from the second emerge Clytemnestra and Helen of Troy. (Another version of the myth pairs Castor with Clytemnestra and Pollux with Helen.)

Dali equated himself with Pollux, the immortal son of Zeus, and Gala with Helen. He identified his deceased brother with Castor, a mortal, and in one version of the myth, the son of Leda and her husband, King Tyndareus. In the "twins" he was finally able to assume his own identity, no longer overshadowed by the memory of this dead brother. Citing Darwin, Dali noted that his brother was too weak to survive, and this made it possible for him, Dali, his successor, to thrive.

Although wildly eccentric, Dali never succumbed to madness. "The only difference there is between a mad man and me, is that I'm not mad!" After a fascinating, colorful life and a prolific career, he died on January 23, 1989.

Ultimately, one can say that being a replacement child was a "positive" for Dali. His experiences shaped his art. As a result, he became his own greatest creation. His genius finds expression in the way he invented himself—an over-the-top, eccentric, flamboyant, provocative work-in-progress.

Katharine Hepburn

Katherine Hepburn was born in Hartford, Connecticut in 1907, the second of six children. Her father was a successful urologist; her mother a feminist and leading supporter of women's rights. Kate's father encouraged independence, competitiveness, and athleticism in his children. Kate was a tomboy, sporting short hair like a boy and referring to herself as "Jimmy." She took a keen interest in golf and swimming, but early on was also drawn to the movies and put on plays for family and neighbors.

In 1921, while visiting family friends in New York City, Kate walked into the attic room where her fifteen- year-old brother, Tom had been sleeping. She found him hanging from a makeshift noose from one of the ceiling beams. She was thirteen and extremely close to Tom. It was she who cut his body loose and ran for help— but it was already too late.

At that time suicide was a stigma. Tom's death was one in a series of suicides in the family, including Kate's maternal grandfather, as well as one of her father's brothers. Kate's father adamantly denied that Tom's death was a suicide, rather the result of a "parlor trick gone wrong."

Just as these tragedies were never spoken of within the family, there was no mourning for Tom. In fact, the family never mentioned his name thereafter. In large part this was due to the fact that Kate's father thought of depression as a "contagious disease" and by denying its existence he sought to banish it from their lives.

But the loss of her brother instantly and completely changed Kate's life. She had adored and idolized her brother—he was her best friend and confidant. After Tom's death Kate grew withdrawn and moody and it was decided that she should be home-schooled by tutors.

She coped with this devastating loss by keeping Tom alive within herself, even taking on his birthday, November 8 (while her date of birth was actually May 12). She vowed to herself and her deceased brother that he would live with her always; she would live a life for two. And along the lines of sharing birthdays, she stated that "the real date of his death would not be until the day I died."

Kate went on to attend Bryn Mawr. It was during that time that she decided to become and actress and appeared in many school productions. Her illustrious career needs no discussion. The long-standing relationship with Spencer Tracy may have served both of them well. Tracy was often depressed, a sometime alcoholic, whom Kate referred to as "tortured." She was there to help him, to make his life easier; perhaps to make up in part for what she could not do for her beloved Tom. Tracy helped Kate be a girl again—something she had been robbed of from the day Tom died.

Kate died in 2003 at the age of 96. It's said that just before her death she had a dream about the day Tom died. Everything played out as it had on that fateful day—until Tom smiled at her. He loosened the noose around his neck and told her that he had figured out what he had done wrong on that day so long ago.

Peter Sellers

If you ask me to play myself, I will not know what to do. I do not know who or what I am.

–Peter Sellers

Richard Henry Sellers was born on September 8, 1925 near Portsmouth, England. His parents called him Peter, the name of an older stillborn brother. A British film actor, comedian, and singer, Sellers is best known for his uncanny ability to assume the identity of the characters he played. When he was acting, he became the person he was portraying. When he wasn't acting, he was Richard Henry playing the role of Peter.

Sellers' parents, Peg and Bill, were vaudeville entertainers. Peter joined them on the stage shortly after his birth. As a child, he traveled with his parents on the vaudeville circuit and grew to love entertaining. Sellers became a radio personality on "The Goon Show," a British radio comedy program. He began his career as a film actor in the 1950's. Many of his most-loved films were comedies, such as *The Pink Panther* series, but he excelled in more serious roles as well including *Dr. Strangelove, Lolita,* and *Being There.* Sellers demonstrated his versatility, playing many kinds of characters, skillfully using different accents and disguises, and sometimes playing many roles within the same film (*The Mouse That Roared* and *Dr. Strangelove*).

He had extreme insecurity and struggled with depression. Sellers was known to be difficult to work with, which presented a challenge for his costars and directors. Although considered a genius, colleagues found him to be unbalanced and manipulative. By the mid 70's, Sellers had many issues with his physical and mental health, along with alcohol and drug-related problems. He refused to get help.

Sellers made the claim that he had no personality. Perhaps he needed to play very strong characters in order to gain an identity. In 1978, appearing on *The Muppet Show,* he decided not to appear as himself but rather, to play characters wearing various costumes and assuming different accents. When Kermit the Frog remarked to Sellers that he could just be himself, Sellers replied, "But that, you see, my dear Kermit, would be altogether impossible. I could never be myself... You see, there is no me. I do not exist... There used to be me, but I had it surgically removed."

Sellers was married four times and had three children. He had great difficulty relating to his children, purportedly insulting and verbally abusing them. There was always the threat of being abandoned by him. Sellers and his son, Michael eventually reconciled, but sadly, the closeness they achieved did not last long. Sellers confessed to his son that "he hated so many things he had done." Sellers died of a heart attack on July 24, 1980 at the age of fifty-four in London, England.

John Coltrane

John Coltrane was born on September 23, 1926 in North Carolina. His father was a tailor by trade but loved music and played several instruments. When Coltrane began playing the saxophone at age thirteen, it was clear that he was enormously talented.

In an article, "John Coltrane and the "replacement child" syndrome," author Bertrand Lauer hypothesizes that Coltrane's family history had a profound influence on his personal life as well as his professional life as a musician. The stage is set from the beginning: Coltrane is a replacement child for his mother's first child who died in infancy, shortly before Coltrane's birth. "Maybe less than a year. Too short a time for the mother to finish off the mourning of her deceased firstborn child." [15]

Lauer describes what we will hear over and over again—that hastening the end of mourning by prematurely replacing a deceased child may have far-reaching consequences. In this case, the author puts forth the idea that Coltrane's mother was most certainly still in mourning, but further notes that mourning can become melancholia.

Quoting Freud, "In mourning it is the world which has become poor and empty; in melancholia it is the ego itself." [16]

Possibly, Coltrane absorbed his mother's depression—her incomplete, unresolved mourning, and her sense of guilt—and this may explain in part why he remained close to her his whole life. In addition, his maternal grandmother had also lost a firstborn child and mourning was never completed for that child.

Tragedy struck in Coltrane's teenage years with a series of deaths of significant people over about a two year period: his grandfather, Reverend Blair (his mother's father), Coltrane's father, his maternal grandmother, and Goler Lyerly, his uncle.

Lauer further proposes that what remains unspoken within a family, may eventually become a family secret and this, in turn, might negatively affect a child psychologically. Such were the events surrounding the unresolved mourning of the first child born to Coltrane's mother.

He was a class musician, a gifted jazz saxophonist who played with the best in the business such as Dizzy Gillespie and Miles Davis. But he was profoundly self-destructive, addicted to alcohol, cigarettes, and heroin. He was known to practice obsessively, "maniacally" for hours on end. But while staying with his mother in May 1957, Coltrane had a spiritual awakening and gave up drugs and alcohol.

Sadly, Coltrane would not find the "answers" he was seeking. In 1965 he began using LSD. Addiction followed. And in July, 1967 Coltrane died of liver cancer.

Elizabeth Montgomery

Born on April 15, 1933, the actress Elizabeth Montgomery was the second child of actor Robert Montgomery and Elizabeth Allen. Their first daughter, Martha Bryan, named for her aunt, was born on October 13, 1930 and died at fourteen months as a result of spinal meningitis.

Elizabeth became a successful actress in her own right and is perhaps best known for her TV show, *Bewitched.* A 1965 magazine article, "Witches are People Too" written by Jackie Thomas, explains how Robert Montgomery was totally devastated by the loss of his first child, suffering from severe depression that crippled him for months. In fact, he never really fully recovered.

Elizabeth had a complex, often difficult relationship with her father, especially in relation to how strict he was in her younger years. Perhaps in part, this was her father's way of controlling Elizabeth's life when clearly, he had had no control over what had happened to her sister. His critical attitude toward his daughter continued through the years and eventually gnawed away at Elizabeth's self-esteem. Perhaps too, Elizabeth believed that she was never able to match Martha in their father's eyes.

In a recent book about her personal life, *Twitch upon a Star*, author Herbie J. Pilato reveals that Elizabeth had a "dark side," looking for the "bad boy," choosing to be involved with troubled men, some of whom abused her. The conflict with her father is evident—while trying to please him, she also rebelled against him. Elizabeth seemed to have what the author calls a "father complex," falling in love with older men, some deeply disturbed. Married four times, Elizabeth never seemed to find real happiness. She died of cancer in 1995.

Barbara Walters

Barbara Walters was born on September 25, 1929, the youngest of three children. Her older brother, Burton, died of pneumonia before she was born. Her sister, Jackie born three years before Barbara, was mentally challenged. In her memoir, *Audition,* she candidly speaks of the enormous role her sister's condition and limited life played in influencing and molding her into the person she would become.

Barbara's relationship with her sister was complicated and difficult. In large part, she became her sister's caretaker early on, including Jackie in many of her own activities and foregoing many things that might otherwise have been a part of her life were it not for the fact that Jackie wouldn't be able to do those things. Barbara was embarrassed by her sister and felt guilty that she would be able to fully experience life while Jackie would never have this experience. And she understood early on that ultimately, one day, she would be the one responsible for Jackie. Thus the ambition; the need to achieve.

Sometimes things come our way and we know they are meant to help us. For Barbara, finding the book *The Normal One: Life with a Difficult or Damaged Sibling* by Jeanne Safer explained so much about her own life. Within its pages she recognized much of her own experience—"the prematurely mature child; the looming responsibility for a sibling's care and well-being; the compulsion to be an over-achiever; the fear of failure." [17]

This need to achieve, however, was way beyond sheer ambition and the recognition that she would be the one responsible for her sister's future. It was rooted in the practical role of a highly capable daughter who saw the writing on the wall as life unfolded. Her father was a famous show business entrepreneur. Barbara and her family lived in the lap of luxury—until her father lost it all. Barbara knew it was up to her to support her family.

There's no doubt that the events of her life set the stage for Barbara's future, or at least influenced what she was to become. She did achieve, well beyond what even she might have imagined—as a journalist, broadcasting personality, author, and pioneer for professional women in a man's world. Perhaps the events of her life sharpened her skills as an interviewer extraordinaire of so many notables from so many walks of life. Her ability to capture the essence of a personality in her interviews is uncanny.

Although not a replacement child in the classic sense of one born after the death of another child, the picture she paints in her memoir has many of the elements descriptive of a replacement child; carrying her parents' grief of a lost son and a challenged daughter, the burden to succeed was placed upon her shoulders early on. Barbara was not free to live her life on her own terms; there were many limitations and responsibilities superimposed on her own life.

Her personal life was complicated as well with several marriages and relationships. After three devastating miscarriages, Barbara and her husband adopted a daughter. They named her Jackie for Barbara's sister. In her memoir, Jackie's troubled years growing up are revealed. Perhaps, Jackie carries some of the legacy of the second generation replacement child.

Barbara's achievements and accomplishments are legendary. What often goes hand in hand with the role of a replacement child is perfectionism, the need to be the best, perhaps in part to make up for parental grief over the loss of a child. Barbara had to assume adult responsibility for her sister as a young person. Although this was imposed upon her by her mother, it's very likely that she took this upon herself as well, as a way to make up for her own survivor guilt: Why am I healthy and thriving, given so much, while my sister suffers and is challenged every day of her life?

Famous Twinless Twins

The article, "Leading to the "Elvis Story"" by Peter O. Whitmer, Ph.D., discusses how five incredibly creative artists of the 20th century were profoundly influenced by the deaths of their twin. Elvis Presley, Thornton Wilder, Philip K. Dick, Liberace, and Diego Rivera were each one of twinless twins whose sibling died at or very near birth. Each man was possessed with key elements of the "twinning motif": great drive and exceptional ability. Each endeavored to create something special and new through their creative talents. Whitmer postulates that "they are attempting—for a lifetime—to seek a more fuller understanding of why they lived while their twin died. It is their attempt to replicate, in life, what can only be accomplished in death. Ultimately their life's most profound driving force is toward becoming re-united with their dead twin."

Elvis, a pioneering musician who fused many musical forms, was born a twin; his brother, Jesse Garon, was stillborn. Elvis was deeply affected by his brother's death feeling that a major part of him was missing. He questioned why he had survived while his brother had been born dead. As a child, he would talk about his brother to anyone who would listen. Elvis felt a sense of guilt that he might have been responsible for the death of his brother.

Elvis and his mother, Gladys, had an extremely close connection. From the beginning of his life, people close to the family noted that Gladys was overprotective of her son, worrying that something would happen to him. Certainly, he acknowledged that his mother was the most important person in his life. But in fact, the lives of Elvis and his mother were intricately intertwined rather than having a healthy connection.

At the start of Elvis' career, Gladys spoke of her son's talent and energetic drive. She believed that it was his birth as a twin and his brother's death that set the stage for Presley's incredible success—Elvis' "destiny is to do great things. He is living for two people. He has the power of two people." Elvis longed to reunite with Jesse and pursued this desire through various channels including meditation, studying the Bible, numerology, and other spiritual avenues.

The prolific writer Thornton Wilder was a twin whose brother was stillborn. Having never really "known" his brother, it's fascinating that he carried his twin with him throughout his life. Jules Glenn's paper, "Twinship Themes and Fantasies in the Work of Thornton Wilder" highlights two main themes in Wilder's literary works—the survivor theme and the rescue theme. It's been suggested that Wilder had survivor guilt over the death of his stillborn twin. As for the rescue fantasies, this literary device may have been Wilder's way of seeking atonement for his survival while his brother died.

Wilder was fascinated by twins and wrote about them in his plays and fiction, most notably *Our Town*, *Such Things Happen Only in Books*, *The Bridge of San Luis Rey*, and *Theophilus North*. In fact, although the latter work is part autobiographical, it also fictionalizes the imagined life of Wilder's deceased twin. Whatever guilt Wilder might have felt about his brother's death, he chose to keep his brother's memory alive through his creative works.

Philip K. Dick was a science fiction writer from whose works the movies "Blade Runner" and "Total Recall" were adapted. He was troubled and driven his whole life by the loss of his twin sister, Jane, who died at five weeks of age. "She (Jane) fights for my life and for hers eternally... My sister is everything to me." A life of panic attacks and a failed suicide attempt were the result of Dick's identification with his sister that was so tightly bound up with her that he had difficulty forming his own identity apart from her.

Liberace, a talented showman and musically gifted performer, was a twin whose brother died at birth. A child prodigy, he learned to play the piano by ear at the age of four. He was recommended for a scholarship to the Wisconsin Conservatory of Music by age seven, and by eleven was playing piano in movie houses and burlesque clubs. Liberace felt that the death of his twin had much to do with his own great desire and need to perform. Interestingly,

Liberace's flamboyant style and dress was said to have greatly influenced Elvis.

Diego Rivera, a Mexican painter who established the Mexican mural movement, started drawing at the age of three, one year after his twin brother Carlos died. He worked compulsively, often to the point of exhaustion. Rivera became internationally known and his work served as a vehicle for social reform. But no matter what his success, loneliness and a sense of failure followed him.

Inherent within all of these lives are the many themes of the replacement child—dead siblings, unresolved parental grief, identification with the deceased, identity confusion, the need to achieve attention and/or individual glory, and the desire and struggle to become one's own person.

PART TWO

Psychological Dynamics

What lies behind us and what lies before us are tiny matters compared to what lies within us.

—Ralph Waldo Emerson

IV. Idealization of the Deceased Child

It's easy to idealize someone that you don't know.

—Craig Bruce

◆ The Fantasy Is Better Than Reality

We're all familiar with the concept of idealization; we utilize it throughout our lives in various situations and in varying degrees. Idealization may be directed at the self, at another person, or at an experience. It's when all of the positives—the best, the most superlative, the perfect–are used to describe an individual or an experience/event. On a personal level, the aim of idealization might be the attainment of perfection in beauty, intelligence, power, and so on.

We can fantasize about what having or achieving a certain someone or something might mean to our overall happiness and well-being: the perfect mate, the best job or place to live, the ideal self-image. Many of us imagine that when we acquire what we idealize, we will have achieved our ultimate goal and all will go smoothly thereafter.

When a person is in conflict and unable to reconcile dissonant feelings, a defense mechanism may be set in place in order to cope with the difficult situation. Splitting is a defensive maneuver that divides what one is conflicted about into either all good or all bad. Idealization represents the all-good side (of self, other, or experiences) where everything associated with it is seen in a positive light. Conversely, devaluation represents the all-bad side where exaggerated negatives describe the person or experience.

Idealization is considered a healthy mechanism in childhood; it's a part of normal growth and development. Hopefully, in the course of maturation, the individual comes to recognize the good and the bad that exists within everything—every person and every situation. In her classic *Our Inner Conflicts*, psychoanalyst Karen Horney makes an essential distinction between ideals and idealization, "In contrast to authentic ideals, the idealized image has a static quality. It is not a goal toward whose attainment he strives but a fixed idea, which he worships. Ideals have a dynamic quality; they arouse an incentive to approximate them; they are an indispensable and invaluable force for growth and development."[18]

Beyond this basic description, idealization has a more specific application within the context of the parent/child dynamic found in the replacement child phenomenon. Idealization of a deceased child is a defensive element found in the experience of not all, but certainly many replacement children. While idealization of a deceased person may not be all that unusual (we often tend to see people in the best possible light once they're gone), taking it to the extreme may prove detrimental to parents, remaining siblings, but most especially to replacement children.

Not every parent who loses a child utilizes idealization, however. So what could contribute to the use of this defense? Many researchers have suggested that pathological idealization may be rooted in certain factors: how invested the parents are in the deceased child, preexisting parental psychopathology and/or dysfunction, unconscious negative feelings toward the deceased child that can never be acknowledged (for example, anger toward the child for dying and depriving them of their parenting role), and deeply ingrained guilt about the death of the child (could they have done more or prevented it).

Then, of course, what must be taken into consideration is the age of the child at the time of death. Obviously, the death of a child who has had a life that everyone has shared, who is known as an individual, may have more of an impact on parents and siblings. The attachment to the child has been firmly cemented within the family. There are simply many more memories.

Early research had suggested that attachment to a deceased infant may not be as strong as it is to an older child. While there may be few to no memories of a child who dies shortly after birth or is stillborn, parents may instead turn to mourning the hopes, dreams, and expectations they had for that child. The difficulty, however, comes when parents are unable to move on with life after mourning these losses, remaining instead in an arrested state of grief.

In part, the replacement child may help mourning parents to cope with the death of another child. But the real downside for the "substitute" child is the lack of parental recognition that this child is an entirely separate individual, not someone who has come to fill the place of the "real" child who must be kept alive. Comparisons to the deceased leave the replacement child in an impossible position—they can never fill idealized shoes. Unrealistic comparisons undermine a child's sense of self and erode self-esteem.

I'm Not Bobby

The privilege of a lifetime is being who you are.

— Joseph Campbell

It's hard to imagine which is worse: being the replacement child of an infant or toddler who is still unformed and yet full of promise, or replacing a fully-grown individual who has his/her own personality and history.

Since she was very young, Rita had always felt that in her mother's eyes, she was supposed to be somebody she wasn't. But she didn't understand who it was she was supposed to be and was unaware, until much later in life, where these demands had truly originated. It was only when she examined her life in the light of her replacement child status, that the pieces of the puzzle started to come together.

My mother, basically a kind woman who meant well and worked hard to give me all the advantages, was always supercritical in dealing with me. I could never be relaxed or comfortable with her, and she probably never felt completely comfortable with me—or even really knew me for who I was.

It was only as an adult that I was finally able to understand that the reason behind my mother's behavior, and my own feelings of discomfort, stemmed from her unresolved grief for my brother, Robert (Bobby), who had died at the age of fourteen. I was born eighteen months later, as his replacement. I was even given a name that began with the initial "R" in his memory.

When Bobby died, there was no such thing as grief counseling, nor was there any real support to help people through the trauma of profound loss. And, in my family, the loss of my brother was further compounded by the death of my father before my second birthday. My mother not only did not have time to process the grief of either loss, but had to take over my father's store and scramble to keep a roof over our heads while, at the same time, she had to care for me, a toddler.

For the replacement child whose parents have not had a chance to work through their grief, there is a high price to pay. From birth, it is about who you are not. I was not Bobby. The person I was born to be was not compatible with who I really was.

If I could not be Bobby, my mother needed me to be the "perfect girl," yet another fantasy child who did not exist. When she talked to others about me, she was discussing a girl I did not recognize. This was extremely confusing to me as a child. I was being spoken of in glowing terms to other people while being constantly criticized at home.

Growing up, I was always aware that I had a brother named Bobby, but he wasn't a real person in my world, and I had no genuine sense of who he was. My mother and aunts always referred to him as "Poor Bobby" with a combination of great reverence and extreme sadness. My cousins and I, as young children, had no sense of who he had been. He was a ghost child, as the adults around us never offered us anything else that might have connected him to us in a more human way.

In fact, it seemed that to my mother, Bobby was indeed a super hero, a character in a movie: the perfect boy who never did anything wrong and never would. I, on the other hand, was the changeling: the baby who had been left in his place. And I simply could not measure up.

When I was eight years old my mother and I moved from New York to Texas. The move separated me from my much loved and greatly depended upon older half sister, who was a young adult by the time I was born. It also took me away from cousins who were peers, friends, and the rest of my extended family. It meant leaving a school where I felt happy and successful. All had provided me with a warm network of support and a sense of balance.

I began a new elementary school in Texas in the middle of the year, arriving as the "new kid on the block" when school was in full swing, which made forming new friendships challenging. The teacher was less than welcoming and the lack of support fed into my feelings that I was not good enough. This set the tone for a difficult few years. I soon felt I could do nothing right, either at home or at school.

At home, I heard how Bobby always succeeded and felt constantly compared to him. The invisible "someone else," who always seemed to walk steps ahead of me, made me feel awkward and incompetent. At school, daydreaming became an escape from feeling lost, lonely, and powerless. Insensitive to my struggles, teachers pegged me as lazy and disinterested. To be seen as successful was conditional. Everyone had expectations that I did not meet. In a world of sink or swim, I was drowning.

Years later, when I was pregnant with my first child, I had not even heard of the term replacement child. I only knew, from very early on, that my mother had huge hopes that our first child would be a boy. While she expressed that hope often, I was unaware of the real significance behind her wish and how it was so totally connected to that long-ago loss of Bobby.

With Kevin's birth, the pressure was relieved. I had finally done what it was "I was supposed to do," and it caused a healing of sorts for my mother, though I was unaware of the true impact of it at the time. If I could not be born a boy and couldn't grow into being that particular lost boy, I had at least finally produced a reasonable facsimile, and my mother took great pride in her grandson, who could do no wrong and was never compared unfavorably with anyone. And at around the age of five, Kevin was officially given my brother's set of Lionel trains, which I had only been allowed to play with as a child.

My second child, Arielle, never experienced the pressure of having to be anyone else and could be celebrated in her own right. I remember thinking at that time how much easier it was on everyone to have had a son first "for my mother," but I was still unaware of the real reasons behind her fervent wish for a grandson. Later, as I began to understand the term "replacement child," everything began to fall into place. It would take many more years for me to fully comprehend the life-long consequences for a replacement child and how little is understood of the syndrome. It was only when I examined my life through this new level of awareness, that the pieces of the puzzle started to come together to form a complete picture of my family's situation. Finally, things began to make sense.

We are all biologically hardwired to respond to perceived threats or danger in three ways: we either flee, fight, or freeze. Like a deer caught in headlights, Rita froze. After she moved, she no longer shined on her own—and too easily relinquished her power to others as a child, and later to various external sources in adult life. Viewing her life from a replacement child status has given her a whole new level of awareness of why things unfolded as they did. She realizes now that she was subconsciously afraid to be too visible as herself. She made choices out of fear of disapproval and possible criticism. This was an early set up for "people pleasing"—putting others first, but that meant always coming in second. It was only later, that she became fully aware of what she was doing.

Before and After

Johnny was a replacement child for his brother, Matthew, who died at two. At the time of Matthew's death, their mother was eight months pregnant with a daughter, Noelle.

When the tragedy occurred, their father, who is of Cuban descent, owned a hunting club. One day, when he was out of town, their mother was taking care of the dogs running around the yard. Matthew loved to play with the dogs and followed one to a nearby pond where he fell in and drowned before anybody could find him.

The father was furious and blamed their mother. He moved out of the house and refused to have anything to do with the new baby, Noelle, when she was born one month later. Her father did move back home after a number of months had passed, but Noelle feels that it was difficult for her father to have a connection with her.

Johnny was born eighteen months after Matthew's death. Both father and grandfather were named Juan, (John). Matthew was Matthew John. Johnny was named John Joseph and called Johnny. Their father very much favored his new son, giving him anything he wanted.

However, if Johnny brought home bad grades, his father and the whole extended family would come down on him, telling him they were very disappointed. If Johnny was in trouble at school his father would say, "I wish Matthew was here—he would show you the right way to do things." Johnny was criticized for behavior that was not up to the family standard, for after all, he was carrying on the family name. This was a very big responsibility for him.

His father's family placed a lot of pressure on Johnny to be perfect since that was the way his father viewed Matthew—even though Matthew was only two years old when he died. Johnny felt that he was expected to do everything right, but no matter how hard he tried, in his own mind he never measured up to Matthew.

While their mother keeps Matthew's memory alive especially on holidays and special occasions, such as his birthday, their father speaks about him constantly, saying how much he wishes Matthew was here. The father's extended family speaks about him too, recalling how similar he was to the father and that side of the family. Their grandmother still can't come to terms with Matthew's death—talking about him constantly, keeping his clothes, and crying for him.

Noelle feels that she was basically ignored by her father. Although he did spend some time with her and taught her how to ride a bike and to drive, he didn't make time for some things that were important to her. A professional dancer, Noelle's father came to only one of her dance performances. Although in line to be the replacement child, she was "passed over" for the male replacement and was not compared to Matthew.

Their parents divorced when Johnny was eight years old. He remembers constant fighting and arguing between them—each blamed the other for Matthew's death.

Johnny tried to achieve, to be smarter and not to disappoint; he would do extra things to try to be noticed. But no matter what he did, he knew that to his father, it was never good enough. Needless to say, Johnny felt discouraged and suffered low self-esteem.

Johnny is sad that his brother wasn't around, that he missed out on not having a big brother and envied friends who did. Over time, he found himself trying to connect to Matthew spiritually. Johnny's take-away from all of this is that when he has children of his own, he'll raise them differently. They will be praised, they won't be pressured to achieve (other than for themselves), and they will not be subjected to family fighting.

There are pictures of Matthew around the house and some in his father's office, along with a teddy bear that belonged to him. His father talks about Matthew in a time that connotes 'before and after'—"this happened after Matt died; this happened before Matt died." Matthew's death measures the meaning of time for his father.

For some parents with unresolved grief, idealization of a deceased child may reflect the static nature imposed on life after the death of a child. It's the sense that time stands still, that life is arrested after the death of a child. Life is not lived in forward motion but in the memory and reverie of the past.

Angel/Devil

Maria was born as a replacement child for her sister, Maria, who was burned in a fire in their home in England. It was on a January morning and four-year-old Maria was playing on the floor with her twin sisters, Elsa and Margaret who were six-years-old at the time. Their father lit the fireplace and went to work. But there was no screen in front of the fire and a spark ignited the young child's nightgown.

Their mother, Nina, was upstairs feeding her newborn son and thought the children were only playing when she heard their screams. Young Maria, covered in flames, somehow crawled to the bottom of the stairs where their mother found her and tried putting out the flames with her bare hands. But Maria died in the hospital, 95% of her body covered with burns.

Their mother never recovered from the tragedy. She blamed everybody: her husband for lighting the fire and not putting up the fire screen, and the six year-old twins were accused of not doing enough to save Maria and, in turn, were beaten and sent away to live with relatives. Only her brother, John, escaped punishment. His status was eventually elevated as the only son in the family.

For many months after the tragedy, Nina would spend the day in the cemetery at Maria's grave, while rocking her newborn son in his baby carriage. Nina's doctors told her that the best thing she could do was to get pregnant again as soon as possible, which she did. When another baby girl was born, she named this child Maria. At the point of this Maria's birth, her twin sisters were nine years old and her brother was three.

Still in deep mourning for the first Maria, this new baby girl, though bearing the same name, could not take her sister's place in their mother's mind and heart, although that was exactly what she was expected to do. The new Maria then bore the full brunt of her mother's deep depression and disappointment.

Early on, Maria remembers that in her mother's heart and mind, she was never good enough. Her mother was detached from her, completely emotionally unavailable, and

Maria always felt neglected and unloved, seeing herself as an ugly duckling. Nina did almost next to nothing for Maria's care, even neglecting her daughter's basic needs. It was her father who made breakfast for her and helped her get ready for school. But he did not know how to be emotionally there for her or how to protect her. He never spoke about the first Maria.

Maria was constantly told by her mother how wonderful and perfect the first Maria had been and, as a "substitute," she grew up feeling unworthy, unprotected, and insecure. Her mother was physically abusive and constantly let her know that she was a poor substitute, at best. Maria was shy and withdrawn, totally lacking confidence in herself.

Every Sunday, Maria was taken by her mother to the cemetery to put flowers on her sister's grave, bearing her own name. Her mother would kneel and cry at the grave stone that was affixed with the smiling image that Nina had chosen—that of a four-year-old child with blond curly hair—while the Maria who stood solemnly by, was the dark one with brown hair and eyes. Her mother would say to her, "God has taken away my angel and given me a devil in her place."

Maria remembers thinking that it would have been nice to have known her sister, although if her sister had lived, her own birth may have been uncertain. As for bearing the same name, Maria believes that that actually made her feel closer to her sister.

It was a difficult house for all. Maria's escape while young was to daydream and to play with the local farm animals near her home. She knows that she had a talent for tennis but was never encouraged, so gave it up, and instead became obsessed with going to the gym. Although not outwardly rebellious as a child, Maria was caught shoplifting when she was fifteen. Her mother told the police that she did not want her back.

It is no surprise that Maria often got involved with men who were controlling and some were verbally abusive. She believes that her low self-esteem and lack of confidence allowed them to walk all over her. She's very conscious of the problem and is still working to better understand the issue, as well as her behavior.

To get away from her unhappy home, Maria married at eighteen and, by nineteen, had twin boys, Nicholas and Richard. She divorced her first husband eight years later. Her third son, Oliver, was born during a second marriage. But that marriage and the next one also ended in divorce.

For most of her life, Maria has been dealing with the fact that her mother didn't love her for who she was, a unique individual in her own right, and that she was simply born to replace another Maria, who achieved a level of perfection when she died that could never be equaled.

Now in her fifties, Maria is still dealing with issues of self-esteem, for herself and in her relationships. To her credit, she has developed some very nice friendships, people who encourage and care about her. She now enjoys good relationships with her sons; this is to her credit as well, since Maria was not mothered herself, and had no role model.

She is a gregarious woman who runs her own interior design business in Halifax, West Yorkshire and is starting a cake baking business, expanding on yet another talent she's always enjoyed. To Maria's way of thinking, having been treated so badly as a child helped develop a fearless approach to things, such as starting new ventures and taking personal risks in business.

Maria feels that the family might have had a chance for healing and coming together in a healthier way if there had been counseling, but that was not a common thing to do in those days. Her mother, Nina, was most likely suffering from depression even before the tragedy struck, since she felt trapped in a marriage that she thought held promises that were never delivered and was very resentful.

As a devout Catholic, Nina felt that she could not leave to go back to her family in Italy and was resigned to her life in Manchester. She never fully acclimated to life in Britain, never felt fully comfortable with the English language, always spoke with a heavy accent, which was difficult to understand, and had few friends.

Now in her nineties, Nina is suffering with Alzheimer's. She still has a photo of the first Maria near her bed, and still cries over the memory of her deceased child, even though her memory for everything else is all but gone. Although feeling love for her mother is very difficult, Maria feels she's closer to forgiving her.

This is a life story in the extreme. We have much to learn from Maria's life and her experiences growing up. The story is almost textbook for the worst that can happen to a replacement child. No child should ever be born just to take the place of a deceased sibling. No child should ever have to experience a "dead mother," one who is detached and emotionally unavailable, one who is incapable of nurturing and giving love. No child should ever be devalued or face ridicule and judgment simply because they are not the desired "other." When a child's identity is undermined, when basic trust is denied, when love is withheld, it's highly probable that a child will have difficulty establishing future healthy relationships—unless the cycle is somehow broken.

I Am Not Alone

Trevor's story (not his real name), like Maria's, is one of extremes and certainly not usual or typical. Beyond parents' unresolved grief after the loss of a child, what sets these stories apart from many others is very probably pre-existing pathology of one or both parents. Grief often lights a fire under issues that were already in existence, making those issues even more intense.

My name really doesn't matter. I could be the kid down the street or a co-worker, your cousin or a prisoner, a taxi driver or successful business mogul; it really doesn't matter, because I lived under a false identity my whole life.

I lived with constant and incessant anger, jealousy and resentment over the physical and emotional abuse my mother rained down upon me while my father turned a blind eye and barely even acknowledged my existence. I am an unbearable perfectionist, correcting everyone around me, and I have control issues that are simply out of control. My siblings were doted on and have become powerful and hugely successful people, while I floundered through life, unable to keep a job for more than a few years, blaming myself for failure after failure. To say that my depression was constant would be like saying the ocean is wet.

Through a fluke, I searched the Internet for the term "replacement baby," a name I had given myself years ago as I slowly became aware of the circumstances of my sibling's death six months before my birth. I very quickly discovered I suffered from Child Replacement Syndrome, and that my forced role in life was to assume my dead sibling's identity and endure enormous pressure in pursuit of this impossible goal. Of course, I failed, and my mother made sure that I remembered that I was a failure countless times.

My older sibling died after his second birthday of a fatal illness that was diagnosed six months prior to death. I was conceived during this period as my parents watched their son die. My parents never allowed themselves to grieve and our dead sibling was rarely talked about; my father turned guiltily inward to himself while my mother exploded with rage, rejecting me early in life, never holding me unless she had to, as if love was out of the question. Consequently, I suffered several suspicious injuries that put me in the emergency room multiple times before my fourth birthday and endured false accusations, whippings, beatings, scape-goating, verbal abuse, ostracism and shunning nearly every day of my life after that at the hands of my mother. The memories of this undeserved violence and hatred have haunted me my entire life, and I have blamed myself for causing this, thinking I had done something so horrible in my past that I deserved this treatment, but I had no idea what my crime was. I reacted very badly myself, resorting to anger and violence to nearly everything around me, because that was all I knew.

Somehow, I survived my childhood. I stayed as late as I could after school before going home, joining student government and sports teams to prolong my day. I hid in my room with my door shut, avoiding all contact with my four other siblings and my parents so that I could not be accused and punished for any made-up offense. I graduated with a 3.6 GPG that was the lowest of all my siblings save one, and was punished for the three "C" grades I received in high school with loss of car privileges, grounding, and days of verbal abuse. I went 3000 miles away from home to an unheard-of school at my father's suggestion, and went there in an attempt to please him and escape my mother's wrath. I paid my own way through college without my well-to-do parents' assistance while they put three of my other siblings through college out of their own pockets. And on and on and on and on... I finally ended all contact with my family years ago when the last, unrepeatable verbal assault occurred, with my family's wrath and coldness directed towards my loving wife, son and daughter as well as me. It was the hardest thing I've ever done, to admit failure and defeat because you cannot get along with your family.

But you're not a failure until you stop trying, and I was on a lifelong search to find the "why" of all of this; I actually screwed up the courage and asked my loving grandparents if I was adopted at age 10, and they assured me I wasn't. But I'd never lost that feeling and now I know why; I never was allowed to be who I really am, a loving, giving and caring, extremely bright and talented person. But I grieve over lost decades of depression and the knowledge that it was my mother that destroyed my relation with my family while punishing me for her son's death, and that I never had a chance.

I have found peace and forgiveness in knowing I was not the source of my family's collective sorrow and ostracism of me, and I have begun to reach out to one of my older siblings who, unfortunately, was one year old when the death occurred and may suffer from Child Replacement Syndrome as well. I will be attempting a slow, cautious reconciliation with my siblings, as their disdain towards me is a programmed behavior and a result of the incredible violence they witnessed; it is not their fault and I have found unconditional love and forgiveness for all of them, despite the fact that some will have a bias against me for the rest of their lives. As for my parents, the people that raised me, my forgiveness towards them has stalled and I may sadly never see or talk to them again. But I believe my real mother and father died that day as well, and when I look at family pictures from before my birth, I see two loving and wonderfully happy people with the world by the tail. I forgive those people, those people my parents were before tragedy struck, for those two people did not kill my sibling either.

My name doesn't matter, because I am the replacement baby I had always darkly called myself, and I am not alone. I know that a vast number of people in this world are in their own darkness, anguished without truly knowing why. I am one of the fortunate ones; I can finally live my life as myself, and I have allowed myself to restore my dead sibling's rightful, truthful and honorable birth order place in our family, and I am blessed with incredible friends in my wife and children. My anger at the unfairness of my life falls off in chunks as I forgive the many assaults that were directed at me, and I replace that anger with newly found love.

I miss my older sibling. We would have been the greatest of friends.

Trevor's parents used him as a vessel to relieve their guilt, sadness, anger and disappointments. Not only was he severely devalued for who he was, but a wedge was driven between him and his siblings, further isolating him from everyone in his immediate family.

Though Trevor acknowledges that he still struggles with issues from his earlier years, his story is one of triumph. He realized that the identity his parents tried to force upon him, of being unworthy and "less than," was not who he is. He has drawn on his own inner strength and resources, and this has enabled him to become visible as himself and to value himself as the bright, talented and caring person he always was.

V. The Replacement Child's Search for Identity

If you try to view yourself through the lenses that others offer you, all you will see are distortions; your own light and beauty will become blurred, awkward, and ugly. Your sense of inner beauty has to remain a very private thing.

—John O'Donohue

◆ Who Am I?

The identity disturbance seen in the replacement child is often tied to incomplete parental mourning and its consequences. In their paper, "The Replacement Child: Variations on a Theme in History and Psychoanalysis," Anisfeld and Richards note that when the first child is not adequately mourned, the parents may fantasize that the deceased has been "magically restored to life by the birth of the second."[19] It may prove detrimental to the replacement child if he/she replaces a deceased child too soon, before the grieving process is completed, because the deceased child still exists—not here, but still exalted and occupying emotional space as if they were.

The danger in this scenario is that the expectations held for the deceased child may be fully transferred to the replacement child, thereby robbing them of their own identity—the right to their own set of expectations and hopes that would naturally accompany them from birth. The Cain study pairs a *pseudo resolution* of parental mourning with a *pseudo identity* for the replacement child.

The denied loss of a child can be likened to a corpse kept alive subconsciously by the parents. It's as if the deceased cannot truly rest in peace while the grief surrounding their death remains unresolved. Full acknowledgment and resolution of grief allow for the very necessary emotional burial to take place. Unconscious attachment to the deceased must be released in order to allow for attachment to another child. "Substitution inevitably fails to heal the loss it is supposed to erase, or the emptiness it is supposed to fill. Pain, psychoanalytic concept maintains, cannot be skipped; it can only be repressed and displaced or lived and transformed." [20]

To understand the concept of identity more fully it's instructive to turn to the work of Winnicott, most specifically, the notion of *true self* and *false self.* For Winnicott, the true self is the core personality. From his work, *Ego Distortion in Terms of True and False Self,* "Only the True Self can be creative and only the True Self can feel real."[21] True self can be thought of as one's authentic "experience of aliveness." It's the principle that defines who each of us is to our self, the being we individually recognize as having our own unique ongoing experiences.

The false self is the way the individual learns to adapt to the environment. The false self can be viewed as the protective shell surrounding the core personality or true self. It's the part of you that has learned to comply with what the environment/society/parents requires of you in order to survive. So you learn how to please people, to push your own needs aside, to act in a way other than what feels true or real for yourself, and to repress your feelings.

But it's not all black and white where true is good and false is bad. Positively, the false self can protect the true self by establishing healthy boundaries, allowing the individual to adapt appropriately in social situations without revealing all of their real thoughts and feelings. The pathological false self requires that an individual comply with environment/society/parents in an unnatural forced way. This is often seen in replacement children who must comply with unrealistic or idealistic demands to assume an identity that is untrue and fraudulent; as such, a pseudo-identity.

Throughout his work, psychiatrist Vamik Volkan draws upon the concept of the replacement child to illustrate how transmission of trauma, as in the devastating loss of a child, plays out on the individual level. He postulates that the mother deposits the idealized image of the deceased child into the replacement child. It's now the child's task to find a way to deal with what has been transferred, all the while trying to establish a sense of themselves as a separate individual—one's self-realization.

As for the replacement child, there are several possible psychological "solutions" to this situation, or shall we call it, dilemma. In the best-case scenario, the replacement child may be able to successfully integrate the deposited or transferred identity of the deceased child into his/her own self-representation. On the other hand, the replacement child may struggle with a "dual identity" of self and other, working double duty to maintain both individuals (even though one is dead). Finally, the replacement child may attempt to buy into competing with the idealized image of the deceased through perfectionism and overachievement in order to prove their worth—almost always a futile effort.

Ideally, the *only* solution is for the replacement child to be able to individuate, to establish an identity that is true self, real, authentic, creative and alive in its own right.

A word about identity confusion needs to be included here. Siblings share a common experience within the family, different from the other relationships. In *Children's Encounters with Death, Bereavement, and Coping,* Balk and Corr note that, "A period of identity loss or identity confusion is another part of the grief process for many sibling-bereaved children... When a sibling dies, a child's self image and sense of self is called into question." [22]

The family unit is left to deal with how to be a family without the deceased child, and as such, how to fill the hole left by the loss. Bereaved siblings may feel the need and the responsibility to "fill in" for the deceased child. Identity confusion may occur when a bereaved sibling feels she must somehow be not only who she was before the death but a "surrogate" for who their sibling was as well.

Balk and Corr suggest that, "Reorganizing the family system requires family members to reconstruct what the family means to them and their sense of identity as a family. In addition, family members must reapportion or abandon activities and roles formally assigned to the deceased... Open, honest, and supportive communication within the family system is essential to all of these tasks."[23]

So in order to avoid the dilemma of the replacement child, a few essential things must happen:

- Parental mourning must be completed.
- The subsequent child must be allowed to be who he is in his own right.
- The family must reorganize the family unit, accepting the loss while holding a place in memory for the deceased child.

An Adoptee's Search for Identity

I feel that because I am adopted and was always told that, I was 'special' which meant 'different,' because I was actually two people. One was AnnMarie Touchette, born in a Catholic Home for Unwed Mothers. The other one came into being when, at age two weeks, I was placed in a home in a Massachusetts Norman Rockwell Community in the Berkshires. I was given the name of June Marie Sembenotti and took on the script of that family.

It was a cold bitter winter night in a small Western Massachusetts town in December 1944. Marie was home with her fourteen-year-old son, Edwin (nicknamed Tookie). Her husband, Bill, was working the 3-11 shift at the paper mill. Edwin had a classmate, Susan, over to study and she stayed for dinner. After they finished their homework and had eaten dinner, they sat on the front porch talking. It was starting to get dark out and time for Susan to go home.

Now in most situations, Edwin would have been the person to walk Susan home. However, Marie told Edwin that he had to stay home and clean up the dinner dishes and that she would walk Susan home. When Marie returned, the dishes were sitting in the soapy sink water, but Edwin was not in the kitchen. Marie called for him and looked all around the house. Edwin didn't answer. Marie called over to the mill and Bill came home and together they searched for Edwin. They found him out behind the barn; he was lying on the ground, a pistol beside him. The ambulance came, Marie rode with them, and Edwin died in her arms of a self-inflicted head wound.

The Catholic Church, family and friends felt Marie needed something in her life to help her overcome this tragedy. Bill had his job at the mill to occupy his time, but Marie was home alone. They had moved to the other side of town, away from the home where tragedy happened, and were ready for a new beginning.

March 1946, the adoption agency called to tell them they had a baby girl available for them. Bill was excited. Unfortunately, Marie had wanted a son, attempting to replace the one she lost. She didn't want a girl, but Bill insisted. They brought the baby home. Tension started the minute the baby was placed in her arms.

Everyone in the small community knew they were adopting. They didn't want to keep the name AnnMarie because of the popular comic strip "Little Orphan Annie." They decided to change the baby's name to June Marie, since it was the month they were married, as well as the month that Edwin (Tookie) was born. If Marie couldn't get a boy she would do her best to keep a connection to Edwin.

Marie was even keeping all of Tookie's possessions in the closet of the bedroom, which was now June's. They told June never, ever to open that closed door, all the while idealizing Tookie by telling stories of his life.

I was never read a storybook, never treated with any show of affection; never held, hugged, or given any show of love. Marie wanted to do anything that took her away from me. They were good Catholic church-goers and had no guilt over leaving me home, as an infant, alone in my crib, when they went to early morning Mass. Evidently I must not have behaved well in Church so I had to stay at home.

This went on for quite a while until I was old enough to walk and talk and got out of the crib and went into my parents' room and picked up the telephone. In those days, there was the "Operator, number please," friendly voice on the phone. She asked enough questions as I chattered on in baby talk, to figure out that I was home alone. The town was small, so the operator knew my parents and had to have a talk with them. After that, they made sure my bedroom door was locked, so that I couldn't get out, or to the phone.

As I got older, Marie got over being reclusive; anything to get away from me. She joined a bowling league and it became her passion, bowling three-four times a week and leaving me with my Dad who even had to take me to work with him. I became "Daddy's Girl." Marie really didn't like it when I got old enough to join my own bowling league.

I wasn't allowed to have a social life. Not supposed to play with the neighbor children. Once in school, I wanted to join the Girl Scouts. I was only allowed to go to the meetings but was forbidden to go overnight camping and had to drop out when they wanted me to go sell cookies. I was allowed to take piano lessons because Marie and Tookie were both musical and I guess my Dad figured that if I could be musical, Marie and I might have a common bond. Unfortunately, after years of lessons, I really never was good enough for her to play her violin with me.

At age fourteen, going into puberty was not a pleasant time. I wasn't allowed to have outings or go to the movies or parties, like the other kids. I never celebrated a birthday with a party. I was told I had to 'give that up for Lent,' which always seemed to fall right around my February birthday.

I tried to commit suicide by taking a bottle of aspirin. This was the same age that Edwin had successfully committed suicide (and Edwin became idealized when he committed suicide). I never felt anger towards Edwin—I felt that he probably had to put up with a lot from them. They were so restrictive and strict by nature. He had no choice. I didn't die, so I had to be strong enough to survive and vowed I would get out of the house as soon as I could.

I ran off and married the first guy that had the nerve to defy my parents and ask me out on a date—I was sixteen and not allowed to date until I was eighteen. We actually ran off and then allowed to get married. I was seventeen and he was nineteen. He turned out to be a drinker and physically abusive. I stayed married to him for three years and the blessing was a son.

Marie was also happy that I had a son and became very possessive over my child.

I had to get a job and relied on my parents to babysit. Marie was all too eager to babysit, and very reluctant to hand my son back. She accused me of being an unfit mother. There were many battles. Marie would also call my son 'Tookie,' the nickname of her deceased son. In her mind, he was hers. Life does get better with age and when my son and I were able to move away, Marie stopped talking to me. Whenever I would call home, if she answered, she would just hand the phone to Bill without saying a word.

In 1995 Bill passed away and it was then that my sense of reason prevailed and I returned home to take care of Marie. There just wasn't anyone else that could take care of her. There were grandchildren but they had their own lives. Finally, in July 1995, Marie died, after telling me that she never, ever wanted to adopt me. The final stab was to write me out of her will.

That same year for my birthday in February 1995, I journeyed to Egypt where I had a life-changing experience and reclaimed my identity, changing my name from June to AnnMarie. I had done a birth search and met my birth mother, who petitioned the courts for my original birth certificate. Today I am re-born as AnnMarie Touchette.

In *The Primal Wound: Legacy of the Adopted Child,* therapist Nancy Verrier addresses the consequences of separation from the birth mother for the adopted child. It's not just about a baby, but rather a mother/baby unit that has spent forty weeks together and that shares an intimate bond unlike any other. Verrier wondered why little attention was being paid to this essential fact. Adoption has always been defined by a triad: a birth mother who can't keep her baby, the baby, and adoptive parents who want the baby. What seemed to be implied was that caregivers were interchangeable.

After much personal research, Verrier hypothesized that this mother/child connection is a profound one and "that the severing of that connection between the child and biological mother causes a primal or narcissistic wound which often manifests in a sense of loss (depression), basic mistrust (anxiety), emotional and/or behavioral problems, and difficulties in relationships with significant others.... The awareness, whether conscious or unconscious, that the original separation was the result of relinquishment affects the adoptee's sense of self, self-esteem, and self-worth."[24]

In situations such as AnnMarie's, one can see what happens when there is ambivalence about the adoption to begin with. And further, one can imagine the consequences for the adopted child who must deal with the fallout from parental ignorance and insensitive treatment.

The Man Who Had No Life

Jack is seventy-eight, grey, well spoken, very intelligent and lives alone in a four-bedroom home he once shared with his deceased father. He had been his father's caretaker for thirty years. An Irish bachelor, he is uncle to a large crowd of nieces and nephews. They are often confused by his not having work, other than caring for grand pop who was lively, ambulatory, and had a girlfriend. He seemed to be a lost soul and was referred to as "not having a life." Jack was seen as hidden away, getting a free ride, lonely.

Jack had daily rituals that were almost monastic. He rose, went to mass up the street from his home, prepared breakfast, read the paper, and did odd jobs around the house. His visits to doctors with his elderly father, as he aged, were his main occupation. He read voraciously, watched TV, and went to bed early. How did he get this way? Did he not have ambition? He was a college graduate. What was the block?

Jack was born the third child of two very poor Irish Catholics who had married at nineteen. His parents were the children of immigrants from Ireland, escaping poverty and famine. Jack's parents were thrilled when their first child turned out to be twin boys. Talk about the "luck of the Irish!" They named them Jack and Hugh.

For six months, they were the talk of the small street on which they lived. Six months passed and they were smiling and playing with each other in the crib. They cooed to each other. These babies gave their mother joy and pride. The grandfather would sing to them and bounce them around on his lap. "Two for one, two for one," he'd say. One day, their mother, concerned about their constant cries, took them to the doctor. An intestinal obstruction of a genetic sort occurred and, within a few weeks, both babies died.

A pall hung over the home for months as the young people mourned this loss of both sons. The grandparents were heartbroken. One, in fact, died shortly after that. It was into this pit of grief that Jack, the second, named also after his father, was born about eighteen months later. He was a towhead, lively, and bright.

Expectations for him were high. The story still is told about how he almost died with the same intestinal problem as his brothers, but his frantic mother took him immediately to the hospital where a new procedure had been developed and he was saved. He was to be the light, the replacement for all the pain and loss. Jack, as eldest, was held to high demands. He had to be great in school, to do well in college. He was even given the middle name of an old English castle that was the link between the poor Irish and the rich Irish in the family. If he did well, he might be left a fortune by the unmarried aunt. This myth was destroyed when years later, she committed suicide and nothing was left to anyone.

The story of the twins was not openly discussed in the family. No one visited graves; it was as though nothing occurred. His sister was scolded one day when she told the nuns that her mother had twins. The teacher sent home a note saying that the sister was lying and needed to be watched, since there was no record of twins.

All eyes were on Jack as he moved out into the world. When he failed swimming in a Naval academy, he was sent home as a seaman rather than an officer. Jack was publicly humiliated by his father for his failure. It was as though it was the end of the world. Jack was made to feel as though he had caused shame and death in the family. He was supposed to give life, show the way, and be Jack and Hugh. It was all riding on him.

After several years of living as a seaman, Jack tried the business world and California. His mother always felt he should be a priest because he was good and kind. He began to have problems with his need to control. He dated inappropriate women. His efforts to create a life kept getting stymied. He projected his own need to be perfect onto others and they did not like it. Though he loved California, he was lonely.

When his mother died in an auto crash, he flew home. He made the pronouncement that he was staying at home. His father did not want this, but Jack firmly felt he had to step into his mother's place. He had learned to be the "replacement." His father and he were often at odds over who was in charge. Even when his dad had a new woman friend, Jack stayed on.

The early years of his father's retirement were often referred to as Jack's retirement, too. They lived almost as twins, doing everything together. Jack did not date or see other people. His father did. As the father aged, Jack became his essential caretaker, much to the relief of the rest of the family, some of whom lived at a distance. Jack felt he had a purpose and his father was now grateful and kind. His father lived to be almost a hundred.

Jack came into life at a time of profound grief and death. He lived amidst ancient Irish energies of loss and famine. His twin brothers literally almost starved to death because of the intestinal obstruction. He tried to fill that emptiness with his knowledge, his kindness, his caring for everyone, but himself. In his later years, he lived alone, relished his books, his faith, his house.

Young Jack could never quite step into the shoes left when the twins died, much to his father's disappointment. Jack's life seems to have been arrested in adolescence or in young adulthood, even though he did leave home and did attempt to make a life for himself in the adult world. A life's purpose seemed to have been missing until Jack saw himself as his father's caretaker. In this role, he could be appreciated for his efforts. But the price he paid for gaining his father's favor was the relinquishing of a life of his own.

Sweet Alison

Sometimes, identity confusion for a replacement child has little or nothing to do with parental expectation or pressure, but is rather the result of the thoughts and feelings of a child who is highly sensitive to her life circumstances. Trisha can imagine how her parents must have felt when they lost their daughter. But it's been very difficult for her to express to them how deeply the death of a sibling has affected her over the years. Even now, she believes that her father must think that when she expresses how she feels about her sister, she's trying to say that she wasn't desired or loved for who she was, and is, as an individual. But that's not the case at all. Her conflict had little to do with her relationship with her parents, but rather her relationship with herself. Trisha has survivor guilt. It would take many years for her to feel that her own life was truly separate from her baby sister.

I was born into a family with two older siblings, John and Hillary, on March 17, 1965 on the outskirts of Sheffield, England. My "baby" sister, as I always called her, Alison Jane, was born on February 9, 1964. From the beginning, she had problems retaining her food and with projectile vomiting. She was hospitalized at the age of eleven weeks old and diagnosed with a heart defect. Both parents were with her when she died on the evening of May 11.

I was conceived shortly after Alison's death. My mother told me that she had always wanted three children. My father later remarked that my mother was extremely anxious while she was pregnant and after my birth. She would check often to make sure that I was breathing while I slept.

I remember my mother speaking to me about Alison when I was very young. She once told me she had planted flowers in her garden and for years I thought they were called "White Alison." They were, in fact, White Alyssum.

My mother kept a photo of Alison, which was delicately placed in the Bible in her bedside drawer. When I was about six or seven, I would go often to look at the photo. I would say to Alison, as I looked at her image, that I was sorry to have taken her place and hoped that she would forgive me. If I heard footsteps I would rush out of the bedroom as if it was forbidden.

My mother spoke to me of Alison's funeral and would take me to the Peace Garden, where Alison's ashes were laid among the beautiful scented roses. My siblings do not remember ever being taken there.

I am not sure I had to fill in for Alison, but I felt I had to be alive, keeping my mother's head above water and keeping her happy. I always tried to please her. Teachers reported that I worried too much, got upset easily, and always tried very hard. I feel that my mother's anxiety influenced my life. I had little confidence in myself, was always a worrier and afraid not to give my best. Often, I had feelings of guilt.

My mother said that she was never able to cry for Alison. When I was already married and living in France years later, my brother-in-law committed suicide. My father said my mother had screamed with pain. I think that on that day she also cried for Alison.

It was from that day that all my childhood thoughts and memories of Alison, my "baby sister," came flooding back. I could not even mention her name without feeling as though I was being strangled. I became anxious and was unable to sleep. I had blocked her out of my life for so many years but, unconsciously, she was within me—a part of me.

I felt that our paths came together and I could not let her or our mother down. I had to live "our" life. I had been given the chance to live; she hadn't.

Along with this came guilt and depression. My role in life seems to have been to help my mother get through her bereavement.

I can now accept that Alison is a part of my story, but that we are two separate beings. She is beside me—but I feel I can let her go and be me. I can now listen to my own emotional needs. I felt I had given birth to Alison during a dream I had. It was after that dream that I was able to let her go.

Beyond individuating from Alison, being able to understand herself as a separate and unique person from her deceased sister, therapy has helped Trisha to work through the strong and often difficult emotions she's had to deal with virtually alone over years. Family members have had a hard time understanding Trisha's personal struggle with her identity apart from her sister. At times, she has felt as if they think she's "talking rubbish" when she tries to explain her feelings—she wants her family to understand what she has lived with. For Trisha, it's important to tell her story so that other replacement children who have similar thoughts won't feel that they are alone or crazy.

Lightning Strikes Twice

Michelle was born on September 10th, the same day that her five-year-old half brother, Aaron, her father's son from a previous marriage, died of leukemia in a different hospital in the same city. On the day of Michelle's birth, her father traveled back and forth from the hospital where her mother was giving birth to the hospital where his son was dying. They waited for a few days to tell her mother that Aaron had died. From that day on, her father became emotionally distant. Michelle's mother and father divorced when she was only three years old. Both of her parents remarried within the year of the divorce.

After years of trying, her father and stepmom had a son, Christian, when Michelle was fourteen. They lived several hours away from where she was living with her mother and stepdad. Michelle's father would come at least once a month to take her to her second home.

Michelle describes it as a confusing time. At the age of four, she was known in town by her mom's new last name, which was the name her mother used to register her for school. When Michelle was with her father and stepmom, she was known by her "real" last name. She had a double last name and learned to play the role of both, depending on where she was and whom she was with. She never felt like "daddy's little girl" to either her biological dad or to her stepdad. That added to her confusion. Her biological dad missed out on coming to her birthdays, recitals, and games when she was a cheerleader. Her mother tried to make up for her father's absence by always being present for her daughter. However, Michelle craved her father's attention.

Michelle hated her birthday because she would think how sad her father must be on that day. She knew that he had always adored his deceased son and was very close to his younger son, Christian, Michelle's half brother. She felt she had to work harder to be accepted, especially since she didn't live with her father and did not see him that often.

As an adult, Michelle once asked her father, "Were you afraid to love me?" He answered, "I never thought of it that way," and then the subject was dropped. She then asked him, "Why couldn't I be your little girl—daddy's little girl?" There was no answer. In some way, Michelle feels she was being punished for being born on the same day her brother died. She's seen pictures of her father holding her as an infant but his face lacks expression; the look in his eyes is empty. Her father said that he was just not good with infants. But Michelle knew that he was much more of a hands-on dad with Aaron and Christian. As an adult, she now understands that look.

There was a lot of inconsistency in her life. Michelle lived in two different worlds: her father and stepmom lived out in the country, while her mother and stepdad were very social people living in a big Texas city. From the outside, things looked perfect. Her father never mentioned Aaron, but kept pictures of all three of his children on a wall in his home. Michelle was very proud of her dad for many reasons—for one thing, he had built his home with his own hands and could fix anything.

Michelle and her ex-husband, parents of a daughter, eighteen and a son sixteen, are divorced after seventeen years of marriage. Their son, James, was an identical twin, but his brother was stillborn. Michelle had a feeling, a "mother's intuition," that something wasn't right shortly before her son's birth. The doctor covering for her own doctor was having difficulty finding a heartbeat. He explained that he thought it was there but that it was hard to detect. This explanation didn't sit well with Michelle.

While undergoing a weekly sonogram, Michelle was able to detect that something was very wrong by the expression on the technician's face. A doctor confirmed that there was no second heartbeat. Michelle felt great sadness but strangely, almost a sense of embarrassment. People had given her baby showers for two. She thought about the fact that she had two of everything, ready for two babies, and people were expecting her to have two babies.

When the babies were born the next day, Michelle kept thinking, "I have a dead child and a live child." She took photos of the deceased baby and they had a funeral for him. When driving to her son's funeral, she saw a sea of people—people who were there for a child they never knew. The first person she saw standing by a tree, was her dad. When she got out of the car, she ran to him. They held each other and both cried. It was then she realized the ripple effect of her relationship with her friends and family. The irony about her son's death is that it brought together her birth parents and her stepparents. She said she felt her heart smile as she experienced the great unconditional love that all four parents had for her and for all three of her children. Michelle remembers the funeral was heart wrenching, but beautiful.

On her nightstand, she treasures the white lace baby blanket and silver cross given to her at the funeral. On top of the blanket is an engraved crystal box containing the hair of her deceased son. Her ex-husband, like her dad, was in so much pain that he did not know how to be open about the baby's death. They were not sure how to discuss it with their children or when it would be the right time to tell them.

Michelle believes now that the situation was handled poorly. She finally forced the issue of telling her son, then ten, and daughter, twelve, about their little brother. Michelle felt strongly that they needed to know that there had been another child. It was especially important that they would hear it from their parents and not from somebody else. She hated that it was handled as if it was some dirty little secret.

Michelle and her ex-husband told the children together; they all were able to share their feelings and express their emotions. Michelle was extremely grateful when the children's father explained to them that she had wanted to tell them about their brother long before this. It had been a heavy weight on her shoulders.

When the children were very young, Michelle would frequently take them to the cemetery. She found this to be healing, to have all her babies at the same place at the same time. They would picnic under a nearby tree and the children would play happily, not understanding what a cemetery was. When they were old enough to understand, Michelle wanted to visit the cemetery as a family, to honor and acknowledge this child. All five of them gathered together, finally as a whole family. She had dreamed about this moment for ten long years. The children brought flowers and it was a very emotional experience for all of them.

The twins' names were already chosen before they were born. Her living son is James Daniel. The deceased child was to be named Jacob Aaron—Aaron in honor of the brother who died the day Michelle was born. However, she couldn't see burying a second child named Aaron, so the second twin's name was changed from the original choice, and carefully chosen—Matthew Thomas; Matthew meaning gift from God and Thomas meaning twin.

Michelle has great regret that the children weren't told about their brother when they were younger and that it was not handled in a more natural way. She also regrets that the children don't feel that they can talk about their deceased brother now. James has asked if he was the firstborn twin, which he was. He expressed that he always wanted to be a big brother. When Michelle asked if he ever thinks about his brother, James says that he does and always felt that something was missing.

Michelle senses that it's more difficult for other members of the family to connect to the idea that this child was a real person, since he was born dead. But as his mother, she felt a strong connection to her twin babies for the thirty-six weeks before they were born, so the loss is still difficult for her. Often she would look at James and think, "There should be two of you."

The fact that her ex-husband had not been able to talk about this child freely, and did not share the loss emotionally with her, made the experience even more devastating and lonely. Michelle advises that anyone going through a situation similar to hers should talk about it right away, making it more of a natural part of life.

Identity confusion is pervasive in Michelle's story. Growing up, she lived in two separate worlds: two sets of parents living very different life styles. Her relationship with her father is painful to observe in her story. There was nothing Michelle had done that could explain his detached relationship toward her—except that her birth coincided exactly with the death of her brother. It's clear that her father hadn't recovered from his son's death. His incomplete grief seemed to find expression in the idealization of his deceased son versus the devaluation of his daughter.

Michelle married a man whom she believes, not unlike her father, would have benefitted greatly from professional help to process the loss. Her insistence on finding a place in the family for her deceased twin son was a courageous act. Michelle had learned all too well what can happen to a living child when a parent has not fully grieved the loss of a child and she was determined to break that cycle.

The Need to Be Seen and Heard

Writer and publicist Patti Hawn reflects on how her role as a replacement child influenced the person she became; how being a replacement child helped to shape her individual identity.

I'm from the generation that felt psychotherapy was the "answer." Even if you didn't know the question–it was the answer. I have done everything from EST, analysis, group therapy, marriage counseling, workshops and ALANON. I've gone from blaming my mother, to understanding my mother, to forgiving my mother. It seems mothers hold the key to most everything. And there doesn't seem to be an expiration date on any of so-called "mother issues." When I was asked to write a chapter on my experience as a "replacement child" I was reluctant. Do I really have to go back and revisit my experiences once again? My mom left this earth twenty years ago–and to tell you the truth, the thing about my mother that I most wish for–is simply one day more with her.

That said, there was something intriguing about the commonalities that these so-called replacement children purport to have in common. THE NEED TO BE HEARD.

My mom lost her mother when she was three years old. Raised by her aunt, who provided a loving family, she nevertheless felt "different." My mother gave birth to a son shortly after her marriage to my father and lost this child at three months old. I was born within a year and a half. My firstborn was given up for adoption and I gave birth to my second child within the following year. We are all replacement children in our own way. I have never quite understood, until recently, why much of my life has been lived with the burden of never quite being satisfied with taking a seat in the back of the room. Sometimes this trait has been troublesome and other times it's served me. But, clearly it exists as an integral part of me.

I assumed, in my ongoing quest for "what makes me tick," that my personality was somehow most likely wrapped around the fact that I have a famous sibling. However, I am now rethinking this.

In my earliest memories, I recall needing to be reassured consistently that I was being heard. I remember cupping my small hands around my mother's face to make sure she was paying very close attention to whatever I needed to say. I obviously dropped the act of hands-on-face as I grew older–but time and time again it was apparent that I sought out any and every opportunity to be heard. I learned quickly to identify the people who could give me undivided attention. I spent much of my early childhood with my Aunt Sarah, my great aunt, who took on the role of my grandmother. Much of my childhood memories were of being in her house with her. She made me feel special, something I rarely felt in my own home.

My life has taken me to many places and I've done many things with a variety of folks. I've worked in politics, social work and the film industry. But the reoccurring theme has been the need to surround myself with a cast of a variety of people. If this is not happening I often feel something is missing. The need to be seen and heard is probably inherent in most replacement children. Although it may show up differently in all of us—I'll bet it's a trait shared by most of us.

Patti is correct. The need to be seen and heard is taken up a notch for the replacement child, simply because they frequently are invisible as themselves. The inability to see a child for who they are in their own right may result in a child's seeking out people and situations where they will be seen and heard. Sometimes, this is beneficial; for example, when a child attempts to set themselves apart through some kind of achievement or accomplishment. On the other hand, gaining attention through risk-taking may have consequences that aren't in a person's best interest.

As we've observed, when parents and other family members are incapable of providing a child with nurturing and the space to be who they are, it is often someone from the outside (another family member, a teacher, a neighbor down the block) who is able to provide this. The recognition that members of your immediate family may never know and acknowledge you as you are is enormously painful, but it may also be just a fact of life, and one that may not have anything to do with you at all. Finding someone who can provide a "corrective emotional experience" can be very healing.

VI. The Replacement Child's Need for Perfection

When perfection is driving, shame is riding shotgun and fear is in the back seat.

—Brene Brown

◆ When the Best You Can Be Is Not Enough

Most of us would agree that there are certain essential factors that nurture healthy growth and development within a child: a feeling of safety and protection, a genuine sense of warmth and caring from parents and significant caregivers, an appreciation of the child as a unique individual, and a real commitment to encourage and support that child's developing potential. If the way a child perceives herself is based on the notion of "real self," then the child's ability to explore and live up to her full potential can be realized.

However, if these basic factors are lacking, the child may develop certain defenses that are recruited to compensate for the anxiety produced by feeling unsafe, unappreciated, and unloved. In other words, the alienation from the "real self" prevents the child from knowing and expressing her own authentic feelings.

Self-realization is the healthy desired goal for all humans. A less healthy alternative exists when identity is dictated by *self-idealization*. What this means is that the idealized self tries to compensate for a sense of inadequacy, low self-esteem, and the inability to acknowledge one's true nature.

According to psychoanalyst Karen Horney, self-idealization inevitably manifests in the *search for glory*[25] where the individual creates a persona for himself that exemplifies all that is right and perfect; this in spite of the fact that the individual unconsciously feels that he is flawed, deficient, and imperfect. The quest then, is for the individual to live up to an ideal that may have nothing to do with who they really are—*the tyranny of the should*.[26] This means that they're driven to do what they personally believe they are supposed to do. There are even times when this directive is non-verbal; there's a tacit understanding in the family that this is just the way things should be—this is what is expected and nothing less.

Let's clearly state, though, that perfectionism is not always a negative thing. In fact, many personality theorists including Maslow, Adler, and Murray have examined the positive aspects of perfectionism. Healthy perfectionism may be thought of as the desire and/or need to overcome obstacles and to achieve one's goals on the way to realizing one's full potential. This describes "being the best you can be" but in a way that mirrors what is true and real for you, the individual, and that brings satisfaction to the self from the inside, as opposed to from outside of one's self.

Replacement children often respond to the enormous demands placed upon them with perfectionism. And if parents remain invested emotionally and psychologically in a deceased child, the hopes and expectations for that child may be transferred to the replacement child who may be silently (or verbally) coerced to fill the shoes of the deceased sibling.

But it doesn't stop there. Often there are unrealistic and idealistic comparisons to the deceased that a replacement child can **never** adequately fill. Interestingly, the *idealization* of the deceased child is a fantasy brought to life by bereaved parents, while the *idealized self* of the replacement child is a response to the fantasy of the 'larger than life' deceased sibling. The striving for perfection is a way of competing with the idealized deceased. Replacement children may be frequently reminded that they can't match up to the excellence of the deceased and that they never will. And even if they could excel in reality, their efforts would still be seen as lacking and inferior.

For some RC's, perfectionism finds its expression in the desire and goal to make up for their parents' devastating loss. "If I am perfect will that alleviate my parents' grief?" Many replacement children believe that it's up to them to achieve and to excel, to be the best at whatever they do, so that their parents will have a reason to feel life is worth living; in essence, they create a role for themselves within the family—to be the savior of their parents. Sometimes a replacement child will even do double duty, taking it upon themselves to achieve not only for themselves, but for their deceased (or incapacitated) sibling as well.

For many replacement children, the striving for perfection is the act of going around and around and really getting nowhere. It's simply exhausting to be constantly front and center, attempting to live up to the unrealistic expectations of their grieving parents. And the fact is, that while there is unresolved parental grief, the replacement child cannot be seen for who they are outside of the parents' fantasy. What follows for many replacement children is an erosion of self-esteem and confidence, at times accompanied by anxiety and depression. And yet, the need to overachieve, to handle everything and every situation in perfect order and control, and to be "the best," may continue.

We should mention that in addition to replacement children, bereaved siblings may take it upon themselves to adapt behaviors intended to console their parents for their great loss. Balk and Corr note that a bereaved sibling "will usually try to suppress her grief or hide it from the family members. She is hard on herself, tries too hard not to get in trouble, and strives for perfect grades, athletic achievement, or other markers of success. Striving for perfection helps her to feel less out-of-control, as if by being extra-good she can somehow soothe her parents' pain and compensate for her sibling's death and for all the pain and turmoil the family is experiencing."[27]

The goal for the replacement child, or for that matter any child filling in for a deceased sibling, is to move away from the idealized self-image and the self-hatred it generates. The goal is to relinquish the need to doggedly control life through perfectionism, to give up being "the good one" all of the time, to please others at the expense of one's own true feelings, and to "save" the family from past and future pain. The goal is to move toward adaptability, flexibility, and spontaneity to one's real feelings—a true return to the real self.

A Substitute for the Original

Barbara teaches what she knows. Her writing is instructive and inspirational. Having struggled to find her own identity, her own expression, and her own voice she understands that this is a problem for many, not just replacement children. We all want to be seen for who we are and what we stand for in our individual lives. It's a challenging task for many people, but when you carry the extra baggage of a replacement child it's all the more difficult to find your way on your own path.

I am an English professor, specializing in teaching composition, teaching developing writers to find their writers' voices. It is quite ironic, then, that I have spent decades searching and ultimately finding my own voice. As the replacement child, I have learned to over-compensate in many areas of my life, working tirelessly toward a stronger self-confidence, self-esteem, and self-worth. My own writing in my book, The Replacement Child's Journey: One Woman's Search for Her Own Voice, *recounts the ultimate acceptance of my legacy as my brother's replacement and my rightful place in all areas of my life: as a wife, mother, daughter, and educator. My writings also relate to others who are on their own journeys of discovery.*

I am the replacement child, a permanent stand-in for the original—a substitute for my older brother Jeffrey, who died at age two. His photos embedded around my childhood home reflected a healthy, easy-going, jolly baby. Sadly, he contracted meningitis, losing his capacity to see, hear, talk, or think and died within six weeks. My distraught mother, who lay in shock, was paid a visit by the family doctor, who slapped her across the face to stop her hysteria. He then told her to move on, to think of her own worried parents, and to attend to her other son who needed her.

Thus, my devastated mother, without any therapeutic support, was told to try again for another baby, as if she were playing the lottery or trying to win another goldfish at a carnival. Three months later, she was pregnant with me; thus, I entered the world with my despondent mother spending most of her days in bed, and my father nurturing me when he could, when he was home from his tireless days at the office. Despite the relentless sadness that held my mother as the fog held our city, my foundation was one of love; my father's love was complete and absolute while my mother's was conditional and sporadic.

Within her uneven love for me were tremendous trepidation and anxiety, especially when I was sick. In fact, her fear that yet another child could die manifested into anger upon any cold, flu, earache, or childhood illness that I contracted. I would often try to hide how sick I really was, for I didn't want to upset my mother, worry her needlessly, or even worse, send her to bed, where she announced she would go when too many people and too many events had exhausted her—when I had exhausted her. It was a dance I learned to play. I suppressed any negative feelings, emotionally or physically, in the hopes that my mother would remain more at peace while I suffered silently, always repeating my soon-to-become lifelong mantra—I'm fine. No problem.

Thus, I sensed early on, the fragility of my position within my mother's world, that I was second best, that I wasn't the planned original, and my legacy was sealed. I became a tireless people-pleaser, willing to do anything and everything, and as I aged, such people-pleasing was often at the expense of my own energy, time, and needs. First and foremost, though, I wanted to please my mother. I always knew I could depend on my father's love, for when he saw me, he beamed. However, he was often very preoccupied with his business and the exhaustion that overtook him upon his return home after work from his twelve hour work days. My mother was the one person whose love I could not quite capture in its entirety, yet I continued to seek her complete attention and devotion all the more, for almost our entire lives as mother and daughter.

I was almost always the good little girl, doing whatever my mother wanted me to do and being the sweet child that would secure my tenuous position in her heart. I naturally extended this goodness to everyone—other family members, my friends, teachers, and anyone else in authority. Thus, my needs and desires were second to those of others. I became a Gumby, of sorts, twisting myself into whatever position and form was needed. No matter what I did, though, it wasn't quite enough for my mother.

While she would occasionally acknowledge my accomplishments—my academic achievements, a new position at work—such comments were always couched in tones that belied her disappointment in my one monumental decision for which she could never forgive me. I left the home of my birth—I left for college—never to return home to live, but as she saw it, I left her. The message was clear; as her only daughter, I should not have wanted my own life. The implication was equally as clear; she had me to replace Jeffrey and now I was leaving her, which was especially unacceptable as a female. She told me that she never would have left her own mother.

As a result of my 'understudy status,' I became an astute reader between the lines, lines my mother would often repeat in various ways, "I only wanted two children." "I didn't plan that Jeffrey would die." When I became pregnant with my third child, with shock and disgust upon hearing the news, she asked whether I had heard about that surgery they do to prevent this from happening again, for she believed that two children were enough. Stunned, I asked her where I would be if she had chosen that surgery after Jeffrey was born. Again, she repeated, "That was different. I only wanted two children. That's enough, Barbara. I don't want to talk about it."

My older brother Stephen, who is almost seven years older than I, has no memory of Jeffrey and incredibly, no memory of loss. Despite the photos showing the two of them in matching coats, holding hands, Stephen has no recollection of his little brother or of that time period. Stephen grew up, then, without the inheritance of replacement; his birthright was to wake up in the morning and be quite perfect in his own skin and in our mother's eyes, a legacy that continued throughout his life. He had nothing to prove to anyone, most of all, to our mother.

Yet, for me, as a result of being the replacement child, I never felt good enough, smart enough, thin enough, and over the years, my self-esteem, my self-confidence, and my self-worth were compromised. Early on, I wanted to become a medical doctor despite my challenges with math. I was reminded that I was a female, that I wasn't supposed to understand numbers, and that I certainly couldn't be a good mother if I were seeing patients while my children were home alone from school. I also wanted to work in the Peace Corps, but my mother's fear of my going far away, even of my driving, of my being hurt in any way, underscored that there was no way I would be able to leave for another country when I wasn't permitted to drive alone through Golden Gate Park.

I wanted to eat the foods I loved, but I was told early on, as a round ten-year-old, to watch it. The meaning of those simple words, was actually you are fat, and they catapulted me into a slow, but consistent, life-long eating disorder, at first limiting my calories, then my self-esteem. Recovered from the most severe symptoms of my teenage anorexia, even today, while I am thin enough to indulge in the foods that I have spent a lifetime avoiding, I still hear her voice reminding me to watch it and I stop myself from eating what I truly want.

I have approached many areas of my life with trepidation and an underlying hesitation that I was not as smart as or quick as others despite data to the contrary—in the form of grades and degrees. I instinctively felt that I had to study harder than others to make up for my limitations despite my strong academic standing in various forums. I found, though, that despite my limited self-confidence in my intellectual abilities, I excelled in school. My education was the one area in which I was very successful without huge comparisons, probably because education, while respected, was not a priority in our household.

In fact, I was the only one in my immediate family with the desire to pursue higher education. My father encouraged me while my mother reminded me that college should provide me with my MRS. Degree, and to that end, she advised me to study at either the law or medical libraries in order to find a prospective husband. At that time, I never questioned that those areas of intense study could have been for me, that I could have studied either of these disciplines successfully, and that I could have become a lawyer or a doctor. Still, I fought against and eventually through, my issues of low self-esteem and carved out a noble and rewarding career as an educator. Even with my three degrees, and a fulfilling teaching position in my chosen field, my mother shook her head in disbelief and incredulously asked me one day, "What do you want, a career?"

As a result of never quite being enough for my mother, I, too, internalized these feelings of never being enough in my own eyes. I could not completely own my outstanding grades and advanced degrees, for I did not truly feel that they were connected to my intelligence. The admirable raising of my three sons still fell short of what I felt other moms had accomplished; my long-term marriage filled with respect and love still could have been improved. My devoted friends held pieces of my heart, yet I often felt alone.

It really wasn't until later in life, with my children almost grown and with more time to myself to think, to go deep within, that I began to acknowledge that I did not have to work so hard to show up in my own life. Through this internal process of reflection and introspection, writing, and therapy, I learned to accept myself, to actually feel completely enough in my own eyes despite how my mother felt about me.

During the last conversation my mother and I shared, two weeks before her death, I found my self-acceptance despite her disapproval. She was lying in bed, sharing her disappointments in life, of which I was one. I told her that I was sorry I wasn't the daughter she wanted, the daughter she needed, but that I loved her so much and I always would. Even then, at what could have been considered to be one of the last profound moments of cathartic honesty between us, I imagined her stating that not only was I the daughter she wanted, but that I was the best daughter in the world, that she was so happy to have had me after poor Jeffrey's passing. But, her only comment was, "We don't always get what we want." Such a comment would have devastated me in the past, but I was fortified by the knowledge that I had done my best, that I had loved my mother and I finally believed that her limitations were not my own.

As the child born in exchange for another, Jeffrey for Barbara, the unsteady ground of my existence resulted in my continuously having to prove my presence in all ways to most all people. Today, though, I gloriously accept myself. *I am grateful for all that I am and have, for I recognize it has been relentless, intense work; nothing has come easily. My own pathway of such meditative writing took me through a long, dark tunnel, but I have come out the other end, to experience extreme gratitude for what I have been given and what has been taken. I have endured and flourished, and joyfully accept my growth, reclaiming my sense of self, my worth, my confidence, my esteem.*

Second Best

Elizabeth's story illuminates many issues that affect a surviving child when a sibling dies, one of them is survivor guilt, another is the grieving over a lost sibling. Parents in the throes of unresolved grief may leave a surviving child psychologically and emotionally on their own. If parents are unable to deal with their own issues, they are likely incapable of paying attention to surviving children, especially when it comes to acknowledging and dealing with a child's grief after the loss of a sibling. In some instances, a parent may attempt to "mold" a surviving child into the child they lost. These issues unattended have the potential to drive a huge wedge in the most significant familial relationships.

I was not a replacement child. I was not born to replace my sister, but I knew I should not have been the survivor. I was not the precious one. I was not the gift from

God. I was the slower, more reclusive child. They had given birth to the perfect child; the perfect mix of my parents, and I was second best. Rebecca was the child parents dream of. She was beautiful and above all, smart; the dream child to the yuppie family.

Rebecca died when I was six. I had not had time to develop my own sense of being—my own personality. I will not insult my parents. They did not neglect me, nor did they abuse. They just had their own special way of letting me know that I was not enough. Twenty-eight years after my sister's death, I still know I was second best... and here my story begins.

My mother and father were and are more in love than any couple I have ever met. Their love and respect for one another shines through. Rebecca, my elder sister by fourteen months, was born with congenital heart disease. My parents had barely learned how to be parents much less deal with a second pregnancy when Rebecca needed her first emergency surgery. They loved their sick and needy family with all of their hearts. But one child's life was at risk and that was the child they had to focus on.

I was not born to replace my sister, but after her death, I felt as such. I had been a tomboy all of my life. But once Rebecca died, I was all that was left. My father had adored me from a young age; we had a special bond. Once Rebecca died, my mother molded me to her image of the perfect child.

April 27, 1985, was a less than memorable day in South Florida. Rebecca and I played in the house as the weather was overcast. We could not climb our beloved trees or climb the fence to the schoolyard that backed our own backyard. We soon grew tired of each other's boredom and constant attention.

After dusk our boredom turned to agitation and Rebecca shoved me into a wall, as little sisters tend to annoy their siblings. I remember my mother's harsh words to her as she shoved her back, "How does it feel to have someone bigger than you pick on you?" I was so proud and surprised that my mother stuck up for me. But soon I would learn to regret it.

The next day, mama brought Rebecca and me to the Country Club. It was an overcast day, but we loved to swim and my mother was more than happy to have us out of the house and relax with her friend, Tonya, who tagged along. After a few hours of play, my mother and Tonya decided to run to the store and get a few things. They left us in the care of the lifeguard and warned us not to go into the "big pool." We were both excellent swimmers and there was no fear in leaving us in the small community pool with the lifeguard on duty.

The next hour is a blur. At some point, Rebecca went under water and never resurfaced. A doctor who happened to be at the County Club with his family grabbed Rebecca after noticing she had been under too long. The ambulance came; the paramedics worked feverishly to save my sister on the flimsy poolside table. Mama and Tonya got back just in time to jump into the ambulance. Rebecca was pronounced dead at the hospital.

I don't remember any of the next few days. I know I was not allowed to go to the funeral at the insistence of my grandparents and I know my parents changed forever that day. The biggest change in my life was that I had just lost my best friend. Not only did I lose Rebecca, but due to our closeness in age, many of our mutual friends faded away as their parents thought it was too upsetting for them to play with me and remember my sister.

My mother and father changed so much. Daddy was angry and Mama so sad. She began to drink heavily and he spent very little time at home. My grandparents, aunts, and uncles, and godparents were a blessing. They kept me with them and tried to keep our family together.

I can't remember if my mother ever told me that she wished it had been me, not her precious Rebecca, but I know I have felt that way ever since. For twenty-eight years I have questioned whether my mother hates me because I survived, because she defended me the night before Rebecca died, or if she just didn't have the will to parent any more.

My mother and I fought so intensely growing up that I rarely stayed at their home for a week. I would go to my grandmother's, relatives', or our family friends' homes. I didn't want to play the piano, be a proper girl, or be shown off like a doll. I wanted to run wild and play in the dirt.

At some point, my mother came back around. She tried to spend time with me, but by then, I was angry with her. I began to blame her for Rebecca's death and certainly for the neglect I felt after. I didn't understand how she could just stop loving me, but in essence I had stopped loving her.

At eighteen, I married my boyfriend and moved out of the house. I wanted to know what it felt like to be loved and not judged each day, not live in a home where I was second best to a corpse. I continued to run away from the past and my parents for the next few years. I ran from God and my ethics and morals. I acted out in ways that I now regret. I put my family and friends through hell while I tested the waters and took way too many risks.

At twenty-one, I found that I was pregnant with my daughter, Taylor. I was frightened, young, and completely unprepared. My parents were so angry. They did not speak to me until after the child's birth and then only to tell me how stupid I was to keep a sick child. You see, Taylor was born with Down syndrome and the general consensus was that I could not raise a sick child, as I was still a young girl myself.

I refused to listen. Taylor was a gift from God. Yes, she was special. Yes, she needed extra love, but she was mine—all mine. I could raise her to know she was enough and she would love me no matter what. Taylor was due June 25, 2001, but she was born via emergency caesarean on April 27—the anniversary of Rebecca's death.

Taylor and I endured a few very tough years. I was an inexperienced mother with little financial support and even less common sense. I struggled with her illness and her slow progression, but no matter what, I let her know she was the child I wanted and I loved her. She showed me each day how much she loved me and that I was worth loving. She changed me. My life changed drastically.

I went back to college and finished with honors. I met my husband, quit acting out, and reconciled with my parents. You see, all that I needed was unconditional love—

the love I had had from my parents and sister prior to her death.

The replacement child in our family was my little cousin Cristina. Cristina was born the following year and she brought joy back into our lives. She was a beautiful, intelligent child much like Rebecca. She had raven black hair, walked on her toes, and had a huge vocabulary from a very young age—all qualities that my sister had. Not a week went by that I was not with her. She often spent the night with me and I could not wait to see her each day.

Cristina has always had sadness about her, a very serious streak. I wondered and worried about her. The worry came to a head when Cristina turned seven. She became withdrawn and had nightmares. Her mother, my aunt, asked me to speak with her. We walked to the pond by her house and sat on the grass with the sun beaming down. I asked why she seemed so sad and she responded, "I am seven now. Becky died when she was seven. Everyone says I am just like her, so will I die now, too?"

It hurt me so badly to hear this. I did not realize that in keeping Rebecca's memory alive we were hurting this sweet little girl. I assured her that she was not Rebecca. Although she had many similar qualities, she was her own person and would grow up to be strong and healthy.

The death of a child affects more than just the parents. Research shows that siblings struggle throughout their lives with the loss. They always miss their deceased sibling and yearn to know more about them throughout their lives. The surviving child has to deal with not just the loss of their friend and playmate, the only other person on earth that knows exactly what their life was like, but also the grief of their parents, friends and family. The change in the family dynamic and the redefining of roles within the family are a burden for the surviving child as well.

It's important to note that in the case of an accident or illness, a surviving child may need to be reassured that just because they are related to a deceased sibling or connected to another significant child who has died, does not mean that they are in danger of dying at an early age. This may become more of a concern for a child as they reach the age at which their sibling or other significant child died—especially when comparisons have been made between the living child and the deceased. A child who seems sensitive to this issue, is anxious and/or sad, or expresses feelings of vulnerability must be reassured that any comparisons made between themselves and a deceased child account for only a very small part of who they are as a separate individual.

It may be helpful to have this child "think" beyond the age at which another child has died, into their own future life. Talk about milestones such as learning how to drive, dating, getting married and having their own children. Ask questions such as, "What do you want to do when you grow up?"

My Sister's Shadow

Monica's experience is shared by many replacement children. One parent, sometimes both, and often the extended family, compare the replacement child to the deceased, leaving little to the imagination as it pertains to which child comes up short. Who the deceased becomes in *fantasy* far exceeds who they were when they were alive. In a classic situation, the deceased has been elevated to close to 'saint' status and it's virtually impossible for the replacement child to compete.

Monica, now thirty-eight, is a replacement child for her sister, Karianne—the baby of the family, and everybody's favorite—who died during heart surgery at age four. Her mother was pregnant with Monica a few months after Karianne's death. At the time of her birth, her brother was seven and her sister was already fourteen. Everyone was still mourning and missing Karianne when Monica came along and she felt like an impostor; never a full member of the family group.

There were many photos of Karianne displayed in their home and many of her hung in their father's office. The family often spoke about her—and always in glowing terms and in great detail. Monica felt that her father made an effort to be nice to her but was never warm in the same way he was with her sister and brother.

If I did something one way, I was told from an early age, Karianne would have done it this other way, or Karianne was always polite, always smiling, very neat, and so on. I was always competing with an image of a dead sister who was, to everyone's way of thinking, 'divine.'

I felt belittled as myself; that I was not seen or appreciated for who I was or for what I wanted, and my father continued to act like I was a visitor in the house. The one place I felt that I could be myself and be successful was in art class. That was the place I could express myself without anyone being critical. That's primarily the reason I became a graphic artist.

Ever since I was little, I felt I had to be something I was not and was expected to be someone I was not. I felt that everyone in the family was unhappy that I was not Karianne and made that fact very clear to me very early on in my life.

I remember repeating to myself at a very early age, 'I have to be like Karianne,' and, 'How did she do this, that, or the other thing?' Everyone in the family wanted me to be 'as nice as Karianne,' to be 'just like Karianne, to become Karianne'!! I felt jealous when they said that Karianne was 'perfect, an angel'... I felt I was never going to be like her, and I would never be able to satisfy my parents in the way that she did.

Now, as an adult, no matter how I feel about the talents and potential I possess, which is considerable, there is something inside me that is constantly telling me 'that I will never fully achieve and should not expect to'!

The relationship with my siblings, especially with my sister, improved after I had children. It took until then for her to see me in a different light, one as an individual in my own right, another adult, and not just as a rival or poor imitation, to the lost and adored sister, Karianne.

I tell myself that I don't care that I cannot please my mother and know in my heart that I never will. However, I find myself still trying, even though I know that it is an impossibility and it will never be enough! It still gives me a hopeless feeling with her, but it is something that, sadly, I have to accept.

Many replacement children reflect that they have felt like strangers in their own family. Monica felt like a visitor, an impostor, and others have described feeling like an outsider and even an alien, removed from the familiar circle. It's as if every one else in the family shares a common experience, except you, the replacement child. And often, this is the case—everyone knew, if only for a brief period of time, the deceased child, except for you, the replacement child.

VII. Survivor Guilt

True guilt is guilt at the obligation one owes to oneself to be oneself. False guilt is guilt felt at not being what other people feel one ought to be or assume that one is.

—R .D. Laing

◆ It Should Have Been Me

Survivor guilt is a psychological condition that stems from an individual's belief that they have done something wrong by surviving a catastrophic event while others have not. Survivor guilt is thought to be part of PTSD (posttraumatic stress disorder) and may manifest as a result of a natural disaster, during combat, in the course of disaster response, with widespread illness or epidemic, as a result of an accident, and in the aftermath of ethnic or large group catastrophe such as the Holocaust, civil war, slavery, and genocide.

Survivor guilt is also evident in the replacement child syndrome where the trauma has occurred at the familial level. In the simplest terms, if a child dies, or is incapacitated, the parents remain grieving, and another child is born, or designated, to fill the void left by the loss of that child. The replacement child may come to believe that he/she has been allowed to live while another has died. That child may even come to feel that he/she is somehow responsible for the death of the deceased sibling, reasoning that "the other would still be here if not for me." Along with taking the blame for their sibling's death, the replacement child may feel that he deserves to be punished for taking another life.

From a logical perspective, it's clearly not a child's choice to be born, and especially to be born to "replace" a sibling who has died. When parents are absent emotionally because they are consumed with their own grief, a child may be left to his own devices. The unconscious thoughts and fantasies of very young children who don't understand what has happened or what is expected of them may run rampant. In the extreme case, parents may fuel the fire when they message the replacement child about the idealized original child, the one the replacement child comes to believe they can never compete with.

The dilemma of the replacement child is that they are required to live in two worlds: the world of their own emerging identity and the world of the imagined identity of the deceased through the parents' eyes; as such, a double identity. The survivor child's guilt may center on feeling like an impostor, having taken the place of the other preferred child. There may also be a modicum of guilt that accompanies unconscious resentment toward the sibling whose shadow the replacement child must walk in.

In "Life after Death: The Replacement Child's Search for Self," Kristina Schellinski notes that, "Guilt may also arise from the fact that the "I" is not truly "I," that the replacement child is not free to live his or her own life, and may therefore feel a sense of guilt toward his or her own self realization." [28] Of course, too, the atmosphere is permeated by the guilt the parents surely feel at not having been able to prevent their child's death.

Symptoms can run the gamut in individuals who suffer survivor guilt and may include anxiety, depression, nightmares, and low self-esteem. Social interactions may be awkward and uncomfortable and may serve as a vehicle for the "punishment" the child survivor feels she deserves; for example, being bullied and/or singled out for group ridicule or ostracism. Ultimately, breaking the cycle of survivor guilt requires that the individual comes to understand that he was not responsible for the trauma, but has suffered as a result of it.

Consolation Prize

Adam is the first child of his father's third and his mother's first marriage. In the mid-fifties, his father had two sons from his first marriage. The older son, then six or seven, was hit in the head by a rock while playing with friends, and died. Eventually, his father divorced his first wife and "disconnected" from his younger son, not having any contact with him since the early sixties.

Remarried and divorced once again, his father married Adam's mother in 1969. Adam was born in 1973 followed by his sister in 1975. Adam feels that this second pair of children, a son and a daughter, disappointed their father because they didn't duplicate or measure up to the two sons of the first marriage. Adam believes that he is a replacement for his deceased half-sibling.

A retired attorney, Adam remembers his father as always distant emotionally, except for openly expressing anger. He describes his mother as an "emotional and psychological wreck," especially since his grandmother's death. His parents divorced when he was about nine or ten years old. Adam went to live with his father while his sister stayed with their mother. After the divorce, his father remarried for the fourth time and his mother eventually remarried, divorced, and remarried again.

There was a total lack of stability through Adam's childhood; his parents were always fighting. They never talked about the dead son, even though the father felt closest to that child. There was no remembrance of this son—no discussion about the anniversary of his death, no birthday remembrance, no shrine, and no "wall of pictures." Adam has never been to his half-brother's grave, and he does not think his father has ever visited his son's grave since Adam was born. The only real thing his father continually emphasized to Adam was that he had to be very careful because "accidents happen," and people could be killed in tragic, unexpected accidents or violent incidents such as shootings or stabbings.

In memory, Adam was given his brother's middle name as his middle name. Adam recently attempted to find his surviving half-brother from the first marriage but was unsuccessful, perhaps because that brother was adopted by his stepfather. A major issue for Adam is the way his father has been able to cut off contact, to break close ties with his children. Aside from totally disconnecting from Adam's surviving half brother, his father has broken contact with his daughter for a couple of years and, at one point, for three years with Adam.

It's very clear that his father never got over the death of his first son. Adam always felt like a replacement child; felt inadequate, felt that he always did things wrong, that he was a disappointment. Adam has always felt undeserving of positive things such as happiness, pride, and success. He has always felt uncomfortable (and undeserving) when receiving gifts, and each year he feels guilty on his birthday. As a child, Adam remembers showing his father gifts that his mother had given to him and remembers his father always responding in disgust, commenting about what a waste of money the gifts were.

He had trouble socializing with kids in school and, even later in life in the working world. Adam now realizes that he has engaged in self-sabotage throughout his life so that he could fail to live up to his potential. Though considered to be a bright child, Adam felt little motivation to succeed in his studies and did the minimum required to get grades that were well below his ability. Adam would then criticize and belittle himself, telling himself what a loser he was for not graduating at the top of his class or for not getting into a top university. Similarly, Adam feels as though he subconsciously sabotaged his career development by quitting or causing himself to be fired so that he would be able to tell himself what a loser he was for not having advanced to a position that was suitable to someone with his abilities.

Adam believes that his "job in life" was to be a replacement for his father's dead child, but he felt like he was never able to measure up or to fit in. He always thought of himself as a flawed "consolation prize," that was inadequate and undeserving of the positive things that life has to offer.

In his childhood, he was terrified of dying, or getting killed, or getting “erased” by his father, as his father had done to his half brother. Adam was fearful of everything, especially accidents, and he suffered with terrible nightmares on a daily basis throughout his childhood. He didn’t want to disappoint anybody and especially didn't want them to think, “What are we doing with this crappy kid?” He was bullied and despised in junior high school but never told his parents about any of it. While his mother loved and supported him, his father continued to withhold emotion and failed to express affection and praise. Adam felt that he could never measure up—and that he should never measure up.

Issues bubbled up when he had children of his own. Adam wondered how his own unresolved problems might affect them. Since he had been constantly reminded that accidents happen, he worried excessively that something could happen to his own children. After beginning to experience frequent panic attacks, Adam started seeing a therapist, which has helped him address the issues of his traumatized youth—anxiety about death, the threat of abandonment, the fear of success, and poor self-esteem.

Adam paints a portrait of a very frightened young person, uncomfortable in his own skin. One can’t help but wonder where the adults were in the picture. While the notion of parents missing in action because of unresolved grief is allowable to some degree, the ongoing behavior of parents who are insensitive, uncaring, and aloof to their own children is inexcusable. Some parents, perhaps unknowingly, use the death of a child to remove themselves from their remaining children, or are mostly present for the purpose of judging and criticizing.

As we’ve seen, in many instances the replacement child is told, or is somehow signaled, that he/she will never measure up; all of their efforts will never be good enough in comparison to another. But if that were not enough, some replacement children suffer more profoundly because they are ignored; they are messaged that they’re not worth the time of day to be involved with, to be paid attention to, to be invested in emotionally, and most especially, to be loved.

◆ Trans-generational Transmission of Trauma

Many agree that there is a permeability that exists between a child's psyche and that of the mother (caretakers), a kind of "osmosis" that allows for the passing of ideas and affects from the mother/caretaker to the child. While much of what is transmitted may be healthy and normal for the developing child, that is obviously not the case with trauma. In this scenario, what is transmitted to the child from the mother/caretaker may interfere with the child's psychological growth and developing identity.

Vamik Volkan's dynamic concept of *deposit representations* sheds light on this phenomenon. These are "representations of self or others deposited into the child's developing self-representation by traumatized parents. It is in the form of such representations that replacement children carry the legacy of a parental or generational distortion of mourning after traumatic history." [29]

Volkan and Greer describe how "a mother has an internalized formed image of her child who has died. She deposits this image into the developing self-representation of her next-born child, usually born after the first child's death."[30] The replacement child then serves as the "reservoir" where the deceased child will be kept "alive." The replacement child is assigned (mostly unconsciously) specific psychological tasks in order to preserve what is deposited.

Inevitably, this presents quite a dilemma for replacement children whose own identity has been hijacked—they can't be who they are in their own right, they obviously can't be the dead person, and yet somehow they're expected to embody the representation of the deceased child from the parents' perspective.

In addition to what is unconsciously deposited into a child's psyche from its mother, there is well-documented research to indicate that the developing fetus receives not only nutrients from the mother's blood but may absorb excess cortisol from a chronically stressed mother. This may describe the existing circumstance into which a replacement child is conceived and nurtured, especially following the death of a child, or if there is long-standing unresolved parental grief.

Trans-generational transmission on a societal level utilizes a similar mechanism, except that here the transmission occurs on a larger scale; the transmission of group trauma from generation to generation. Volkan has extensively studied larger group dynamics, such as ethnic groups, and has found that, when a group suffers a catastrophe at the hands of an enemy, the self-images of individuals within the group are traumatized by this common event. The second generation then becomes the recipient of these traumatized images.

The second generation and those generations that follow are "assigned" specific tasks as well; for example, mourning for the losses of their parents or ancestors, or taking revenge on the present group representing their parents' enemies. Volkan emphasizes that, "It is this trans-generational conveyance of long-lasting "tasks" that perpetuates the cycle of societal trauma... Whatever its expression in a given generation, keeping alive the mental representation of the ancestors' trauma remains the core task. Further, since the task is shared, each new generation's burden reinforces the large-group identity and keeps its complexities '*alive*'." [31]

So whether on the individual or societal level, the issue seems to be about breaking the cycle of trauma altogether, and thus freeing all participants from having to identify with a traumatic and/or unresolved past. On a societal level, this would certainly have a healing effect on a world full of "holocausts"–wars, slavery, and genocide. On an individual level, breaking the cycle of depositing parental trauma of any kind would free children from the burden of carrying the "unfinished business," and hence, the guilt of their parents.

From the perspective of the replacement child, breaking the cycle of unresolved parental grief and the consequences that result from it, would allow subsequent children to be who they are, to own their own identity, without the encumbering load of pathological and unrealistic parental expectations.

Analytical Psychologist, Kristina Schellinski understands the replacement child from the inside out and has the unique perspective of a replacement child who now treats replacement children.

Being born as a replacement child can affect one's life emotionally and relationally in a deep, long-lasting way. While millions of individuals may suffer the repercussions of being replacement children, many a replacement child may not be aware, even as adults, of the conditions surrounding their birth and the potential life-long consequences to their mental and physical health.

And it may not stop there. Children born to replacement children, and even grandchildren, may still bear traces of this syndrome, with projective patterns, identifications and the transmission of self-representations being passed on from generation to generation.

The replacement child deserves help and recognition in the consulting room, with adequate analytical and therapeutic understanding of the condition in order to help the individual discover their own path of individuation, finding their way back into their own life. Despite half a century of research and efforts to raise awareness for the specific suffering of the replacement child, the replacement child syndrome often still goes unrecognized by the individual concerned and by the treating therapist.

I was born six months after the death from appendicitis of my two-year-old brother, held and raised by my still-grieving mother whose child was buried in the cemetery across the road from where I grew up. This fact was hardly touched upon in my own training analysis until I was able to formulate its effects on all aspects of my life in my thesis.

Since then, I have worked in my practice with many replacement child clients/patients. I can attest to the life-bringing quality of offering the replacement child deep understanding and empathy, helping the adult replacement child, even when they are much older, to uncover their true identity from the ashes of the "dead other." Exploring new self-representations and discovering the inalienable source of the unique human being alive within, amounts to a virtual re-birth into true life.

The Big Secret

Gabriele Schwab, drawing upon the work of Hungarian analyst Terez Virag (*Children of the Holocaust and Their Children's Children*) notes that key pieces of information can be transmitted, can be passed down, without ever speaking about them. "...unconscious identification with the persecuted or exterminated members of the family was clearly observable... the symptoms, the play activity, the dreams, the fantasies of the children made it very clear that they knew about the family's secrets." [32]

In *Secret*, psychoanalyst Philippe Grimbert writes about his life as a young man growing up in post-war France. The story weaves fact and fiction in a semi-autobiographical account of his family's history prior to his birth. In essence, Grimbert had to reconstitute the family story, taking the little he actually knew about his parents and their life and imagining the rest. All of this, twenty years after his parents jumped to their deaths from their Paris apartment. For all of that time Grimbert had been in mourning, trying through analysis to make sense, to come to terms with the hidden truth of the "secret."

As an only child—one he describes as a thin, pale, and bookish boy, somehow not a fitting offspring for his athletic parents—he creates an imaginary older brother. In addition to his invented brother, Philippe creates a family story from the little he has been able to piece together.

In fact, what he imagines about his brother is true—a half brother lived and died before Philippe was born. He learns that this brother was his father's child from a first marriage and that his parents had had a passionate love affair, even as their spouses were lead away to die in Nazi camps. Eventually Philippe learns about his Jewish past, something he had always known, and learns that the family name had been changed from Grinberg to Grimbert to better fit into life in France as a Catholic family.

Philippe is a replacement child. In *Secret* we can feel his pain as he paints himself as a weak, wimpy specimen of a son compared to what he imagines his brother to be. He disappoints his father; his brother is the son his father wanted. Philippe is the carrier of the hidden family history—the secret never to be acknowledged. But he knows. And it is only through confrontation with the harsh truth and the guilt, exposing the past for what it was/is, and grieving for that tremendous loss, that he is finally set free.

Following in My Mother's Footsteps

Good Girls Don't is the debut literary effort of entertainment publicist Patti Hawn, who is the sister of the legendary film actress, Goldie Hawn. Her book is a deeply personal first-hand account of what it was like to be trapped in an unwanted pregnancy at the close of an era where home economics took precedence over sex education. Her story starts in her childhood home in Takoma Park, Maryland, where as a teenager she became pregnant by her high school boyfriend. In the typical "solution" of the era, she is sent away to have the baby in secret and gives up her infant son on the day he is born. This is where the typical adoption story begins… and ends.

In my sharpest memory I am surrounded by dark. I sit at the top of the stairs and listen. Sounds are harsh. Angry voices rise and fall. I am compelled to stay huddled into the corner of the hallway night after night, commanding my post like a small sentry. Wrapped in a blanket, I huddle against the banister straining to hear every word; I tuck my bare feet under my white flannel nightgown dotted with yellow daisies, and strain to hear. Her voice, loud and commanding. His, softer, yielding often slurred. My breathing feels shallow. They must not hear me. If I am discovered I may be devoured. I store their rage in my tiny body and hide it away in a secret place to be protected at all cost. If my hiding place is revealed, I will surely vanish and never be seen again.

The details of this, my earliest memory, remain etched in my mind as though it were a movie I saw yesterday. I was born a year and a half after the death of my infant brother, the firstborn of my father, a talented musician, celebrated as a child prodigy who was born in the South; and my mother, a dark curvaceous small-town beauty raised outside of Pittsburgh in an Orthodox Jewish family. They were married when my mother was almost five months pregnant. My parents tested every aspect of the institution of marriage.

I sit on the edge of the tub, watching you put on your make-up. A ritual I never tire of being witness to. The color is always bright red. The tube touches your lips boldly, outlining first your upper lip and carefully tracing the full line of your lower lip. Your dark eyes gaze into the small bathroom mirror with the fixed stare of a surgeon. My mouth moves automatically with yours and in that moment my transference to you is complete. You smile and your perfect white teeth glisten. It is usually at this point that my comparison to you begins. I am thin and angular with straight, red hair. You are small, curvaceous with curly dark hair. You are the ideal. I am the counterfeit. I linger in the bathroom after the make-up session is over and take your place at the mirror. I secretly try to imitate your seductive smile and your hooded dark eyes, but all I see is a pale, thin little girl, and wonder where I have really come from?

My mother discovered the body of her three-month old baby boy early one morning when she lifted him out of his crib where he had died during the night of an enlarged thymus gland. We never spoke of my brother's death. Although it was not a secret, it would be many years before she gave me any details of the depth of her despair. My mother's own mother, my grandmother, died in childbirth when mom was three years old. She was raised by her mother's sister and her husband. Although she never said this I think she always felt a bit of an outsider in this large and loving family. She never referred to her aunt as mother and shared her with seven other children.

I learned the details of this horrific experience in bits and pieces throughout my childhood. Although mom was a vivid storyteller who colored in all her life stories with amazing details, she left this one a little vague. Her stage was our knotty pine back room, as we called it, and I was her audience. Her props were a coffee cup filled with instant Nescafe and a pack of Camel cigarettes. Fragments of her still rush in upon me when I least expect it. There was a time when my mother's stories became mine and I wasn't sure where hers ended and mine began. It took me many years to claim my own stories.

Mom loved my sister and me with a fierceness that excluded almost everything in her life. She lived for and sometimes through us, ready to protect us from all and any suspected dangers. I suppose losing an infant child through something so shocking, and the loss of her own mother at three years old seemed good reasons for her desires to keep us safe at all costs. Her intolerance for our pain often took strange turns. Once when my sister was about a year old she tumbled out of her high chair onto the kitchen floor. She was unhurt except for a few scratches but it upset mom so greatly she grabbed the high chair and threw it down the cellar steps breaking it into pieces.

When I was about ten years old, my dad bought me a two-wheel bike for Christmas. I began to suspect something was up when routinely I found a flat tire every time I wanted to ride it. I spent more time fixing the tires than I ever did riding the bike. It wasn't until years later I found out mom regularly took the air out of the tires after I left for school. It was her way of keeping me safe.

The course of my life was drastically altered when I became pregnant by my high school boyfriend and was sent away to live with a kind family member. Secrets and lies became my reality until I gave birth and surrendered the child for adoption. I was unaware at the time that my mother had also become pregnant prior to marriage to my father. In her case, her baby died. Mine was given away. I remember the day, some fifteen years after the fact, that she shared this information with me.

We both knew the point of her confession on that day was not about the tragic loss that she endured, but her way of telling me, after fifteen years, that she, too had become pregnant before marriage. She handed it to me, like a gift, to let me know so many years later that I had not been alone. I never knew why she chose this time to reveal this to me. In my quest to continue family tradition, I also became pregnant a year and half after my firstborn was given up for adoption, once again creating a "replacement child." I couldn't help but think of my own life and wonder if behavior, like an heirloom, could be passed from one generation to another.

Many years have passed since this conversation. My parents have long ago left this earth and today I remember it in a new way. How hard it must have been for mom, after the death of her baby, to re-live such a hideous time of her life through me. Who knows what I would have done under the same circumstances. She did what her aunt said to do and I did what she said to do. It was the natural order of things, just the way it was. Secrets and lies were so imbedded in that era that to do anything different was unimaginable. Mom's ill-timed first pregnancy was kept a secret at all cost, even from me, and I perpetuated the secrets by doing the same.

In the light of today, the absurdity of this kind of thinking just made me want to comfort mom. I couldn't imagine what her pain and guilt must have been to discover her baby dead in a crib. I wanted to let her know that we simply didn't know better, that I understood. It was nobody's fault. We had all been replacement children of a sort–my mother, my son, and myself. We all wear the scars of those experiences.

I strongly believe that most of the decisions that we make throughout our life are based on early trauma that lead us through a lifetime of choices unknowingly borne out of early experiences. I think this is what creates our uniqueness and is what we call character. As for me, I've spent much of my life in search of answers—without ever really knowing the questions.

Patti's story is an all too familiar one. Time and again, children reenact a family drama without having conscious awareness that it's been played out before. And all too often, the consequences of the drama could possibly have been prevented had parents been up front about the circumstances. Ultimately, it's only when the secrets are uncovered and brought to light, and when the pain is acknowledged, that healing can begin.

The Secret Child

In this very short but incredibly poignant description, Rita Catherine describes what she calls the "aura" of her experience as a child. Her poem, *Dust*, follows.

Suddenly my parents lost their firstborn at the age of three—a son. A couple of months later my mother gave birth to a daughter—me. Mom and Dad thought it necessary to keep forever silent, and my deceased brother was mentioned only on very rare occasion by my grandmother. As a small girl, I was impressed by the sense that even grandma knew she was not to speak of the baby. If not for Grandma and a few remnants of my brother's life found tucked away in drawers and closets, I might never have known that he lived. The secret child. Despite my parents' efforts to hide him away, I shared my childhood with that little boy. A seemingly happy childhood wrought with an undercurrent of uncertainty, obscurity, ambiguity and fear. A personality influenced purely by an impression left by the reality of my parents' loss. Who is this little girl beneath the grief? I remain hopeful that someday I will find her.

Dust

Do we walk alone today
Or with the ghosts from far away
It's said they're gone with their last breath
Yet they stay much past their death
Their presence looms forever strong
So could it be that I am wrong
That I believe the dead are here
Tucked away inside my mirror
For when I look, I can see
That they are there inside of me
Open up and look around
You will see what I have found
If you peer inside the mirror
You will see that they are there
You cannot hide them in your heart
As if to think they have no part
They listen to our every word
And influence what's said and heard
No different from the rest of us
Except that they have turned to dust.

—Rita Catherine DiRenzo

◆ Children of Holocaust Survivors

There has been so much written about the children of Holocaust survivors, and yet controversy remains regarding psychopathology in this unique population. From the literature, we can ascertain that there appears to be a profile, clearly not "written in stone," to describe many children of Holocaust survivors, but certainly not all of the population and not definitive.

Generally, studies show that some Holocaust survivors are overly involved in their children's lives. These children are precious commodities beyond the "precious" most children are to their parents, for they are the living embodiment of all that has been lost. The pressure to be high achievers and to assume certain roles within the family is pushed hard on many of these survivor children.

Survivor parents may be overly protective of their children, overly concerned with their health and safety. The world for these parents is not a safe place, and trust, beyond the immediate family, is often lacking.

Separation-individuation is difficult for some children of survivor parents. While parents may encourage children to stay near so that nothing can happen to them, children may feel that separating from the family is tantamount to betrayal and abandonment. Further, survivor children often feel they are their parents' protectors, buffering them from further suffering.

With many publications about trans-generational transmission of trauma, researcher Natan P.F. Kellermann set out to review the existing literature on the mental health of children of Holocaust survivors. In the paper, "Psychopathology in Children of Holocaust Survivors: A Review of the Research Literature," he presents the findings of thirty-five comparative studies on the subject, published between 1973-1999.

Kellermann summarizes his findings, "This extensive research indicates rather conclusively that the non-clinical population of children of Holocaust survivors does not show signs of more psychopathology than others do... The clinical population of offspring, however, tends to present a specific "psychological profile" that includes a predisposition to PTSD, various difficulties in separation-individuation and a contradictory mix of resilience and vulnerability when coping with stress." [33]

He suggests that problems seen in families of Holocaust survivors may not be unique to this specific group but may, in fact, be seen in families where the parents have been traumatized by different circumstances, for any reason. But, Kellermann has identified a specific clinical subgroup of survivor children who are at risk for psychopathology beyond the general population:

- Only or firstborn children
- Children born soon after their parents suffered trauma
- Both parents are survivors
- Replacement Children
- Survivor's trauma and loss were so devastating that psychological damage resulted
- Symbiotic relationship between parents and children
- Too much or too little discussion about the trauma [34]

Failure is Not an Option

The problem with surviving was that you ended up with the ghosts of everyone you'd ever left behind riding on your shoulders.

—Paolo Bacigalupi

A survivor may have been the only remaining member of their family and as such, had to start life all over again. Some survivors married other survivors; perhaps in part, because there was a connection, a shared knowledge and experience of tragedy, loss, and grief hard to fathom by someone who had no first hand experience of what had happened. Many children of survivors are replacements for children who died. Replacement children of survivors often have the added burden of having to compensate for *all* of the losses that their parents suffered.

I was born in Romania. My parents are both Holocaust survivors; they lost their parents and siblings. I was born after my mom lost pregnancies due to her many chronic illnesses. My brother was born eighteen months after me.

I had a happy childhood. My parents lavished me with everything. I was a serious child and not demanding. Later on it was difficult for me because I could only date Jewish girls and there were not too many left. I was reminded at all times of what my family went through and I could not marry a non-Jew.

My mom depended on me for everything, from taking her to doctors, to telling me her problems; she was my friend and I was her parent. She told me about the Holocaust when I was twelve. My father never talked about it but before he passed he left us a letter. All of our friends immigrated to Israel and a few to the U.S.; we were among the last Jewish families left. It was hard to know that we do not have grandparents.

We grew up knowing that we are Jewish, a very small minority, and that we had to excel in everything. I was first in my class from kindergarten to high school and in medical school. I learned early on that "Failure is not an option."

The only friends I had were leaving, one after the other. We were lonely and isolated. Life in Romania became more and more difficult under Ceausescu's dictatorship. After years of good economy, everything was exported; food was scarce and the informers were everywhere. Anybody who would say one bad word about the authorities would end up in jail. We stayed because my mom was chronically ill and was afraid to start a new life.

I studied since age fifteen to get into medical school, where I was first in my class, as usual. The burden of leaving the country first fell on me, as the older sibling. I immigrated to the U.S., leaving everything behind—my family, my home, my first love—for freedom of speech and religion. I endured almost two years of Securitate interrogation, my father was forced to retire, and everything was censured. It was a life of terror.

When I arrived in the U.S., I was no longer the Jewish minority but I was a foreigner. I had to prove myself over and over in my work. I lost my confidence but I did not give up. I was determined to succeed and eventually I did. I finished my training in great residencies and fellowships.

I met and married a woman I did not know well. We have a wonderful child but the marriage ended on very bitter terms. At the same time, my family came over and I helped them. They were against divorce and initially they advised me to be a martyr and to take what life was giving me. For the first time, I did not listen.

I lost everything in my divorce. I nearly became homeless, and I was forced to start over. I worked 24/7 for many years in order to pay the lawyers, giving up a line of work that I was passionate about, all the while helping my family. Soon after their arrival, my father became ill and died. My mother faulted me for his death, for being a doctor—I did not help enough. I became, yet again, the head of my family, a position that I deeply resented but I had to be there for them.

I joined a second generation peer group where I understood and learned a lot about how the Holocaust affected us. I became strong and independent. I remarried six years after my divorce.

I am still helping my family; I feel it is still my responsibility. My wife, albeit far from perfect, agrees with me. I could not imagine leaving them behind. It is something that all my friends who were raised like me still do.

Although she had a very hard time, my child is doing very well; she has been the force and inspiration that drove me to get through everything. I love my work now and I still help my mother and brother. My child is also a strong, determined and wonderful human being. So after all, I did not mess her up too much.

Children of survivors such as Eric are often forced into many roles within the family that they would not have chosen on their own—head of the household, parent to the parent, confidante and friend, caretaker—and there's little room to refuse.

But with all of the emotional and psychological issues brought to bear on survivors' children, it's clear that "positives" have emerged from the tragedies and suffering of their parents. Many survivor children are extremely capable people, exhibiting qualities that stand them in good stead in the world—responsible, adaptable, resilient, and resourceful.

VIII. Family Dynamics and the Replacement Child

◆ Birth Order, Gender and Family Roles

As social beings, part of many social circles during our lives, we will have or will be assigned, various roles that we'll be expected to fill. Many of these are necessary for the healthy functioning of a whole group. Think tribe. The tribe functions smoothly when members know their place and responsibly fulfill whatever their particular role requires for the common good of all.

On a more personal, smaller scale, think family. As members of a family unit, individuals are assigned roles in accordance with age, birth order, gender, and importance of function within the family. Good parental role modeling prepares children to step into and fulfill adult roles when the time comes.

Dr. Kevin Leman is a psychologist who has studied birth order for several decades. In *The Birth Order Book: Why You Are the Way You Are*, he postulates that the birth order in a family determines the differences in the personalities of siblings and further, that parents will deal with each child according to the birth order of that child. It's expected that firstborn children will be quite different from their second born siblings. Firstborn, middle, last born and only children demonstrate various characteristics and traits that set them apart as individuals as well as within the family structure.

In addition to birth order, gender may determine how a child is treated by the parents—why one child is favored over another and why one child may acquire a specific role within the family over another (sometimes even taking on a role usually meant for a firstborn child).

As might be expected, some situations present exceptions to the general rule—adoption, blended families, and twins, who may view themselves as their own family unit separate from the other siblings. Another interesting exception is when more than five years elapses between children. In this case, the birth order starts from the beginning—a new baby becomes a firstborn.

Then again, there are roles assigned that almost invariably represent dysfunction, such as when a child is highly favored, overly valued, and put on a pedestal. From an archetypal perspective, this is the Hero or Golden Child, a child whose light shines on everything he/she is and does, a child who can simply do no wrong. Conversely, the Scapegoat is the child who is ridiculed, criticized, and devalued; who just can't seem to do anything right in the eyes of their parents. There are other roles thrust upon children and in some instances, it's the children themselves who take on a specific role, such as the family Mascot.

There is the phenomenon of *parentification*—the roles are reversed and children are turned into the parents. From an emotional perspective, these children may be required to take care of their parents' emotional needs and sometimes the needs of their siblings as well. Sometimes this role extends to taking care of the physical needs of a parent, as might be the case when a parent is unable or refuses to function as an adult due to any number of reasons.

Children forced to become adults way before their time, are certainly robbed of their childhood. The level of responsibility and obligation they face day in and day out may create resentment and anger and may negatively influence future relationships.

The replacement child often finds him/herself in a difficult and strange bind. The individual role of this child within a family may be usurped and replaced by a totally different one. As we've seen, in the extreme, the replacement child may be expected to take over the role (including the talents, behaviors, and interests) of a deceased or disabled sibling. Their job in life is to fill the shoes of the idealized other child. But inevitably, the replacement child comes up short; simply never as good as what the "other" child would or could have been.

Conversely, the replacement child may be cast in the role of the family savior, the only hope remaining for the family. Pressure may be brought to bear on this child to excel and to achieve in order to compensate for their parents' loss. No doubt, in either case, the responsibility and obligation to fulfill the role of a "deceased or impaired other" severely diminishes a child's capacity to just be who they are in their own right.

Sometimes a child becomes a replacement within the family even when there is no death of a sibling. The "death of an ideal" may impact the family dynamic and one child may be cast in the role of replacement child to compensate (and often, over-compensate) for this loss within the family. These children carry the burden of over-caretaking for family members, especially siblings, in an effort to assuage the hurt and pain for traumas suffered by them.

A replacement may suffer birth order confusion when an older sibling dies, and as a second born or subsequent child, must assume the role of the oldest in the family. Sometimes, the family dynamic is altered when a child of the opposite sex is born after the death of a sibling. This may not be what one, or both, of the parents expected. A replacement child may be "punished" for not being able to fulfill a parent's fantasy of how things should have been by being ignored or paid little attention to, or by being made to feel "less than" they deserve, simply because of the unfortunate circumstances of their birth.

Life, with all of its inherent requirements, is hard enough to figure out. A replacement child may be given no choice but to assume a role in which they have little or no say and, in many instances, no clue about how to be or how to walk in the shadow of another.

But it's important to present a balanced view, to emphasize that the fate of many replacement children is often not the doom and gloom of the most extreme cases. In fact, many replacement children who would place themselves in a "middle of the road" category along a continuum (how they were treated, parental demands, expectations, and so on) have done quite well, navigating through many of the issues confronting replacement children and coming out on top, more resilient, more compassionate, and more aware of who they are as individuals. It just might have been better for them had they known earlier on what it means to be a replacement child, and that there are others just like them.

The Big Sister

The firstborn may be more of an achiever according to birth order theory and may exhibit a tendency to be more cautious and controlling, while being conscientious and reliable. In a way, the firstborn lives in two worlds: the adult world where the imprint of the parents may be more evident, and the world of the child. By the time a second child arrives on the scene, the parents have hopefully, worked out the kinks and perhaps are more relaxed.

More than sixty years ago, a young couple, very much in love, married. The young bride was just nineteen and the groom was twenty-four. Within their first year of marriage, they learned they were expecting a baby. The baby girl that was born to them was by all accounts, an angel. She had the face of a porcelain doll. Her white-blonde hair formed a curly halo. Her dazzling blue eyes sparkled. They named the baby Betsy.

The young mother and father doted on their angelic bundle of baby bliss. The young mom started a scrapbook for Betsy, full of adorable pictures with funny captions.

They dreamed of teaching her to horseback-ride since horses were their passion.

One day, when Betsy was not quite two years old, she and her young father were outside their apartment building. The father was in charge of watching Betsy. But in a fleeting moment when he was distracted, the couple's landlady backed her car over Betsy, crushing her skull. Betsy died a few hours later.

The young parents were, of course, devastated. They would never be the same. How could they be? Not long after Betsy's death, however, they learned they were expecting another baby. This baby was the only one of their four eventual children that they hoped would be a girl. They wanted a little girl who would fill the hole in the hearts left by Betsy's death.

They were troubled that the new baby's due date fell exactly a year to the day of Betsy's death. But mercifully, their hoped-for baby girl was born a day earlier than that tragic anniversary. That baby was me.

And so it was that I eventually became the eldest of three living children, but, of course, not the firstborn. I never felt like the eldest child. I always felt I was meant to have—not be—a big sister. I longed for Betsy's presence in my life as my big sister. I so ached for a big sister that when I was seven or eight or so, I fervently prayed that Betsy would come back for just one day and be my big sister. Later as a teenager, I pined for a big sister who could show me the ropes about things like applying to colleges.

I tried to be the big sister, though, for example, by teaching my middle sister to read. My role—or perhaps the role I tried to fit into—was reflected in the imaginative games my sisters and I played as children. When my sisters and I played "house," my middle sister was the mommy, my little sister was the baby, and I was always the big sister.

Meanwhile, my mother never truly forgave my father for what happened to Betsy, and he never truly forgave himself. He began to drink excessively and seek comfort in the arms of women who wouldn't judge him. My parents divorced when I was thirteen.

Plenty of children end up playing roles they would not have seemed born to play. We've all heard of kids with irresponsible or absent parents who take on parental roles with their younger siblings. Other children are conceived specifically to replace a dead sibling, with their parents placing a huge burden on them to stand in for the deceased child.

But in reflecting on my confusing role in my family, I do not intend to in any way suggest that I have been a victim of Betsy's death or of living a life as the eldest but not the firstborn.

We often have roles thrust upon us in life that do not feel comfortable, do not feel as though they were meant to be. Perhaps in my striving so hard to be the eldest, to be the big sister, to take the place of the firstborn, I learned to work hard and try to make my mark in the world. Maybe in trying to be a big sister, I learned to be a teacher.

I never knew Betsy, of course, but I cannot remember a time when I wasn't aware of her as part of our family. When I said my prayers at night, I would say, "God bless Mommy, and Daddy, and Robin, and Carolynn, and Betsy-up-in heaven."

In her less than two years of life, Betsy gave my parents great joy. Her presence lived on in our family among her sisters who never knew her. It was a tragic presence; yet there was something about a baby's goodness and innocence that bound us together and gave us ideals to aspire to. Yesterday was Betsy's birthday. She would have been sixty years old. This tribute is my gift to her.

When a firstborn dies, the parents must start all over again, except that the relationship they've had with the deceased first child is carried over into the order of the subsequent children. The child that follows, the second born as Katharine was, but now the eldest, may then "inherit" the role of the firstborn. In essence, this child may be deprived of the family role that is rightfully theirs according to birth order. Although the memory of the deceased is a reminder that someone was here before them, the responsibility to fill this other role shifts to their shoulders, and what they should have been on their own terms becomes a distant memory.

Finally Free to Find Myself

Lena is a "sandwich" replacement child. On one side, she sensed early on that she had to be the "perfect" daughter—to be strong, independent, and to avoid bothering or upsetting her parents at all cost. In addition, she saw the need to take on the role of caring for her younger siblings; in essence, she became a parent to them, protecting them and providing what her parents could not. This caretaking on both sides carried huge consequences; she couldn't take care of herself and her own needs. It wasn't until her siblings were on their own that Lena finally was able to take the time to focus on herself.

Up to now, I thought I was making a "big" deal for nothing. I mean how can I be so affected by the death of someone I didn't even know? Many people have had worse and are doing fine. A lot of children die. Too many. And that's horrible for the parents. I really understand that and I understand that the concern is on the parents. But in most cases there are also siblings involved. But as there's not much on it, I always felt alone and that the other siblings were doing fine. So reading all the stories on your site was such a relief. There's even a name for people like me! :-) That's why I also want to share my story even though it's very similar to the others.

My parents had a baby boy who died at a couple of weeks old from the sudden infant death syndrome. I was born a year and two months later. My mom explained it to me when I was very young and we used to look at pictures of him and talk about him. Growing up, I tried to be the perfect daughter. But not enough to make my parents happy. Good at school, never sick so as to not worry my parents. Very independent from a very young age not to bother them. I played my big sister role to protect my sister (four years younger) and my brother (seven years younger). My mom wanted three children (despite many miscarriages and against doctors' advice) so in case one of us died, we'd still be two. I carried the whole family on my shoulders. My parents never showed any affection towards us and never told us they loved us.

There's one place though, where I was not very good. Food has always been a problem for me and the subject of many fights with my mom. Apparently even as a baby, I was very difficult to feed and didn't want to eat much. Food is still a problem today and I'm just starting to work on it, so I don't really know if it's related or not, but apparently food is the connection to the mother...

After I left home, I started to live!!! After so many years of worrying and taking care of others, I could finally take care of me and do whatever I wanted. I guess I was an adult as a child and am now a child as an adult. :-) But, it's only once both my sister and brother were married, meaning they have someone else to take care of them, that it all came down crashing on me. Everything came back to me and I started to do some research and thinking and work on myself. If he didn't die, I wouldn't be here. Now, that I'm out of home, what is my role? What am I supposed to do? I failed to make my parents happy. My own parents don't love me so who could? Why aren't they proud of me? I can't die because it would kill them. (I don't mean I wanted to, it's just to show how much pressure I have and that I'm not even free with my own life.) Is that why my dad drinks so much? And drives with us in the car? Is that why I could never get along with my brother? Is my phobia of vomit linked? Those are a few questions I remember asking myself.

Today, I'm 38 and still a work in progress!! But I'm happy! And more relaxed and calm. I understand now, that my parents did the best they could. I don't blame them. But as I'm still in the middle of all this, I try not to see my mom too much. I have to take some distance for a while. I have to find myself. I know it hurts her but I'm too fragile right now to take care of her. She's still leaning on me a lot and I just can't. I still have a long way to go.

Caretaker Extraordinaire

As a result of severe trauma suffered by family members, Lara became the replacement for that "loss of an ideal" within her family, and through her constant caretaking, attempted to assuage the hurt and pain of her family, particularly those who were suffering the most.

Lara is one of five children within a very closely-knit family where, from early on, all of the children were taught to stick together. The personal tragedies suffered by members of her family included events both known, and shared with others within the family, as well as events unknown. All of these experiences carried far-reaching consequences and dramatically changed her family's life. Although Lara was unaware of the facts while growing up, she still intuitively realized that something was not right. Lara quickly learned the things she could do to help balance the pain and suffering within the family.

Caretaking quickly became a full time job in her efforts to try to "rescue, repair, and fix" her family members' traumas and ensuing problems. This soon became an unsustainable responsibility and over the years she realized she could not continue assuming that kind of burden on herself, emotionally, physically, and financially. She also realized that it was not in the best interest of those suffering to continue doing so. In recognizing this pattern of co-dependency and enabling, she realized she could be keeping them from becoming more self-sufficient and more proficient in their own capabilities.

Lara's focus on her family began to overshadow her own needs. Her caretaking role soon became her primary identity, so much so that when she left for college she experienced a great deal of separation anxiety. These feelings of anxiety have remained with her, to varying degrees, throughout her adult years. It is only recently that she has acquired the therapeutic tools and insights to cope with stress in a healthy way and make the necessary changes. The family members, who had become her "projects," kept her from focusing on herself and living her own authentic life. She had a clear idea of what her role was within the family, but lost touch with her own identity and life goals. She also lost touch with the simple role of just being a normal sibling within the family. Her caretaking duties overshadowed the sweet simplicity of just being a daughter and sister.

However, she still continued to be the problem solver and the person who was always "there" for her family. And her role grew more demanding as they grew older and had bigger things to "solve." Over-caretaking set up an expectation that was difficult to stop, as was the anxiety that went along with it. This dynamic eventually became unhealthy, unbearable, and unsustainable.

Today, Lara realizes that this kind of behavior is very dysfunctional. While it can be extremely detrimental to the person doing it—physically, spiritually, emotionally, and financially, it also can affect the growth of the person that you think you're helping. In some cases it can erode their self-esteem since they don't exercise their own muscles. In other words, if you take away their reason, their opportunity, and their responsibility for using their own skills, they run the risk of not being able to fully function on their own. A popular phrase in Recovery that illustrates this point is the following: The person helping someone should not be working harder than the person who is being helped is working for themselves.

But on the positive side, the same skills Lara used to make "other's lives better" was also something she could draw upon for herself. In a way, it was a stage for her to build her talents, sharpen her senses, and design her own life.

Today, Lara has learned much about the replacement child syndrome, the effects of trauma, establishing healthy boundaries, about positive healing modalities, and most importantly, about the transformational opportunities on the other side of trauma. She's learned that while there are many paths to growth and evolution, our challenges provide us with our greatest opportunities to make positive changes in our lives.

In recent years, she has shifted her focus away from fixing family problems into helping a larger audience through her work on a series of documentaries. These documentaries were inspired by the challenges she personally faced in her life as well as a variety of important issues that impact so many people.

The Realities of Gender

Gender sometimes forces certain roles upon us. This is especially true in some cultures where gender roles are more traditional and fixed. Although much of the world has advanced, still today, there are restrictions and prohibitions based on gender that are placed on individuals in parts of the world.

Gladys was born in Buenos Aires many decades ago. When she was three years old, her mother had a son who died shortly after birth as a result of an RH blood problem. After the baby's death, her parents felt the lack of a male child. In their culture, having a male in the family was extremely important; if not, "Who would take care of the family finances?"

After the baby died, Gladys' mother became sad and very distant. She kept silent much of the time, always sewing with her head down, only speaking to her husband and when she needed to tell the cook what to do. She was not able to connect to three-year-old Gladys. No one talked about the baby's death; it became a big secret. He died before he was named.

Even as a very young child, Gladys felt that she was not what her parents wanted or valued. She was very sad, but playing by herself made her feel better. Eating became her compensation and made her happy—like a comforting pacifier. Gladys didn't feel appreciated for anything she did. She loved reading and writing, but that "might not please the boys; they don't want a 'clever girl'." Her self-esteem suffered. She believed that her parents didn't value her capabilities. They wanted her to be the “perfect bait girl”—to look pretty, wear nice dresses, and the like.

Her parents divided the world between what they thought women were supposed to do and what men should be capable of doing. Gladys was intelligent and excelled at things they associated with men and so she was reprimanded for those capabilities and talents. For instance, men were supposed to be intelligent and women were not supposed to be as smart... or to show they were, anyway.

In her parents' mind, women were supposed to please a man and not compete with him on any level. Gladys was always held back by her parents. When young, she was not allowed to run and climb trees because only boys were supposed to do those things. She was just supposed to be beautifully dressed and ladylike so she would be able to marry well when she grew up. She understood from her parents that this was to be her main job in life.

Every single day Gladys' mother would bring to the table stories about women who were “working almost like servants” because their husbands left them or divorced them. Nothing was said directly, but it was a ‘matter of fact’ that women always seemed to come up lacking; it was a given that “this is just the way things are.”

Gladys' grandfather held a special place. He was the powerful caretaker of the whole family. Everybody respected him and feared him, but the family felt very protected by James. He died at fifty-eight, when Gladys was eleven years old. Her parents probably lost their hopes and dreams and fantasies of the boy—“the future savior,” the family's protector-to-be, when their son died.

A sister, Stella, was born when Gladys was eleven and a half and a brother was born a year and a half after that. He was named very quickly because he also suffered from the same blood problem that had caused the death of the first son. This boy had a blood transfusion and survived. They named him Julio in memory of James.

When Gladys' father died, Julio took care of the family finances. Gladys married a hard-working man, very similar to her grandfather in many ways. Ironically, the meaning of

James' last name, Stone, was carried in her husband's nickname, Lito (*lithos,* which means stone in Greek).

It has taken Gladys many years to come into her own as a person and as a woman. It's no one's fault that a woman's role was severely limited, where what she was expected and allowed to do was narrowly restricted. That's just the way things developed along societal lines, and still do in many cultures.

But it's hard to ignore the fact that people suffered (and still do) because of their gender. It may be very instructive to apply what we now understand about the replacement child to issues of gender, where the individual is not seen for the person they are in their own right but rather for what others need them to be.

The Replacement Stepchild

This story presents a very interesting twist on the phenomenon of the replacement child. Here, a young girl is expected to assume the role of a deceased child from outside of her biological family. It's not so much that she's asked to carry on the role of the child born before, but rather to fill the hole left by the deceased child for a parent and grandparents who lost their only child and grandchild.

Ashley's parents had a contentious divorce when she was ten years old. Shortly after that, her father, Ruben, married Tina. Unable to conceive in her first marriage, Tina and her ex-husband had adopted a baby boy. He was born with major heart issues that required several surgeries and many hospital stays. However, when Geordy was five, he passed away while undergoing another surgery. He was Tina's only child and the only grandchild of Tina's parents.

After the marriage, Ashley felt that Tina was trying to take over as her mother and that Tina's parents were trying to take over as her grandparents. Ashley was resentful; she had a perfectly good relationship with her mother and her mother's parents as well as with a grandmother on her father's side. Complicating matters further, was the fact that her parents were not getting along after the divorce and Ashley felt that her mother was being treated unfairly by her father.

Her father didn't help matters, telling Ashley that she had to consider his new wife, as well as her parents, as blood relatives. From the beginning, the step grandparents were very demanding of Ashley's time with them. Because they lived nearby, they wanted Ashley to come and spend nights with them and invited her to do her homework at their home. When she would complain about the pressure placed upon her by the step grandparents, her father and Tina would tell her that she should feel differently about the situation and instead, appreciate them.

Ashley, now a young teenager, feels bombarded by their unreasonable wants, desires, and needs but she's not allowed to have her own feelings about any of this. If and when she speaks up, Ashley is told that she's being unappreciative and disrespectful. Her father invariably takes the side of her stepmother and step grandparents. Ashley resents that the step grandparents are included in everything she does with her father. These "relatives" feel entitled to give Ashley their opinions about the way she lives her life—what she's doing, what she's wearing, and so on.

Interestingly, the stepfamily is far less invested in Ashley's older brother. Perhaps, there's less pressure on him to comply with their wishes because he was a teenager when his father remarried and by then had more of a life of his own. To Ashley's way of thinking, the stepfamily expects her to take the place of the dead boy they lost years before Tina married her father. She resents that her father "goes along with the program" and that the step grandparents, who are not her grandparents, are so demanding of her time and her affection.

While one can sympathize with Ashley's stepmother's and step grandparents' wish to make up for their tremendous loss, it's evident that they're incorrectly assuming that Ashley would want to take on this role, and are making a worse assumption that she has no say in the matter. Obviously, children are not interchangeable. Family members who make this mistake, thinking their seniority overrides all else, are creating a potentially dangerous family dynamic that may have far-reaching consequences.

PART THREE

Family Matters

You are not a drop in the ocean.
You are the whole ocean in a drop.
–Rumi

IX. What's in a Name

◆ A Blessing or an Albatross?

Your name is your identity. It defines you. Of all the things you own, it's the one thing you carry with you your entire life. When choosing a name for a child, it's important to carefully select a name that will resonate in a positive way. Ideally, a person should feel a deep sense of meaning and satisfaction at the sound of their own name.

A person's name establishes their uniqueness, and may even help determine a specific life path. A child might accept their name as given without question, or they might be interested to know why they were given the name they have. What's the name's derivation? Who are they named for? Is there some story behind how they got their name? If they're named for a specific person, what was that person like and what is their story?

Naming a child should be an extremely conscious decision, thoughtfully undertaken and bearing the child, as owner and carrier of the name, in mind. How will the child feel about the name? Will he/she have a real sense of pride in the name he/she bears, or will carrying a specific name be a huge burden?

Every religion and culture has its own established traditions—its own way of choosing a name for a new person. Biblical names abound in cultures all over the world. Often "family names" are given to remember and honor ancestors.

Other traditions exist for choosing names including using surnames as a given name, popular names, invented names (to honor certain events or occasions unique to the family), secret and/or forbidden names (for example, as used in Aboriginal and Hawaiian cultures), and sometimes, re-used names within the same family, often when a member of the family has died.

Catholic parents are encouraged to choose a name tied to Christianity, such as a saint's name. In Christianity, the practices of naming vary according to the many denominations of the Church, but usually a child is named and blessed a few weeks or more after birth. Mormons often give their children names after prophets and apostles, or Scriptural names from The Book of Mormon, or from the Bible. Some parents choose to combine the names of parents and grandparents to create a unique new name and sometimes parents create a name of their own design.

Jews from Middle and East European ancestry known as Ashkenazic Jews follow ancient Jewish belief when it comes to naming. Traditionally, the Ashkenazi name children after deceased relatives, and the belief is that by so doing, the child is the recipient of the deceased person's soul. On the other hand, Sephardic Jews, whose heritage goes back to pre-Inquisition Spain and Portugal and also includes Middle Eastern and North African Jews, name their children after grandparents who are living and sometimes, after themselves.

There are no specific laws in Judaism governing how a child is to be named, except for the obvious; a child should not be named for an evildoer. Not surprisingly, the same thing applies to Catholicism, and such names as Salome, Lucifer, and Judas are avoided.

From early Biblical times, a person's name was changed when their status was changed. Stories and lore about the special significance of a name abound in Scripture. The changing of a name after a revelatory experience symbolized a radical shift in identity. Abram to Abraham, "for I have made you the father of a multitude of nations" (Gen. 17:5); Jacob to Israel, "for you have striven with God and with men, and have prevailed" (Gen. 32:28), and the conversion of Saul of Tarsus on the road to Damascus, assuming the name of Paul, are some examples.

Another practice going back to ancient times is that of changing a person's name during a serious illness. The idea is that the angel of death will be "tricked" into passing over the sick person whose name is now unrecognizable. Parents may give a newborn a name chosen specifically because it has a protective quality—a way to guard against harm coming to this new child. In a similar vein, a special name can be given to a child after he/she is born if the mother was ill during pregnancy. For example, the name Raphael means "God has healed."

◆ Naming a Child After a Deceased Sibling

Before the 1900's, high infant mortality ensured that many children would not survive past birth, or would die shortly after. Sometimes, when a baby died, the parents would give the same name to a subsequent child. If you recall, several famous replacement children were named for deceased siblings.

Naming a child after a deceased beloved relative may be very appropriate, especially if the deceased passed at the end of a long life and is remembered with love. There is often a deep sense of satisfaction that comes when the name of the loved one passes to a new member of the family; their memory is kept alive. But sometimes, a name can elicit passionate emotions, especially when there is disagreement about it and/or if there is family pressure (and guilt) to give a name that may not be of the parents' choosing.

Sometimes, a specific name is given in the hope that the child receiving it will fulfill a desired expectation, or will somehow embody or emulate the individual he/she is being named for. But that's an adult point of view. As parents, it's essential to think long and hard about this issue so that the name you give your child carries no unnecessary predetermined responsibilities with it. It's important to ensure that the child knows that they're *not* expected to take responsibility for the expectations and comparisons to the "other" they're being named for that might be imposed upon them.

For many replacement children, being named for a deceased sibling carries consequences that may follow them the rest of their lives. The expectation placed upon them by parents that they, the replacement child, will fulfill the hopes and dreams of the deceased child is now compounded and cemented by giving the very same name as the deceased sibling. It's as if the replacement child does not have the right to their own identity. And when that happens, they may not know who they are, why they're here, and there may be real confusion and conflict while navigating the road toward selfhood.

Many adult replacement children believe that it is best to avoid using the same first name as a deceased sibling. Instead, the middle name is felt to be an acceptable place to remember a deceased sibling, still honoring the memory of the dead, yet avoiding the "baggage" and identity confusion that a name carries.

Lifting the Burden

Naming a child for a deceased young relative may turn out to be unsettling for the child. Family members heavily invested in the deceased and unable to let them go, may unwittingly attempt to turn a subsequent child, especially one bearing the same name, into the embodiment of the deceased.

Ethan was born about four months after an older first cousin passed away at twelve years of age after a long illness. His parents had always planned on naming him Ethan. However, they bowed to family pressure and at the last minute named him Martin, the exact name of his newly deceased cousin. They agreed that they would call him Marty, but his name was legally Martin on his birth certificate.

The late Martin's mother and grandmother were still having a very difficult time dealing with his recent death. The grandmother of the two boys started referring to the new baby as Martin, not just Marty as they had agreed, and was always telling Marty/Ethan how much he was like his first cousin, the original Martin.

When Marty/Ethan was about five years old he was told that his cousin was his guardian angel and would always be with him, watching over him. This caused anxiety instead of being comforting and reassuring. He thought that the ghost of his cousin was suddenly going to appear, grew frightened of being in his room at night, and had difficulty sleeping.

He asked that the picture of his cousin be removed from his room and insisted on being called Ethan, the name he knew that his parents had originally chosen for him and which was his middle name. He expressed to his parents that he was afraid of getting sick like Martin. His parents were concerned about the discomfort the name was causing their son. They gave him the choice of having the name Martin legally removed so that he could become Ethan, as originally planned. Once this took place, it made a big difference for Ethan, who was finally able to visibly relax.

Now as an adult, Ethan knows he would never name a child after another who had died. As a young boy, he remembers feeling that he was sharing not only Martin's name but also Martin's identity. This situation was largely due to his grandmother who seemed to become more depressed as the years went by after the first Martin's passing; she was never able to disconnect. She spoke about Martin and constantly compared the boys to each other.

With the legal name change, Ethan felt that the weight of the world was taken off his shoulders. Ethan feels that using his cousin's name would've been fine as a middle name, especially if people would not have made an issue out of it when he was a young boy. Using the middle name would have been a good way to honor his first cousin, free of the burden—the expectations and comparisons—that had been originally placed upon him.

A Heavy Name to Carry

There were six children in Paul Joseph's family: Mike, David, Joseph Paul, Paul Joseph, John, and Laura, with a two-three year gap between the birth of each child, except for Joseph Paul and Paul Joseph. Paul Joseph was born one year after his brother Joseph Paul died. All of the boys were named after saints in this Catholic family.

Paul Joseph heard about his deceased brother when he was a child. However, it wasn't something that was really discussed in the family. He was picked on by his other siblings, though his mother was good about not showing favoritism. He felt that if his brother Joseph Paul had lived, they would have been like team mates; this brother would have been on his side.

Paul Joseph identifies himself as the only one of four brothers who didn't become a high-achieving professional. His father, with whom he doesn't have a close relationship, is a surgeon and his mother is a nurse. His sister works in advertising like Paul Joseph, and although they don't hold professional degrees, they're successful. His parents divorced when he was in the seventh grade; a bad marriage that finally came to an end.

Paul Joseph's grandmother passed away when he was in his early teens. The family was living in Texas at the time but went to Chicago for their grandmother's funeral and burial. It was then that he saw his dead brother's gravestone with the name Joseph Paul inscribed on it and his mother became emotional.

Suddenly, Paul Joseph felt the absolute reality of his brother's death.

He felt as if he himself had died; as if it was a previous incarnation and that his former self had died. It was extremely upsetting for him to see his name (in reverse order) on a gravestone. Much too close for comfort!

Retiring a Family Name

Sometimes a family name has lived out its life and needs to be retired. As much as one may want to honor family members, a name that carries baggage or whose story is a sad one in the history of the family, may be replaced by one that connotes promise for the future.

I was born about two years after the death of my brother, Tom at about one year of age. Tom suffered an intestinal twist that medicine could not fix. (A younger sister developed the same condition but it unraveled on its own and she was spared.) I was a sickly child suffering with bronchitis, pneumonia, appendicitis, and ongoing ear, nose, and gland issues. In fact, my family worried that I would not be permitted to enter the U.S. due to a small mark on my lungs as a result of tuberculosis. Somehow or other, that mark didn't show up on the X-Ray that went to the U.S. Embassy. No doubt, this was the work of a kind family doctor. My health improved and life was good to me in the United States. I became a U.S. Marine sergeant and an attorney with a very successful and fulfilling career.

The name Thomas was venerated and honored in my family—my grandfather on my father's side who died at forty-five, my father's brother who died at thirty-one of tuberculosis, and finally, my brother, Tom. There may well have been more since it was the practice to call the first son after the father, but good family records had not been kept. Perhaps, no one paid much attention to that in the old days.

My father's name was William (Bill/Willie). When my own son William (Liam) was born, I knew that the name Tom was a no starter. After all, you don't want to name a child after those who have died young. The Liams in the family have faired considerably better.

There was a photo of my brother, Tom in my bedroom, but it was of no interest—just another photo. All I learned about my family was from aunts and uncles and the most of what they told was how broken-hearted my parents were; my Dad apparently didn't let Baby Tom go until I was born, and how happy they were when I arrived.

I had never thought much about the "replacement children" issue until I heard about it. It made me more interested in Baby Tom and my parents' life before I was born. I started searching at our last family get together. But, alas, the old memories and old people are gone.

As the World Turns

While many are eager to name a new baby after a deceased sibling, there are times when a chosen name may symbolize the nature of the relationship between parents and their replacement child. Lisa describes the "cornerstone" of the hollow relationship that she has with her parents.

My parents were so terrified of my impending doom, that they never picked a name or set the hopes on me while they were pregnant. The story goes that they had to stay in the hospital for two extra days because they couldn't agree on a name for me. They never considered any boys or girls names... at all. 'Never even thought about it,' according to my mom.

Ultimately, I was named after a fictional character from the soap opera As the World Turns. *The character is Lisa... I don't know the actual actress' name, and I haven't ever investigated what kind of "person" she was on the television show. I know she has been on it for years and years. Another family joke.*

This is like the story of my life–my parents were so paralyzed and apprehensive about my existence that I was named after a fictional person!! Like I have said before, I feel like I stand behind a veil: they know I am there, but they can't see me. I wasn't even worthy of a name for a real person.

Call Me AnnMarie

AnnMarie's story continues... (See An Adoptee's Search for Identity.)

In 1991 I had to return home to The Berkshires as my Dad had passed and there was no one to watch over Mother. The neighbors were calling. So from 1991-1995, I had to find my own living arrangements, as I was told by mother that she didn't care where I put my bags as long as it wasn't in her house! Fortunately, Dad and I had spent some time together before he passed and he set me up with bank accounts to allow me to be there to take care of Marie.

In January 1995, living in the Berkshires and caring for Mother, I received a flyer in the mail about a group trip with Power Places Tour Group for a two week Past Life Regressions Tour to Egypt, scheduled for February. What a great way to celebrate my forty-ninth birthday!

I was always fascinated with pyramids and visited them in Mexico City and Cancun. I had always wanted to visit The Great Pyramids and never thought it possible. Two weeks before I was to leave, every night when I went to sleep I would close my eyes and "see" in my mind's eye, the three pyramids and the Sphinx.

Even when I arrived with the group of one hundred sixty in Egypt, I would get that image. The experience was amazing and so was the energy there. We climbed inside the pyramid's King and Queen's chamber. The night before we were to leave Giza, I along with a young man in our group made arrangements with the guards to be alone with the Sphinx after the place closed. It was after midnight and as we were meditating, I asked, "Who was I in a past life?" I clearly heard a voice say, "It's not who you were that matters. You have been many! WHO you are in this life is what matters!" I resounded, "I am June."

"NO, you are not," was the reply!

I had to pause and reflect on that. June was the name given to me by my adoptive parents. My birth name is

AnnMarie. In 1986, I had done a birth search and found my birth mother and siblings.

My birthmother, Phyllis, had petitioned the courts for my original birth certificate, but I had never used the name out of respect for my adoptive parents' feelings.

On this night, just before my 49th birthday, I said, "Well, I am AnnMarie." A vibrational energy went through me and when I went to sleep that night and closed my eyes, the image that I had been having for weeks of the pyramids and Sphinx was gone!

The next morning, I woke up with laryngitis, closing me down from talking so that I had to just listen and process. I asked my fellow travelers to call me AnnMarie and the way that name "bounced" off the temple walls and energy went right through me was like a cleansing healing. The energy of the temples of Isis and Hathor we're filled with remembrances of past lives. I had to go within. I re-claimed my true self! I celebrated my birthday; the group leader had a cake made, with the name AnnMarie. It was my first birthday party! Made up for the ones that I never had!

When I returned home, I told everyone I was no longer June and to call me AnnMarie. It was a shock to them, but after hearing the story they completely understood. That trip completely changed my life.

Letter to My Parents

Dear Mom and Dad,

I know this may seem out of the blue for you, but as I continue on this journey of self-discovery and try to make sense of how I got to this stage in my life, I've been forced to look back and try to understand who I am. I didn't realize I'd have to go back to before I was born.

You already had five children when your eldest daughter died at the age of twelve from cancer. Two years later you had me. I have no idea if you tried to have another child in an attempt to 'replace' the one you lost or, as practicing Catholics, perhaps you left that choice in "God's hands." Either way, I was born and if there were one thing I wish you hadn't done, it would be giving me her name.

Intentional or not, by giving me her name, it was like I was put on this earth to finish her journey. What an impossible mission! How could anyone live up to the memory of a deceased child? All I knew for sure was that I was a constant reminder to anyone in our family who knew her.

There are only a handful of pictures of the daughter and sister my family lost, but in all of them she is beautiful. She had such a warm and genuine smile that you just knew by looking at her she was a precious gift from God. And that's when the guilt sets in... and I get angry with myself for being jealous of a memory. And not just any memory, the one of my big sister. The one I didn't get to know. The one no one really ever talks about, but her name is mentioned on a daily basis.

I wish we could talk about her and how losing her impacted the family. Do my sisters and brothers resent the fact that they lost their big sister and then mom and dad came home with a replacement? I don't know because we never talk about it. Sometimes I'm not sure what talking about it will resolve, but I'm hoping it'll prove to me that it's all real—that I'm not making a mountain out of a mole hill.

I want to feel like I'm part of the whole family and that it's okay to talk about your sister and daughter in front of me. In a way it seems like a 'secret.' I mean everyone knew about her, her pictures are everywhere, and yet we really don't talk about her. None of us. Ever. Why is that? Because of me? Or maybe it doesn't have anything to do with me–it's just how everyone protected themselves after her death–what they did to survive and that hasn't changed. But is that the environment I was born into? One where everyone pretended to be okay with her death and then I come along and we pretend I'm not there to replace her? Like seriously–did no one question you on this name decision??? No one?

You are both always so sad. Do you have any idea what it's like to know that every time you look at me, I make you sad? And I know you're comparing, wondering what Grace would have achieved had she lived. I thought about changing my name; even read that it's a good idea. But I feel like I gave away my own childhood, please don't take my name away too. Please help me accept it.

I know you feel guilty about your thoughts. I know that growing up I got away with more than my brothers and sisters. Although I'm only realizing it now, I think I always knew that you couldn't afford to lose me. I was and continue to be your connection with your firstborn and as you get older, I find myself pulling away from both of you. Soon you will leave me and it feels like you're looking forward to being with her again. That means I wasn't a replacement; I was a "filler."

I don't know if I'll ever have the courage to give you this letter, but this is the first step.

X. Sibling Grief: The Forgotten Mourners

◆ Altered Family Dynamics

The death of a child profoundly alters future family dynamics and changes the course of the family's life, as well as the life of each individual within the family constellation. A totally *new reality* follows the death of a child for the surviving family members, in every situation, whether grief is resolved or not. It's an absolute given that the loss of a child will color the life of everyone in the family forever after.

While we've emphasized parental loss and grief thus far, it's just as essential to discuss the grief of siblings, in the context of the death of a sibling at any time, but specifically as it pertains to the replacement child. A baby born after the death of a child will not have known their sibling, but as we've seen, that may not matter very much when the deceased is constantly referred to as if he/she is still alive. The child who 'replaces' a sibling with whom they've shared an intimate relationship, may grieve as much as, or in some cases, more than their parents, so profound is the connection.

There is often a misguided expectation that living children will resume their normal lives while their parents and other close adults grieve. But we must acknowledge that children are far more perceptive about what's happening around them than many adults might realize. *Children need to grieve too, in whatever age appropriate way they can.* From the very beginning, keen attention must be paid to surviving siblings since it's mostly adults they look up to for support and guidance.

Open communication within the family is an essential determinant of how well family members are able to move through and beyond the profound grief, deep sense of loss, and psychological vulnerability experienced immediately after, and for an extended period after the death of a child.

We emphasize this point because we've learned that grieving parents may not understand what the grieving sibling is going through or how to address the needs of their grieving children. Any loss carries long-term consequences but how loss is handled is the crucial piece.

It's essential for parents and/or other very close family members (especially if the parents are unable to do this themselves) to explain the circumstances of the death in simple terms. In fact, parents should be aware that questions and issues surrounding the death will probably need to be addressed many times, not just initially. Be truthful, direct, and reassuring especially with very young children. If the surviving sibling is very young, refrain from using pat phrases or euphemisms (He went to sleep. He was so good that the angels took him.) to describe the death of a child, or even the idea of death itself.

Very young children think in concrete terms and may believe that death is temporary or reversible. A child who is sleeping can wake up. A lost child can be found. It's also better not to create a relationship between a young child and the deceased, such as "So-and-so is your guardian angel or, is watching over you." That can be both confusing and frightening.

For older children, the information surrounding the death can be expanded to include the actual circumstances, for example, an illness or accident. Surviving children need to understand as much as is age-appropriate since some children may feel that they caused the death somehow or are responsible for the family's related sadness. Even older children may feel guilty about a sibling's death, believing they caused the death, for example, by having asked the sibling to run an errand during which time the sibling was killed, or for having survived, by just continuing to live after a sibling died, or by having survived a car crash in which the sibling was killed. An older child should be reassured that he/she is not responsible.

Children should be reassured about anything that might be frightening them, including unstated fears. It might be good to say things like: "Not everyone who gets sick dies,"

"Not everyone is in a car accident," or "Not everyone who is in a car accident dies."

Children learn how to express grief from watching their parents; in other words, parents model behavior for their children. Parents who are capable of expressing their emotions and displaying their feelings positively show their children that they can do the same thing. Parents who can openly express grief, yet are still able to stay present and grounded in their lives, reassure their children that in the midst of profound sorrow, they are still capable of taking care of their family.

Children may cry, feel depressed, and sometimes even show regressive behavior, both developmentally and emotionally, such as tantrums, aggressive, or dependent behavior. Young children can't always express their feelings and so may act them out. Often a child who seems overly demanding is trying to get a parent's attention, sometimes to distract them from their grief and sometimes to remind the parent that they are right there in from of them. When a parent is not there emotionally for a child after the loss of a sibling, it may feel like a double loss. On the other hand, some children may withdraw, showing little emotion outwardly, choosing rather to grieve privately. However a child chooses to respond, be patient, loving, and compassionate, pay more attention, and make extra time for the child.

Most older children are capable of understanding the nuances and the circumstances surrounding the death. But changes in behavior, including withdrawal from usual activities, using alcohol or drugs, sexual acting out, taking risks, and talking about suicide require immediate parental intervention without judgment, and if necessary, professional intervention.

Parents need to include their surviving children in the process of grieving and mourning in the same way they do themselves. Mourning may last for months, or even years if it's complicated, but grief to some degree may last a lifetime, especially around birthdays, anniversaries, and all the events that should have happened but didn't. Children need to be included in all aspects (again, whatever is age appropriate) of family grieving, from attending the funeral and/or memorial service to planning family rituals around the death of their sibling.

Excluding an older child or teen from the funeral and burial of a sibling may be far more detrimental to them than adults may appreciate. This might occur when parents and close relatives believe that they are actually protecting their child. But in reality, missing this crucial piece may cause a surviving child to feel left out, especially when relative strangers are allowed to attend, and may prevent proper closure for a sibling. Consequently, children, especially older children, should be asked and included if they wish to attend, while their decision should be respected if they decline.

Of course, children who do not attend a funeral or go to the cemetery can be given other options so that they feel they are doing something and being included, for example, planting a tree or giving to a special charity in the deceased's name. For many, choosing such options may be the better choice, keeping in mind that the main concern should be the child's feelings of safety and security.

There is one exception to the idea of including children in family grieving, rituals, and remembrances: taking very young children to the cemetery on an ongoing basis. Some parents feel the need to frequently visit a child's grave, beyond the funeral and on special occasions such as birthdays and anniversaries of the death. Adults may want to share their experience with their children "as a family." But most young children's experience of death will be limited. They may be confused and upset to see a parent openly express emotions of sadness and grief.

You might consider giving an older child a choice about cemetery visits. Be honest about what you will do there. Hopefully, they will be better equipped emotionally if they understand what the experience will be like. You may give them the option to visit the cemetery at a later time or perhaps to bring someone along that he/she is particularly close to and comfortable having there.

In some cases, when there are no other caretakers, older siblings may *temporarily* assume the role of parent. At some point, though, children must be allowed to return to their role as children. Professional help may be needed if parental grief remains largely unresolved and the parent's functioning within the family is compromised.

In an excerpt from her book, *Sibling Grief: Healing after the Death of a Sister or Brother*, Pleasant Gill White notes that seven kinds of 'survivor' siblings have been identified:

1. The Haunted Child lives in a family where death is acknowledged but no one talks about what happened, and therefore, the surviving child cannot ask questions.

2. The Overprotected Child is hovered over in an attempt to ensure that nothing happens to them. This may interfere with the child's autonomy and independence.

3. The Lap Child is a variation on the theme of the overprotected child. In this scenario, it's easier for the mother to keep a very young child close by while she is tending to a child who is ill and eventually dies.

4. The Lonely Child may be neglected or left to their own devices after the death of a sibling. This may be the result of parental separation and divorce, living in a single-parent home, or being the only child remaining.

5. Later-born Children are often outsiders, having never known the deceased. These children may fantasize about a relationship they could have had with the deceased sibling.

6. The Scapegoat Child becomes the object of parents' hostility due to their own guilt about the death of a child.

7. The Replacement Child encompasses three separate situations:

- a child born after the death of another may be treated as the reincarnation of that deceased sibling;

- an adopted child may assume the role of replacement;
- a survivor sibling may 'replace' a deceased sibling by taking over the role of that child. [35]

Above all, sibling relationships are among the closest many of us will ever have. The death of a child breaks that unique sibling bond and is irreplaceable. Siblings are best friends, "buddies" through life, protectors, and keepers of the family secrets. The loss of a sibling is the loss of a "life witness," one who knows you in a way that no one else ever will.

Remembering Our Sister

A few months after she recounted the story of her sister Jennifer in The Girl Who Never Grew Up, the first story in this book, Shelly was sitting with her other sister, Joanne, on the eve of her niece's bat mitzvah. She mentioned that by a strange series of coincidences, she had been interviewed for a book on replacement children. She recounts the conversation that followed.

Joanne looks at me for a second and I watch her whole face change.

"Huh," Joanne's eyes widen, "I never thought about the idea of replacement children. I guess you are. I mean, I always knew it, I just never thought about it. So," Joanne puts down the spoon from the pot she's stirring, "Can I ask you... what did you talk about?"

My sister and I don't have these kinds of talks. She's ten years older, and because I knew that witnessing Jennifer's death left her traumatized, I never brought it up. The last time I can remember talking about it with her was when I was nine, when she told me she saw it in the first place.

"Uh, sure." I say. This is a big deal for me. I don't like talking about it either. It's one of those things I brush over in conversation. When people ask me how many brothers and sisters I have, I don't even mention Jennifer. When I do, it comes out as a run-on sentence, jumbled and quick, Uh yeah, I had another sister, Jennifer, but she died way before I was born, it's okay though, I never knew her...

I decide to start with the easiest part.

"She asked me if Jennifer was idolized." I tell Joanne.

Joanne laughs.

"And then," I say, "I remembered that I had never, like ever, heard one bad thing about Jennifer. Do you remember? Was she really that perfect? Was she really as perfect as Dad said?"

My sister takes a moment.

"Well, she was definitely brilliant," Joanne, says matter-of-factly. "It was kind of ridiculous. She could recite whole operas at four years old, and speak other languages and all those things. That part is absolutely true, but she had a temper. She would have these incredible outbursts, real meltdowns that were, frankly, scary."

Neither of us takes the time to mention we have seen my father do the exact same thing.

"Wow. See?" I say, "I never heard that."

"Oh." Joanne grabs a kitchen chair and sits. "What else did you talk about?"

"Well," I start to tell her, "Like the fact that Dad said that I looked exactly like Jennifer all the time."

"But," Joanne looks at me confused, "You don't look anything like her! She had Mom's complexion."

"I know!" I laugh. I had always been jealous of that. My mother and grandmother both inherited a rich beautiful olive tone that none of the other children were lucky enough to get. Instead, we got her rotting teeth.

"And you know," I continue, "the pressure, how I could just never live up to the expectation of becoming an overachiever, stuff like that, even though I never really thought about it at that age. Also about having to look at all the poetry and stuff."

"I had to go through that too," Joanne tells me, "I remember Dad telling me, 'Why can't you write a poem like Jennifer? Why can't you be more like your sister was?' And of course I couldn't because of the dyslexia and all my learning problems. It was even harder for me to do something like that, so I would always end up feeling stupid. I never felt as good as her."

"Me too," I say quietly. "Mom said that when Jennifer died, Dad kind of just broke. She said he was never the same after that."

My sister and I have little in common. She's a schoolteacher in Manhattan, very religious, six feet tall, larger framed, with two kids and dog. I'm an artist living in Los Angeles, who hasn't gone to synagogue since my nephew's bar mitzvah the year prior. I own a cat that I treat like my child. It was weird to sit in her kitchen and hear the same stories come out of our mouths. Slowly, as she gets up and starts to putter around the kitchen again, we swap stories, and I start to see that we both hold the burden of being replacements.

I begin to tell my sister things I have never talked about openly before. "We talked about, and I didn't think about this either, but how I didn't really have an identity till I passed the age that Jennifer died."

"You know," Joanne begins rapidly, "You want to hear something crazy? When I was in fifth or sixth grade, we had this paper we had to write called One Wish. We had to take it home and write down one wish that we wanted. I took it home and I showed it to Dad and he said 'Well you know what you're going to wish for, don't you?' and I thought, I don't know, a million dollars or something? And he said 'Of course you're going to wish that your sister hadn't died.' And I felt so guilty that I hadn't thought of it first. I mean I felt really bad about it. I felt like a bad person, but I was only like ten years old. So I did. I wrote my whole paper about how I wished my sister never died and got up in front of the whole class and read it. Every one else got to wish for a plane or to go to Disneyland. I never got to be a regular kid. I never got to do stuff like wish for a million dollars."

I understood so much about my sister in that moment. During her speech at my niece's bat mitzvah my sister said, "I knew at ten years old I wanted to have a baby girl and I wanted to name her Jennifer." I thought about our conversation in the kitchen, and I felt for the first time that I had never really been alone in my plight. I was just never encouraged to talk about it.

"So let me ask you a question," I say that night in the kitchen. "Were you worried about placing a burden on Jenny... with the name and everything?"

"Well," Joanne says, "I consciously named her Jenny. I never call her Jennifer."

"But," I tread light on this topic, "She went through that weird phase last year though, when she was asking about her."

Joanne doesn't like to talk about this. I think it makes her feel guilty. I don't think she talks about Jennifer much to anyone, particularly Jenny.

"Remember? She was always asking me about her. She kept saying she wanted to know about the person she was named after? Does Jenny still do that?"

Joanne bends down to pull some chicken out of the oven and brushes off the question, "Not with me."

"Well it was a couple years ago." I tell her. Some things are still not open for discussion. "I guess when she was more Jennifer's age. Maybe it faded when she got older. Were you worried about something happening to her, when she got to be as old as Jennifer?"

"Shelly," Joanne says, "You always worry about that." She paused. "What about you? Are you going to name your kid after Josh?"

Josh, our brother, died of leukemia at age twenty-eight.

"Well," I say, "Dad sent me an email the day he found out I was pregnant asking me that if it's a boy to name it Joshua Steven, and it took me two days to realize that that was Josh's exact name. I guess some things never change..."

"Are you going to? Name him Josh, if it's a boy?" Joanne asks.

"Know what?" I say confidently, "I don't think so. I mean I used to think I would, but now I think it's just too much of a burden. It's not like naming someone after Aunt Shirley or someone who lived a nice healthy loving long life. It's naming someone after something tragic and I think it's too much to put on someone. I think it's time someone in this family got a clean slate."

"Sounds like a good idea." Joanne says.

My sister puts the lid on the soup and I help her cut some carrots and put whipped cream on a chocolate pie. The rest of the night is spent talking about politics, children, our mom and our husbands, but everything seems a little different. Somehow, we're a little closer, warmer. It feels a little lighter in the air. Now the air is filled with warmth and the smell of graham cracker crust. It feels after all this time, we are able to clean our slate too.

My son was born six months later. My husband and I named him Oliver. After no one.

Missing Pieces

The idea that if something is never discussed, means it's as good as if it never happened seems to be, for many, an acceptable way to deal with loss, especially tragic loss such as that of a child. It's understandable, yet quite amazing that adults believe that if they pretend that nothing ever happened, it's as good as erasing it out of their lives. That defensive posture may work for the adults involved, but it's not acceptable for some surviving children who often "know" that something bad happened, that something is wrong, as Sarah sensed.

"Purposeful forgetting" is the flip side of the constant, and often distorted, remembering of the deceased. While parents may feel that they may be doing everyone a service by keeping things hidden, that doesn't seem to be the case, as surviving siblings will tell you.

I was born just a few days shy of the first anniversary of my sister's death, at the age of just two years. I have my own first name but I carry her middle name.

My parents didn't tell me about my sister until I was fifteen (and only then at the urging of a concerned relative who thought that it would be awful for me to find out by accident). Until then I had thought that I was possibly an afterthought, as there is a six-year gap between me and my older brother. It was an enormous shock to me of course, and although there were tears at the time and an explanation of how she had died, things very quickly moved on to a place where we just didn't talk about it. I went for many years without discussing it and I still find it enormously hard to talk about her without feeling overwhelmed.

As for my siblings, I assumed that my older brothers knew and so did not raise it with them either. I regret that now; the younger of my two brothers was four at the time of her death and did not remember ever having a sister (which still seems incredible to me). He found out about her in his thirties through a chance meeting with someone who attended the scene. I was so sad that we had both struggled with this and that here was this person who thought he may possibly have had a sister but never knew for sure.

And although the grief of losing a child is impossible for me to begin to imagine, I was angry with my parents for seeming to have tried to just go on as if she never existed, and for not helping their other children through their grief and confusion. I imagine that my brothers dealt with her death in their own way, and would have understood through the example of my parents that she was never to be discussed. This was the sixties and I'm sure that there was little support in the way of grief counseling or family therapy.

My brother eventually spoke with my parents about his need to have his sister acknowledged. Although there was a funeral service for her, her ashes were scattered at a memorial garden and no plaque erected to commemorate her. With my parents' permission, my brother organized a plaque in that same memorial garden and I have since visited it with him and then later with my parents.

Their grief is still absolutely raw and we can't talk together about it for long before it is too much. I have always felt guilty for needing to talk about it, as I tend to think of it as "their grief" and not something for me to be a part of, given that I did not know her and was not part of the family when she was alive.

My mother has referred to her lost daughter as being "like a dream baby," in that her time with her was so brief that it is almost as if she never existed at all. I think I have always hoped that I could offer up my story to a health professional and they would say, "Aha, yes, now that I know that about you I have the key to making you feel better." But of course that has never been the case. I also sometimes feel that I place too much emphasis on it as having a negative impact on my development as a child and adolescent and it can seem self-indulgent to dwell on it (when I cannot possibly understand what my parents went through); maybe I would be an anxious and insecure person anyway.

I have children of my own now and when they were smaller I was terrified of something happening to them. I watched over them constantly because I know based on my own family that freak accidents happen. Now that they are a bit older I am not as anxious and I do also make a conscious effort to let them take risks.

Love is the Most Essential Thing

Melina was twelve when her eleven-year-old sister, Clara, began to have physical symptoms that progressed and worsened, resulting in her death two years later. These siblings were very close while their little sister, Vera, who was nine at the time, was too young to share this bond.

Melina's relationship with Clara was a fascinating one. Clara shared with her sister that she had premonitions; she seemed to have an understanding about mystical and spiritual things that made Melina feel somewhat inferior. When she was with Clara, Melina felt as if she was with an enlightened person.

I felt a huge sense of well-being; that's what people generally say about being close to such enlightened people. What's said about them is that they have re-incarnated so many times, and so have learned so much. It's as if they know everything about life and can connect with heaven and earth. It's a very nice feeling!

When Clara and I spoke, I didn't understand much, but I listened and said, 'Wow! I feel great!' It was such an amazing feeling of well-being, and I kept looking at her in admiration, so surprised and in awe of her—what you would imagine today would happen in the presence of an enlightened Tibetan lama—something like that, very special. Any topic she addressed was touched with wisdom. That surprised me a lot. And I was no fool. I realized that in comparison to other members of my family Clara spoke from a place of wisdom.

When I began to understand what death was, I was furious. In some way, I wanted to accompany Clara. I had such mixed feelings about how I was supposed to respond appropriately to her death. Immersed in my anger I felt, 'Well, now I'm going to do whatever I like or want!' I was very, very rebellious, and I remember I wanted to fight; I fought with my parents. I was mad at life! I questioned, 'Is this life? How can they take a sister away from me? How can they do that?' I was terribly angry.

I remember that when Clara was in the hospital I asked God to give her back to me. When that didn't happen I said, 'I don't believe in God any more!' I couldn't believe in life this way. I was annoyed! But, it was not only about not believing in God, it was about not believing in life, too. I pushed against the "design of life," no longer in agreement about how things happen. I thought that this must have been the way the people in the Holocaust felt. They probably wondered, 'How can this be happening?' My whole foundation, the structure of my life was rocked. I questioned my sister's death—'And this? What do I do with this?'

I was only able to resolve my grief a long time after Clara died. My thought was that life should have taken the less capable of us, and that I couldn't measure up to her. Only when I started seeing good aspects in myself, or virtues that I was not aware of, could I start accepting my own existence. Only much later was it possible for me to understand my complaint to God for not having heard my demand that Clara continue to live.

I'm fifty-six and only now do I understand that it's not up to us to decide our destiny in life or death; that there's something or someone that is in charge of deciding how long we will remain in this state—life as we know it. Because of Clara's existence, life was touched by a magic wand, given that she left us the teaching that love is the most essential thing in life. I had to learn to love myself to be able to love others. The feeling of spirituality that Clara transmitted left an indelible mark on me. Only now have I found the path to spirituality. It was like going back home—finding myself on the road she acquainted me with.

My advice to those who have lost a sibling is to try to understand that in a death there are no guilty parties, nor is death a chance occurrence. Things are managed by rules that bow to a higher order than the ones we can understand. What's left for us is to accept our reality and enjoy life with what we have. That doesn't relieve the sadness we feel when a sibling dies. But there is something else; things happen for a reason, beyond what we would want to happen. We need to accept and love life while we have it.

Two Generations of Sibling Loss

Diana Doyle lost her mother, sister, and four-year-old daughter all to different deaths within thirty-six months. Her blog *Sunshine in a Blue Cup* gives hope to those suffering a loss, experiencing grief, or facing a life challenge.

My daughter and I share a special bond. Both of our only sisters have died. The death of my first child, Savannah, created the same unique loss for my other daughter, Dempsey. Sometimes, we are known as replacement children.

However, I feel I have an advantage over Dempsey because I'm an adult. I can comprehend the 'how' and 'why' and can process my sadness to a greater degree. Dempsey is only a tiny ten years old. She was almost two when her sister Savannah died at the age of four and a half. She never knew her! I'm thankful I had thirty-nine years with my sister, Tarnia.

However, I've learned that no matter the age, the feelings and thoughts after losing a sibling are similar. The only difference is that Dempsey's questions about her sister's death are unfiltered... honest, unlike mine, which I hide most days like a shameful secret.

Yesterday, Dempsey and I had a chat about the loss of her sister Savannah, and my sister Tarnia, as we sometimes do. You see yesterday, my sister's twin daughters, Emerald and Charlotte were over at our house for a swim; the splashing going on in the pool went from giggles to tears in a heartbeat. An argument erupted over a silly game, "Marco Polo," and when the twins left, Dempsey burst into a ball of tears in my arms—crying about the argument, because she loves her cousins. They're sisters like the one she doesn't have here.

I hugged her and we chatted about the silly fight. I told her she has to be kind to her cousins, to forgive them; that one day, Daddy and I will be gone and it'll be important that she has her cousins in her life since she doesn't have her sister here... or any other sibling.

Later, when she was in bed, I thought about our conversation. I always wrestle with guilt that she doesn't have her sister here and that I couldn't give her another sibling. I thought how the death of a brother or sister leave lifetime scars, a cocktail of emotions that linger on years after their deaths.

For me, losing my sister changed my identity. It changed my place in our family from being the baby to stepping up into my sister's shoes and becoming a replacement for her... in many, many ways. I still struggle with some of the fallout of her death. It never goes away—and if anything, as time goes on, it gets harder because she's not here. I think that's the most challenging thing—that death is final.

Some of the things I struggled with and still do are these:

Guilt: Guilt that it wasn't me that died. Why her and not me? Guilt that after some time, I could laugh again and enjoy life... and Tarnia never would again. Guilt that I get to witness her children growing up and not her! It was me that attended her son Alexander's graduation, and me that her other son, Fraser pours his love into. Me that got to take her twin daughters shopping for their first bra... I also have guilt that as Dempsey grows into a woman she won't have her sister here to support her when she needs someone. And I can't dismiss these feelings. I've learned how to accept that this is part of who I am now.

I've managed to channel my grief over my sister's death into something constructive by keeping a journal of memories about Tarnia that's helped me to heal and relieve some of my guilt. Her four children, especially her twin daughters, who were only six months old when she died, will cherish this one day.

Sadness: The sadness comes and goes. On difficult days like birthdays and anniversaries it returns in force. However, for a long time after Tarnia died it was like I was invisible. Everyone was supporting Mom and Dad, and rightly so. Not many people asked the simple question, "How are you doing, Diana?" I was left alone to deal with losing my sister while at the same time morphing into my mother's role, comforting her as she was inconsolable. And because of this I hide my tears from Dempsey when she cries for her sister... it's heartbreaking, but I never want her to feel she somehow has to 'fix' my grief or that she's responsible for my happiness because of her sister's death.

I fear Dempsey will also have guilt as we were praying Dempsey's stem cells from her cord blood would save Savannah... but this wasn't to be and I'm afraid this may play on her psyche in years to come... that she couldn't save her sister too.

Anxiety: Anxiety is now part of my being, like the birthmark on my neck; I carry it around everyday because of my sister and my daughter's death. I've become a helicopter Mom as a result of that anxiety and fear. Because I know in a heartbeat that life can change. I hate Dempsey being out of my sight, and I worry when she wants to be a thrill seeker, jumping off a pier or kayaking on our lake! Sometimes, Dempsey reminds me to "Stop, Mommy!" And I hate myself for not being able to control this evil twin that I live with.

Anger: After Tarnia died, I was angry at her, which was ridiculous! Anger that she caused so much pain to Mom and Dad... to her husband and kids... that she altered my life. Anger at my Dad that sometimes he favored my sister's children over mine. I feel he still does this sometimes. It's a demon I still struggle with.

Wondering: The reflecting and wondering is unyielding, relentless... for me it's the ultimate emotion in the grief process. I know Dempsey always wonders too. She often asks, "What was Savannah like?" "Did she love me?" "What would it be like if my sister was still here?" ...amongst so many questions she longs to know, as do I... and I realize that she'll struggle with this as her life unfolds.

For a long time after my sister and my daughter died the wondering became an obsession. Once I followed a stranger around the supermarket because she looked so much like my sister... I couldn't stop staring at her... and imagining, just for a second it was Tarnia!

And some nights, I watch Dempsey sleep, soaking in the resemblance between my child who's here and the one who's not. I also know I can't fix this part of Dempsey's life... without her sister. It's something I can only give her tools to deal with as she grows. Sibling grief runs as deep as losing my child. It's always there; however different, it's shaped and molded me into a new person.

I feel my biggest responsibility now is to be there for my sister's children, to love them and support them. And then there's Dempsey. She will feel the ripples of her sister's death her whole life... like I do. I can't change that. However, I can take what I've learned through having experienced the same unique loss and provide her with guidance and knowledge that she is her own special irreplaceable being—to never make her feel she is inferior to her sister who isn't here or that she'll never live up to who Savannah was to me.

I can reinforce she should never have guilt, that she's innocent of not being able to save her sister. Instead of sadness she should be happy she had a sister, and that we have photos and meaningful videos and my memories of their time together. And also that anger and anxiety create unhappiness. I teach her we all have choices that will shape who we become, so to always choose to live life to the fullest and enjoy every moment she's blessed with.

However, the wondering; that's something I think she'll learn to incorporate into her life... as I have, a byproduct of grief that losing a loved one, especially a sibling brings.

Yes, Dempsey and I share not just a mother/daughter relationship but a connection; that as an adult she will come to understand and if I lead by example, and demonstrate to her that girlfriends and cousins can be sisters, family you choose for yourself! That all is not lost, and that lessons in losing a sibling teach us compassion and appreciation and that's something I will be grateful my sister left me with forever... like her death.

A Sister Reflects

Jessica was delivered by C-section, two weeks passed the due date, after a normal pregnancy. She began having problems very shortly after delivery and ended up coming home with a feeding tube. After that, it was one thing after another. At eight-month-old Jessica developed cataracts and was diagnosed with failure to thrive. She would stop breathing on a regular basis and had to be resuscitated day and night.

However, Jessica was a bright and happy baby, meeting all of her milestones. She would sing all the time and started reading at a very early age. She was diagnosed with a degenerative nerve condition and problems with her metabolic system necessitated one month in Boston Children's Hospital when she was two and a half. On top of that she had frequent bouts of pneumonia. Her father was in medical school at the time and constantly searched for answers even while going to more and more doctors.

When Jessica was four and a half, she became very ill with pneumonia. This time, they could not resuscitate her and she went into a coma that lasted two weeks. After she finally awoke she was never the same: she was no longer able to talk or walk and came home with a tracheotomy.

In 1998, the family moved to Connecticut and Jessica went to school with a nurse. She was totally aware but could not speak or respond. She stopped breathing many times during the day and night and would need to be constantly resuscitated. Jessica passed away at home one day when she stopped breathing. She was eight years old. Melissa was five years old and a brother was only nine months old when Jessica passed away. Sixteen-year-old Melissa reflects on the death of her sister, Jessica, and the meaning of her life to her family.

If there's one emotion I can remember feeling when my sister was around, it was love. I can't specifically pick out moments where I felt sad for her, or when I wish things were different. I have been surrounded by love my entire life, and I think my sister was a huge part of that. There was no doubt Jessica loved me; I remember her smile and how she used to play with me and look at me. My parents also showed great affection for me and for both of my siblings, no matter what. Love is the first word I think of when I think about my sister and my childhood.

I've tried many times in my life to think back to the morning after she passed away. I don't know if these are memories I made up in my head or if they actually happened, but I have a memory of my sister's room, completely empty, and an empty house. I wish I could remember exactly how I felt when I found out she had passed away, but unfortunately I can't. I think it's for the better that I can't remember. It lessens the pain a little bit.

If I can remember anyone's feelings, it's my parents'. I remember that sometime after Jessica passed away my parents and I sat on my bed, just crying. I didn't really know what was going on or what to do. But I remember that this was the first (and only) time I'd seen my dad cry. I also can recall one night after I went to bed, my dad came into my room, picked me up, and brought me to the kitchen. My mom was leaning on the kitchen sink in tears. I was scared, clutching my dad and not knowing what to do. My dad whispered in my ear to "hug mommy" and so I did as I was told. That is one of the most vivid memories I have from that time in my life.

Now, I find myself often having moments where I just stop and think about her. Even now it's hard to process that I once had an older sister, another member of this family. I do miss her, everyday. I miss who she was and I miss the person she could've been. Even though I know this sadness is still in the back of me and my family's minds, we know we have to move on and continue living our lives.

I think given the circumstances, my parents and everyone who helped did a fantastic job at handling the situation—whether it be my sister's being taken care of, or me and my brother's happiness. My parents never broke down in front of me, no matter how hard it may have been not to. I, my brother and my sister were all given equal love and care.

I definitely feel her loss in a bigger way now, without a doubt. Now that I'm older, I'm able to process death. I've seen similar situations around me in life, and I find myself thinking about her more and more as I get older. The most common vision I have of her now is who she would've been, despite her problems. I think about what kind of sister she would be, had she not had any of these disabilities. I could picture myself visiting her in college, her helping me with my homework, or letting me borrow her clothes. I think the hardest thing now, is hearing about my friends' older siblings. I have a group of camp friends who are all like my sisters.

Coincidentally, about four of them have older siblings who are the same age as Jessica would've been. About a year ago, their siblings were all entering college and they would talk about it a lot. Those were the moments when I felt the most sadness because I know if my sister was still here, I would be able to talk about all of this "older sibling going to college" madness too. Though I constantly think about her and her loss, I know she's in a better place now.

Typically, I try to avoid talking about my sister. Not because I don't WANT to, but simply because it can get kind of messy to explain. For one thing, she did not have a diagnosis. I also don't like the idea of people feeling bad for me. Usually when I tell people about my sister, they react in a dramatic way and I feel as though they think that I'm not okay. The truth is, I'm perfectly fine. Sure I miss her and wish she was still around, but I'm okay.

It's definitely uncomfortable to bring up, though there have been times when it's unavoidable. I'm so lucky to have so many great friends who understand me and can be there for me. My best friend from camp lost her dad when she was eight years old. Loss is something we share and can relate to. I think this is one of the reasons we are so close. We completely understand each other and help each other in any way possible.

For anyone else who might be going through this kind of loss, I would say that I know it's hard now to accept that someone you love is gone, but you have to keep going in life, and just never forget the memories of that person. Things will get better and if you keep a positive outlook on everything, that will definitely help you cope. For example, don't think about everything that person may have suffered, but rather think about their smile and the joy they brought to this world. It's amazing how big an impact people have on others.

I think initially my parents decided to start having a cake on Jessica's birthday. In fact, I can't remember a time when we didn't have a cake for Jessica. She's always with us in our hearts, and it's also a way for us to keep her spirit alive, and to never forget her. I always feel sad when we start singing happy birthday; there's just no way not to.

As I get older I feel as though it gets a little more painful to sing happy birthday, but at the same time I get stronger. It's important for my family to remember that although it is sad to know she's gone, we have to keep our thoughts positive and remember how great a person she was. We are simply celebrating her life each year on her birthday.

I definitely think this experience has made me a much more sensitive and compassionate person. When I see a person with special needs, I feel an internal connection. I think I also have become a more thoughtful person; someone who can connect with others on a personal level, and I feel as though I am more willing to help people. I don't know if all of these characteristics relate directly to my experience, but I'm sure it has helped them grow and blossom. My sister is a big part of who I am today, and I will never forget her smile, her laugh, or her hugs. I love my sister and always will, and I know she's always watching over me and supporting me no matter where she may be.

Through all of the craziness and sadness my family and I have experienced, we all have shared it together. This has made my family closer than ever. I can honestly say there are times when I'd rather be with my family than my friends, which I don't think a lot of teenagers can say. I feel as though Jessica made our family stronger, more together, and positive. She will always be our angel."

Healing the Divide

What happens when grief remains unresolved, continuing for years, when denial and addiction are the chief coping mechanisms, when the family refuses to recognize and/or discuss the feelings of the adult replacement child? Often, it is up to the individual, the "outsider" to find their own healing "solution," which is exactly what Lisa set out to do.

In my recovery work over the past couple years I began to explore the idea of healing the divide between me and my deceased brother. I am essentially estranged from my family of origin—we still have a contentious relationship since I want to talk about this and they say I am crazy. Never mind the fact that I am the only one in recovery and they are all still running from their grief. I suspect there will be no healing unless they can acknowledge this. I do feel crazy sometimes and alone most all the time.

My parents divorced over thirty years ago. My dad has remarried twice. My mom is drinking herself into oblivion and has never had another companion. My sister was infertile and adopted three children. My brother married late in life and has one stepson, but has no children of his own. My three children are the biological "next generation" and my family doesn't even know them—or want to—know them. I ache to know their families, but being around them is so painful for me—to be invisible while in the same room. When they do notice, it is only to criticize me. It is quite sad how unspoken grief and unfinished business has fractured our family.

Perception is reality, and I am at the opposite end of the spectrum from each of them. I feel like I am screaming, "I am right here!!" and they are turning their backs. I am still trying to accept that I have a desperate need for their approval, and I am just trying to live my life without it.

Since I haven't been able to get a direct answer out of anyone for over forty years, I started my OWN healing process by obtaining a copy each of my brother's birth and death certificates. I had to "prove" myself as a direct, immediate family relative. It was much easier than I expected, perhaps because we were both born in the same hospital. Somehow, having these documents makes his existence real, and my reality as their replacement for him more tangible.

What I have realized is that because he was "replaced," he has never had an existence either. He was God's Creation with his own unique spirit, placed on this Earth, even for a short time, for a very specific purpose. When they pretend his death never happened, this denies both of us. He is gone from the physical realm and I stand behind the veil. My family cannot look at either of us clearly because it is simply too painful. If they were to draw back the veil and truly see me, even for just a moment, that would confirm that he really did die. By not accepting his death, they cannot accept me... or him.

I went on to find out the location of his gravesite. His cremated remains are in a mausoleum in a cemetery near our birthplace. We moved away from that place forty years ago and never returned to visit his grave. I have tried to visit, but the cemetery with his remains is currently mired in a lawsuit. Visitation is meticulously limited and it has been closed both times I was in town. Someday, I will make that trip. No family member ever goes there, to my knowledge. Essentially, he has been forgotten.

I still struggle with "getting picked." I am learning that I need to choose myself. I don't need to do flip-flops hoping that, one day, my family-of-origin will see me (and pick me!) for who I am. Ironically, I feel closer to my deceased brother than I do any other family member. Even though we have never met, we have a common bond. I am doing what I can to remember him–give some significance to his existence. Although my parents didn't communicate it well, they are correct that I am alive today because he died. I wasn't making much of my life before recovery, but I have been working hard to create a new legacy for my children. I am grateful for this second chance, and I want for my brother to be proud of the life opportunity I was given, in his place."

Lisa's decision to bring her brother "back to life" is a bold and courageous one. She chose to make him a real presence in her own life, recognizing him as a real member of her own family, even while the rest of the family could not. This is one way that the replacement child can reconcile the past with the present even when family members remain in denial.

Life Changes in an Instant

Beth is a long-time New York City journalist. She is the author of *Ten Minutes from Home,* a memoir of loss. Her book poignantly tells the story of the tragic accident that dramatically changes her family and the course of her life. After years of grief and guilt, Beth ultimately finds great strength within herself and the desire to survive and love.

The year was 1982. Beth was twelve years old and her little brother Adam was seven. They were on their way back from Beth's ballet recital when their car was hit by a drunk driver. Their father, mother, and Beth's best friend, Kristen were also in the car that night.

Beth and her father were injured while Adam and Kristen lost their lives in the accident. Beth learned of her brother's death that night but didn't learn for several days that Kristen had also died. While in the hospital, Beth asked for Kristen repeatedly and didn't understand why she was not seeing her friend.

Beth did not go to her brother's funeral by choice, but wanted very much to attend Kristen's funeral. She was told that someone would take her to the funeral, which was being held on the day that Beth was being released from the hospital. But she was stalled on purpose and missed being at the funeral because "everyone thought it would be too much for her." She felt cheated that other friends who were not as close as she was to Kristen were able to attend the funeral while she wasn't.

Beth wanted so much to attend the last day of her sixth grade year. However, she was told that it wasn't an appropriate thing to do given the circumstances. She had looked forward to seeing her friends and receiving the many awards she had earned that year. The morning after the last day of her sixth grade, several teachers as well as the principal of her school, came to her home to present her with these awards.

Beth finally learned all of the details of the accident after seeing the local newspaper. Before that she had been told very little about what had actually happened. There were many quotes about Kristen from her junior high school friends. Beth read the quotes over and over again. She felt disturbed that she didn't get to give any of her own quotes about her best friend. People felt awkward around her and Beth realized that her accident injury, a broken foot, provided people with something concrete to talk about. "How's your foot?" everyone could ask, instead of, "How is your grief?"

After the accident, Beth felt that her mother was falling apart; she seemed to be disintegrating and unable to be there, as the mother she had been before the accident. Perhaps profound grief was all that kept her mother going. Unable to save herself, she in turn, could not "save" Beth. Beth believed she had to stay around the house much of the time to make sure that her mother was okay. It was her way of keeping everything together for the family.

When Beth returned home from going out, she would often find her parents in puddles of tears and this made her feel as if they were back at the beginning, like the first night in the hospital. Fear of that scenario would ensure that she would never talk about Adam or even mention his name. Her mind felt like a field of landmines; avoiding any single conversation that could in any way be connected to the accident.

In middle school, Beth found solace talking to the school social worker. It was easy to talk to Miss Boyd. Later on, another girl who had recently lost her brother was included in these sessions. The girls were very different, but in the sessions with Miss Boyd, their differences fell away and they could be open and honest with each other and themselves—Beth found a kindred spirit.

For Beth, her mother continued to feel "missing" in so many ways while her father did what he could to be there for her. On one occasion, her mother ran out of the house and Beth was terrified not knowing when her mother would return. Her father tried to reassure her that her mother would be back soon and she did return a couple of hours later.

Her mother's fleeing, even if for only two hours, was terrifying and stirred up something in Beth—a rebellious side began to awaken. Beth felt she needed a better escape, which included alcohol, cigarettes, and some destructive people, and this continued through high school.

Therapy resumed with the school psychiatrist in Beth's sophomore year in high school. A mandatory appointment had been set up for Beth by her English teacher because she had growing concerns about Beth's tendency to wear all black to class and appearing glassy-eyed and distracted. The psychiatrist told Beth that her emotions had been shut down for years, and now as a sixteen-year-old, she was beginning to feel her grief profoundly. Because she didn't know how to express it, she was acting out and depressed.

Going off to college was not, in and of itself, what allowed her to get her life together and move forward, but it was a start (though she says she probably drank more in college than in any period of her life). She thinks that being an English major focused her on her writing, which has always been a help. Home for winter break during her first year in college marked a breakthrough for Beth. It was one of the first times she was able to speak to her parents about all that had happened. This was the beginning of healing the gap between them. But it wasn't until years later, when she started real therapy, addressing the issues of the accident head on, that she was able to truly move forward and feel strong.

Both of her parents read her book. Her dad said that it was amazing to know what she was thinking and feeling about the events of that time. Beth feels that her daughter was definitely healing for her parents. While she doesn't feel she's overprotective of her young child, she doesn't like driving in the car with her.

The biggest piece of advice she can give from her experience is that after a trauma such as this, the child should be taken to a therapist immediately! After the accident, she was asked if she wanted to go to therapy and said, "No," since there was no way for her to be able to judge her own needs at that age or after such a traumatic experience. It would have been very helpful for the whole family to be in therapy at that time; it would have made a huge difference.

A few more thoughts... After the funeral and immediate mourning period, when the daily life begins to pick up once again, parents should keep some things in mind. First and foremost, they have to remember that their children will be mourning, too, so they need to pay close attention to what's going on in their children's lives and to keep the conversation going. Perhaps, at this point, grief counseling or a grief group should be considered. Sometimes the whole family can work together with a grief counselor or therapist.

A point that is often overlooked, applies especially to very young children who have lost a sibling. They may fear that they will not live beyond the age at which their sibling died. Consequently, it is extremely important to reassure them that, despite their connection to the deceased sibling, they are not in danger of dying at an early age. Referencing future events in their lives such as learning to drive, going to college, getting married, and having children of their own may be very reassuring.

Surviving siblings, like their parents, have to find a "new normal." Roles will be shifted within the family and outside the family as well. It can be very awkward and uncomfortable for a child returning to school or getting together with friends after the loss of a sibling. They may want support and acknowledgement that things have changed, or may not want to talk about it at all. Giving your child a "script," ways to direct the conversation or helping them find a way to indicate they're not ready to talk about all that's happened, may help them feel more comfortable when questions are asked and comments are made.

Sibling grief is ongoing and forever, just as parental grief is. But it need not be morbid, and life can go on.

XI. Parents: Resolution & Remembrance

◆ Death Ends a Life—Not a Relationship

All of the books, articles, and studies, no matter how conclusive, can never capture the full impact of the loss of a child on the parents, nor describe accurately the profound grief, the sense of emptiness, and sometimes, the loss of purpose that accompany the death of a child. Many of the stories in this book highlight the major issues and pathological aspects involved in the phenomenon of the replacement child. Inevitable within these stories are the grieving parents.

We frankly weren't sure how parents would respond to questions about a deceased child, or even if they would respond at all. It's clear that for many parents, the death of a child, even a death occurring years ago, is far too painful to discuss; the wound of loss remains open and raw. Our hope was that some parents would write about their experience of death, loss, and grief, and what happens beyond that.

We are so grateful to have these instructive and inspirational stories. Rather than focus on all of the things that can go wrong, they teach us how to get through one of the darkest periods that anyone will ever experience in a lifetime. Each story takes us through a difficult and complex process fraught with emotion, often doubt, and ultimately focuses on the determination to move on, to try once more, to be grateful for everything, and to live life to its fullest capacity.

Ten Minutes for Silvan

Holding Silvan: A Brief Life, is Monica Wesolowska's story about the birth of her firstborn child, a seemingly healthy boy. But soon after birth, there are signs that something is very wrong. Eventually, Monica and her husband are handed the grim prognosis and they make the decision to allow Silvan to die at home in his own time. Although an incredibly heartbreaking story, Monica and her husband demonstrate steadfast courage throughout their ordeal. Only a parent who has gone through an experience of this kind can speak to all of the issues and emotions.

Monica conveys the everyday life while waiting for her son to die with such raw honesty and humanity. She portrays her son and his brief life with love and pride; there is such a sense of integrity about this little boy—he is not just a baby, but a full human being in his own right. One comes away feeling great respect for Silvan.

Here, ten years after Silvan's death, Monica speaks about keeping his memory alive, parenting her two sons, and stepping fully into her decision to live life in every moment.

Sitting at the kitchen table where I write these words now (my children's voices in the background), I once listened in horror as a woman I barely knew gave me these words of advice after the death of my newborn son, Silvan: 'Whatever you do, don't have more children. My parents had me after my brother died, and I could never live up to their expectations.' Her words felt terrible on many levels. For one, I was deep in grief. To think of subsequent children felt a dishonor to Silvan's memory. For another, as we grieved together in our empty house, my husband and I held on to the hope that someday we would be ready to try again. I already knew about grief. I'd lost my father and brother before Silvan. I knew my father and brother were irreplaceable, but I also knew I'd gone on to love others. I had to believe it was possible to raise subsequent children without damaging them. I was sure I had more love in me. Having loved Silvan fully made me want to love his siblings fully.

This didn't make the leap to pregnancy any less scary. Silvan had been damaged during labor, so severely we'd chosen to remove him from life support. This had seemed the loving thing to do, to hold him and let him go. Though we knew he'd been asphyxiated inside me, no one knew why. Now the doctors questioned whether I could carry a healthy baby to term at all. But if I was going to try, my doctor wanted me to try soon because of my age. Mercifully, I got pregnant easily. Once I did, the doctors seemed confident, but still I worried if I'd have the strength to endure another loss. I balanced grieving for Silvan, going through pregnancy again, and worrying that something terrible might happen.

Miles was born one year and two weeks after Silvan's birth. For the first week after birth, I felt removed from him. Not that anyone could see this–I cooed; I nursed; I coddled him–but I was holding back. I was waiting to make sure he survived. A week later, the fog lifted. The same happened two years later with his brother Ivan. Perhaps this is natural. Throughout time, most cultures have waited to celebrate the arrival of a child for at least a week—the life of both mother and child being so tenuous at first. I was sad not to feel ecstatic, not to be able to say that my children's births had been the "best days of my life," but by the end of the week for each boy, the love flooded in.

From the start, my husband and I believed in talking to our children about Silvan. We installed a child-sized wooden bench in the backyard with Silvan's name and dates. As soon as they could crawl, Miles and Ivan climbed onto it. They called it Silvan's bench which led to questions about Silvan. Sitting in the backyard, they could see the naturalness of death all around them–in empty snail shells and curled pill bugs. In some ways, it seemed so easy, so natural to explain death when they were young.

But just when we think we've got parenting down, our children change, or we change. With time, Miles and Ivan began asking harder questions, they worried more about mortality. At the same time, I was growing and one day I felt an urge to write about Silvan. With both boys past infancy and toddlerhood, I had more room for Silvan again. I wanted to remember his newborn sweetness and examine our choice. Knowing that someday our children will need a full explanation of that choice, I wanted to make sure that removing Silvan from life support still felt right. I felt I owed this both to Silvan and to those of us going on without him.

Publishing a book about Silvan challenged our family. It gave him more space than he'd had before. My children seemed jealous. Miles wanted to know why I didn't write a "happy book about me and Ivan." Ivan stapled his own drawings together and called it The Ivan Book. At the end of that year, I missed a hip-hop performance by Miles and a classroom celebration for Ivan because I was away giving readings from my book. I felt terrible about it, but they recovered quickly. And in the end, I think it's been a good thing—I've felt again how much we loved Silvan, and I've seen how much our story has helped others, but also it's been good for the boys. Just as they had to learn to share my love for them with each other, and with their father, and with our extended family and friends, they are learning that there's room in our hearts for the dead as well as the living.

This year, on the 10th anniversary of Silvan's birth, we decided to go as a family on a silent hike. One minute of silence for every year since Silvan's been gone. Without our voices, other senses opened. We saw wild turkeys, tasted miner's lettuce, heard the squeak of eucalyptus trees rubbing limb to limb. The reality of loss forces us to feel lucky for what we have. To think Silvan would have been kinder, smarter, more handsome than our living children, is to indulge in a fantasy that helps no one. Our three children have been so different one from the other. They have each been spectacular in their own way, and they make me see how random it all is, which sperm and egg meet, which zygote implants, which survives until birth. Knowing any one of us could die at any moment, there's barely room for regret. I'll always miss Silvan. But I'd be *dishonoring him not to live fully, not to love fully, because of his absence. Ten minutes of silence in nature may have been hard for our boys at first, they may have only been doing it for us, but by the end they'd decided it was worth it. They even said they wanted to do it again."*

 Her memoir about the brief life and death of her firstborn, HOLDING SILVAN, is available from Hawthorne Books.

Memories of Zoe

Here, too, first-time parents suffer the tragic loss of a child when the unimaginable happens. Complicating matters significantly is Alicia's potentially life-threatening condition at the time of Zoe's birth. The decision and the determination to become a mother, no matter what it would take, serve to help Alicia put her grief in perspective in order to accomplish her desired goal.

This mother and father were able to harness their energies in the throes of their grief, to dig deeply within themselves to find their way to a new beginning while holding their beloved daughter within their memory.

Zoe was born on March 3, 1999. There had been no indication that anything was wrong during the pregnancy. But suddenly, during labor on a night of a tremendous thunderstorm, Alicia's placenta ruptured and "all hell broke loose." An emergency C-section was performed, but Zoe had gone too long without oxygen. A decision was made to fly Zoe to Sutter Memorial in Sacramento.

Alicia's doctor was unable to get to the hospital because of the weather conditions. There was a new emergency room physician from Los Angeles on duty that night. Alicia's bleeding wouldn't stop and the doctor immediately recognized that she was suffering from a condition called DIC (disseminated intravascular coagulation). Very ill, she was placed on a ventilator in a drug-induced coma.

Alicia and her husband had previously spoken about what they would do if the unthinkable happened. Zoe was flown back to be with her parents. Alicia was brought out of the coma and the decision was made to remove Zoe from life support. But Alicia was still not out of the woods herself.

Eventually, she was released from the hospital and allowed to return home—but to what? The hardest thing for her was to walk back into the nursery. Alicia was filled with a sense of emptiness and failure. How did this happen? For a while she blamed herself although she was not sure what she was blaming herself for. She was angry. And then the sadness came. It felt almost like purgatory to her when she had to face the emptiness and sadness.

There was a sudden urgency to be pregnant again right away. But the doctors were not encouraging. They said maybe in a year, or maybe never. She cried a lot during this time. She asked her family to let her have her space. Perhaps three or four months passed.

Alicia decided that it was time to get pregnant again. She saw twelve to fifteen doctors who refused to take her on as a patient; she was just too high risk. Finally, one doctor agreed. For the length of her pregnancy, he watched her like a hawk, monitoring her progress every two weeks. There was bleeding early on and so for several months Alicia was on bed rest. But her doctor had faith that all would go well.

Grace was delivered in May 2000, three weeks early by C-section. Mia was born in March 2002. Alicia was now the mother of two healthy girls. She credits her aunt, who is a delivery nurse, for helping her through the pregnancies and helping her navigate through the doctors. Her aunt believed that Alicia should be a mother no matter what the odds were. She served as Alicia's advocate and in-house counselor.

Alicia has sage advice for parents going through very tough times after a child's death. "Don't let the grief overtake you. Don't get buried by it." She's observed what can happen when bereaved parents can't move on in their lives—there are often marital problems and parents aren't taking care of the children they have. When a parent can't resolve their grief it hurts everyone around them. "You have to step out of the darkness."

Moving on for Alicia was about the ability to continue building her family and to celebrate the family she and her husband are so grateful to have. Although Zoe's death was a tragedy, Alicia wishes to have positive memories of her oldest daughter. That translates into finding something positive in life.

Alicia, her husband, and immediate family were able to see Zoe and say goodbye to her. Alicia held her after she was taken off life support. Although she was breathing for a while on her own, Alicia knew there was no brain function. She needed that closure. She still has a hope chest with Zoe's birth and death certificate, her ultrasounds, and her baby cap.

When Alicia was well enough, she and her husband took a trip to Fort Bragg and went walking on a random quiet beach. All of a sudden, a baby seal popped up and Alicia knew it was the right place to scatter Zoe's ashes. Every year, Alicia, her husband, Grace, and Mia make the trip to Fort Bragg to visit Zoe. It's a time of remembrance and a time for the four of them to be together. They celebrate Zoe and they celebrate their two awesome healthy girls.

Alicia reflects that some people get lost in grief. For some grieving parents, family will help or perhaps some counseling, or maybe having a new baby. Her family gave her the space she needed. Those closest to her didn't criticize Alicia and her husband for the way they handled anything. Alicia feels that it's essential that the family be respectful. Above all, she has deep gratitude for her life. She is grateful every day.

Going Beyond the Unimaginable

Lorri had been told by her original Ob/Gyn that she and Mitch would never be able to have children. They had made peace with that sad fact and gone on to fast track their careers in Art Education. Art was one of their shared passions and teaching could give them a chance to be in contact with children.

Finding Lorri pregnant seven years later was a wonderful surprise for the couple. They immediately moved to a different doctor and after an uneventful pregnancy and natural childbirth, a healthy baby boy was born. They named him Joshua Shannon. He was a tiny handsome baby who was alert and seemed to see colors early on. Lorri says that he would reach out to touch the flowers in the room at the hospital. When his parents were to leave the hospital, however, they were told that baby Joshua had to stay a few extra days because he was jaundiced. The doctors wanted to place him under bili lights to remedy this condition. Lorri and Mitch were assured that Joshua Shannon would be able to go home shortly.

Then the unimaginable happened. An E. coli infection broke out in the neonatal nursery and Joshua became ill. He was never to leave the hospital and lived only for one month and one day.

They were devastated and unable to function. Their Ob/Gyn confided to the couple that he had also lost a first child shortly after birth. He urged Lorri and Mitch to have another child right away, telling them that it was what he and his wife had done.

Mitch and Lorri had realized after Josh's birth how important children were for them. So it was not difficult for them to take their doctor's advice. They were soon pregnant with a second child.

Lorri went back to work despite the fact that she was greatly depressed and even had thoughts of suicide. She knew, however, that when their baby was born, she would leave that position for good and focus on the child.

After their daughter Abigail was born, Lorri was relieved to see that the baby was a girl. Abby was born round and sturdy and was very alert. Josh had had a different body build. He had been thin and wiry and 3 lbs less.

Abby also had jaundice, but Mitch and Lorri refused to leave her in the hospital. They took her home and Lorri laid down with her each morning in the sunlight. They traveled back and forth to the hospital each day for blood work until Abby was cleared. The little girl thrived. She was a smart, beautiful child with a full head of black hair and twinkling hazel eyes.

Later, looking back, Lorri realized that she had not had enough time to mourn for Josh. Mitch had even less of a chance, as he had to return to work immediately under threat of dismissal. She says that she sees the sadness on their faces when they look at the photos from that period of time.

Once Abby was over a month old she had surpassed Josh's life and all her growing and changing were new experiences for the couple. They were in love with her. They also however, realized that they were extremely over-protective of Abby and hyper-alert to her needs and any chance of illness.

Lorri and Mitch knew that they wanted a bigger family. They didn't want Abby to be an only child and they also hoped that a sibling would take some pressure off Abby.

This was very different than how they would have proceeded with their life had Josh lived. They were told that they could not have children. They had been a power couple in their fields and both were working on their doctorates writing their dissertations at the time. They decided that they would have that one child and continue working in their chosen field.

However, after having Josh and then losing him, they realized how important children were to them. Now that they had that option, they started to rethink their lives. It made them step back and think about what was most important to them.

Their son Daniel was born four and a half years after Abby. He was born two weeks early and also had jaundice but again they took him home and placed him in the sun each morning as they had done with Abby. He was a happy smiling child with beautiful blue eyes and his greatest delight was his big sister. After eating, he cried without stopping for long periods of time. When Daniel was three months old, it was discovered that he had a large tumor in his stomach that had to be removed immediately. This brought up all the feelings about Josh all over again. Daniel was operated on in the same hospital and was on the same floor where his brother had died.

When Abby was in the second grade, she made the statement, "Boys die, but girls get to live." Fortunately, Daniel's tumor was fully removed with no bad lasting effects.

While at first Mitch and Lorri wondered if they should talk about Josh to Abby, the answer became clear on one of their first visits to relatives with children. A six-year-old nephew chatted intensely to their new baby about Josh's death. Lorri and Mitch mentioned Josh from time to time, but did not keep his pictures out. Despite trying to hold back, Lorri continued to be overprotective of both living children: spoiling them on occasion and over-compensating at other times. Her attempts at no sweets and no play guns were ended by the reality of not living in a vacuum. She tried to do everything right.

Lorri says that she has never slept through the night after the children were born and would rise several times in the night to check their breathing.

She also worried that the children would feel that they were born just to make up for losing Josh. She wanted them to know that this was not the case. Both Abby and Daniel were planned and welcomed into the world with great anticipation and delight.

Lorri realizes now that she was still very much in mourning after Abby's birth and felt that she was often distant. She worries that she was not able to give complete attention to Abby or Daniel and that they felt that their mother was not all there for them.

The birth of Joshua totally changed Mitch and Lorri's lives and put it on a whole new course. Their priorities totally changed from being on a fast track to get their doctorates and being a power career couple, to totally being child-oriented and understanding how precious a family was for them. Lorri never regretted not getting her doctorate!

The Gift of Kasey

On Sunday, July 26th, 2009, Emma, eight, Alyson, seven, and Katie, five, were returning home from a camping trip in the Catskills in a car being driven by their aunt, Diane Schuler. While on the road, Emma, scared and crying, called her mother, Jackie to say that, "Something is wrong with Aunt Diane." Jackie could also hear her daughter, Alyson, crying in the background. When Diane took the phone from Emma, her words were slurred and Jackie could not get a coherent answer.

Jackie's husband, Warren called his sister to tell her to stop the car and stay where they were and he spoke to Emma again to try to figure out their location. Warren jumped into his car to look for them, but Diane was already driving the wrong way on the Taconic State Parkway. She drove for nearly two miles before crashing into an SUV, killing herself, the three Hance girls, her own daughter and the three men in the SUV. Only Diane's son, then five, survived.

Jackie and Warren had never seen Diane drunk, but toxicology reports revealed that Diane had a blood alcohol level more than twice the legal limit. There was also evidence that she had been smoking marijuana. When this was revealed, Jackie felt raging anger at Diane, her once beloved sister-in-law, since she now felt that her children had been murdered.

Lost in their grief, Jackie and Warren began to fight ferociously. Jackie thought often how she did not want to live and became fixated on seeing her girls again. Dazed with grief, at night she would often wander out of her room or out of the house. Close family and a tight-knit community of friends rallied around the Hances. Friends stayed with them day and night. They delivered meals, dragged Jackie out of bed and encouraged her to take small steps. Warren busied himself with work and projects.

Eventually, friends began suggesting that Jackie try to have another child. Her tubes had been tied after she had given birth to her third child yet again by C-section. However, a chance conversation led her to a leading New York fertility doctor who offered his help at no charge. Jackie agreed to freeze her eggs though she never seriously planned on using them.

It had been sixteen months since the accident and Jackie was secretly planning to kill herself. It was then that she had the dream that changed everything. Jackie saw herself standing at the entrance to heaven. Beyond the gate she could see Emma, Alyson and Katie. As she rushed towards them God did not let her inside the gates. "You didn't do everything you could on earth," he said. "The doctor gave you a gift, why don't you use it?"

The following day after her dream, she went back to the fertility doctor. It had been almost a year since her eggs had been frozen. After only the first try of IVF treatments Jackie found she was pregnant, yet she felt unfit to have this child. Her emotions were so mixed. She felt that she had not been able to protect her daughters so how she could take care of another life? Her guilt was overwhelming.

The pregnancy was a roller coaster ride. Jackie had to handle the usual hormonal swings that come with being pregnant, while having to give up her antidepressants. She went through the pregnancy with a mixture of "guilt and pain, excitement and hope." She wondered if she had the right to bring a new baby into their unhappy home where tension was high and she and Warren were always so sad and arguing. They were only existing—not living. In this state, it even crossed her mind that maybe they should give up the baby for adoption. She felt that this child should be entitled to happy parents.

When Jackie found out that the baby would be another girl, it was very emotional for her, but gave her hope; she felt that her girls were giving her a gift. Jackie immediately knew that she was going to name this new daughter Kasey. The name was chosen even before implantation. One evening while watching the Miss America pageant on TV, Jackie noticed that one of the contestants was named Kasey, spelled with a K, not a C. Jackie had always loved the name but when she saw that it could be spelled with a K she felt that it was perfect—a beautiful name that included the letters E, A, and K for Emma, Aly and Katie. Kasey's middle name, Rose, was chosen in honor of Dr. Rosenwaks, the fertility doctor.

Kasey Rose was born on October 11, 2011. This was two and a half years after the accident and she was the exact image of her sister Emma at birth. For the two years since the accident, Jackie had told herself that her only purpose was to be with her daughters. Now having had Kasey, she made a new choice—to live. She and Warren hoped this baby would restore some of the joy to their home.

Jackie was excited and emotional after giving birth. She felt as if her girls had heard her and she had been granted what she needed. However, she lost that connection almost immediately and she was afraid to attach to her new daughter. When Kasey came home, Jackie had trouble hearing her baby cry because it would trigger post traumatic stress feelings that reminded her of the last conversation with her daughter, Emma, when she heard her girls crying in the car.

The first couple of months with the new infant were very difficult. Jackie took good care of the baby, but went through the day automatically without much connection to Kasey. Jackie felt numb and didn't trust herself. "I did not bond with this baby until months after she was born—I felt it was a betrayal to Emma, Alyson and Katie."

One day when Kasey was a couple of months old, Jackie went to the cemetery and, for the first time, walked over to Diane's grave. Jackie thoughts turned to a man she had seen that morning while watching an Oprah show. His message was that hate is so powerful that it overwhelms any chance for love. Jackie then thought about Kasey who deserved a mother who loved her with a full heart.

She realized that for this to be possible, she needed to reconcile her emotions; that she could not be happy and angry at the same time. If she continued to hate Diane and not let go of her anger and resentment, she knew she could not move forward in her life. Jackie touched Diane's headstone and spoke to her. She told Diane that she would never know what happened that day but that she had always loved her, still loved her, and that she forgave her. Jackie says that she cannot explain the feeling, but it was almost a magical change once she said those words. She suddenly felt an unexpected lightness. "Trying to build a future with love was more important than hate." After this experience, her happiness grew and she was able to begin to bond with Kasey.

Kasey, though still very young, is aware that Emma, Alyson, and Katie are her sisters. She says good morning to their photos and the girls' birthdays and holidays are celebrated in a way that includes all of them. Jackie worries about the pressures that people are inadvertently putting on Kasey when they say things such as "she is a special child" or "she was put here for a special purpose." Kasey is already her own person with a strong personality that differs from her sisters. She likes to test the waters and knows how to get attention.

Certain things are more relaxed with Kasey. For instance, she was allowed to keep her pacifier much longer and the bedtime routine is not as strictly enforced. She also climbs into bed with her parents, a habit that was discouraged with the other girls.

Sometimes people give the impression that they assume, now that Kasey is here, that things are so much better for Jackie. "They do not understand how I am still breaking inside. They are not just "The Girls" but are three individual people who had a special bond with each other and were best friends."

Emma loved being the big sister, enjoyed sports, and being on stage in plays. Alyson was a people person: loving, happy, and empathetic. People gravitated to her. Katie, the youngest, was mature for her age and loved to shine in the spotlight. She kept up with her sisters and loved giving and receiving hugs and affection.

"I am missing three individual people with three distinct personalities. I know I have Kasey, but I want my other girls, too. The pain is so bad. It is hard for other people to fully understand this."

People say Kasey looks like her sisters. Jackie enjoys hearing it when people tell her this, but at home alone it still breaks her heart.

In the beginning, it was Warren's role to hold everybody else up, especially Jackie. While she found release from talking, Warren's way of coping with grief involved physical labor, going to work, and keeping as busy as possible. He built a rock garden and waterfall in the backyard to memorialize the girls. A cardinal was always present while he worked. Warren told Jackie he thought of the cardinal as a sign that the girls were nearby.

About two months after the accident, Warren had a cross tattooed on his chest over his heart. A few months later, he had the last picture drawn by Emma, a peace sign, tattooed on his arm. On his other arm was the cardinal with branches sporting the letters E, A, and K.

Later Warren added one more tattoo—Emma, Alyson, Katie, and Kasey written in cursive with a peace sign. When Jackie saw the tattoos she realized that even though they expressed grief so differently, Warren was as desperate to hold on to the girls as she was.

With the passage of time, Jackie has begun to find her way—she has Kasey to look after, her job, and her loyal group of supportive female friends. But it's more difficult for Warren now. It's easier for him to cope while occupied with work during the day, but his mind races at night and he's unable to sleep. There is still a strong support system, but since it's now years later, people have gone back to their own lives and are not around in the same way.

The Hance Family Foundation was founded to honor the lives of three beautiful sisters—Emma, Alyson, and Katie. The program is dedicated to providing innovative educational programs for children of all ages and abilities. The foundation's central project is "Beautiful Me," a program designed to educate young girls by promoting appreciation for their genuine qualities and accurate self-awareness. These educational programs enhance self-esteem through acceptance, friendship, and community awareness.

"Through the activities of this foundation we celebrate the spirit, love of life, kindness, and joy that embodied our beloved girls." (You may visit their website: www.hancefamilyfoundadtion.org)

While pregnant with Kasey, Jackie wrote an article for "The Ladies Home Journal," which was met with an outpouring of support. This convinced her to write a book in order to help other people who were struggling with tragedy. Jackie's memoir, *I'll See You Again*, spent five weeks on the New York Times bestseller list. It's a truly inspirational story about hope and building a future based on love, in spite of having to live with the sadness of the past. Jackie has become a symbol of hope and strength for women across the globe. Her book helps to financially support the Foundation. Jackie hopes that people will have a chance to get to know her girls and remember the legacy of her three daughters.

Both Jackie and Warren are very involved with the Hance Family Foundation. Warren attends all meetings and events and the Foundation has become a mission for him. He is gratified that they have been able to make a positive difference in the lives of so many children. He wants every girl to feel confident and happy, just as this would have been his goal for Emma, Alyson, and Katie—and now is his wish for Kasey.

A Father Remembers

When a child dies, both mothers and fathers grieve deeply, but differently. Women are given free reign to express their grief emotionally, but less so men. Society often expects men to be strong, to be practical, to protect the family, and to keep their emotions in check. It's far easier to express sympathy to a mother whose grief is visible and palpable. A father may feel like a bystander in the grieving process, suffering silently until he is alone and able to give himself over to his own sorrow.

It's not surprising that much of the literature on the death of a child refers primarily to the mother—her loss, her grief. Many of the stories and interviews in this book seem to corroborate that perception. A father's unexpressed sorrow can morph into anger. And in some situations, a father's grief shuts him down, perhaps protectively detaching him from the onslaught of intense and overwhelming emotions. Clearly, a father's voice and perspective on the death of a child is so necessary. Mark shares his story.

Jessica was the most precious and wonderful little girl. We were extremely close and I always felt we had a special connection, something unique. It was like our brains were tuned to exactly the same wavelength. It is hard to describe, but an example is that she always "got the joke."

I could mutter some under-the-breath, humorous comment in any situation and she was always the one person who would crack up and know what I meant, even when no one else did. We spent a lot of time together and I loved every second of it. She was a truly happy and joyous soul. Her mother and I always said that when she wasn't miserable (suffering physically and emotionally from her ailments), she was always happy. Despite ending up in the most horrific physical state, she was able to find joy in life and receive unconditional love.

Jessica went through so much and over her eight years got progressively worse. She experienced a sudden, massive decline at age four and lost the ability to use her body and to speak. However, she suffered no loss of intellect and was extremely bright. I felt so frustrated and helpless, especially as a doctor, and felt like there was something, some key, to making her better that all the doctors were missing and that I needed to figure out. Even after she died, I felt like it was my fault for not being able to "save" her.

The way I dealt with my grief is hard to describe because there was grief for me even before she died. The feelings of loss began when she had that major decline at age four and things were so horrific and unmanageable towards the end of her life. There was an element of relief when she died for both her and our suffering.

I feel our story is very typical—men usually grieve in silence while women usually share their feelings with others. I grieved mainly in silence and held on tight to my wife and other children. I am a recovering drug addict and I got into recovery some years after Jessica died. For years, a lot of the feelings were simply medicated away. I also felt it was my job to be strong and keep our family going and part of that was not "falling apart." I wanted my wife and the kids to feel secure and I did that with stoicism and reassurance.

While going through the illness, I feel we did really well, in general: we stuck together and supported each other and fought sadness and frustration with unity and love. I know that many people end up divorced in or after a similar situation. Every relationship is different: all I know is that we are a couple who are together for the right reasons and we realize that what is most important in life is what happens when the door closes at the end of the day. The material possessions and trying to impress or please others are not what matter. It's really all about your closest relationships and what you give, in terms of love and support. I guess the same holds true whether it's going through a child's illness or after the loss of a child.

It took me several years to really move forward even though it felt like I was just going through the motions of life while feeling crushed inside. It was important for me to maintain a routine and sense of purpose and responsibility to move forward, emotionally for me in particular. Getting into recovery from addiction really helped me move forward and I learned how to live life on life's terms. One special thing we do to keep Jessica's memory alive is to celebrate her birthday with a cake and sing "Happy Birthday" to her each year. We don't have any other rituals or shrines. We talk about her when it's relevant or something reminds us of her—Elvis music is one example, as she loved to dance with me to Elvis Presley songs.

We have always been open and honest with our children and never felt the need to sugar-coat anything or be evasive. It's that same unity and love I spoke of above, that we share with our children.

No 'Replacement' Here & I'm Nobody's 'Hero'

Often, well-meaning people with the best of intentions may say inappropriate, insensitive, and awkward things after a loss. The fact is, many people are extremely uncomfortable when someone dies and really don't know what to say and how to behave. Many people who suffer a loss may have their own expectations about how they want to be treated and are often disappointed that people don't respond in a way that is truly comforting or worse, don't respond at all.

It's important that people take care when addressing a child directly about loss. Statements such as, "You are here for a special mission," "Now it's your responsibility to take care of your parents," "You have to be a good girl now because mommy and daddy are very sad," "I hope you're going to be a good boy like your brother was," and the like, place undue pressure on a child who is attempting to cope with their own grief and may not understand how shifting family roles after the loss of a sibling will affect them.

My name is Tamara Thomas. I suffered the loss of my only child, Abigail, in May of 2008. This mind-boggling loss and subsequent pain changed me in ways I am still discovering.

The death of my daughter was the nadir of what I have come to call my Decade of Death. I lost my mother in 2001 after eleven months of lung cancer. I lost my father in 2006—cancer took him too—and then my daughter two years later. Grief has become, if not my friend, then at least a faithful companion. Through my conversations with grief, I have come to know it well.

Because most of my identity had become that of "mother," after my birth daughter died, I found I needed to re-create that identity, so I adopted a wonderful eight-year-old girl in 2010. I frequently refer to her as my little "lifesaver." Perhaps we are that for each other. Then, in 2011, I added two delightful teenage sisters to my family.

They had abruptly lost what remained of theirs, so we joined forces. All four of us have blossomed. The teens are now successful college students, and my little one is thriving, as am I.

I am currently in the process of adding two more to the family. One is a teenager currently in the care of the state; the other is a wonderful man who wants to join me and my crew in our life journey. I am busier than ever, but also happier than I have been since–well, since before Abigail died."

I know they mean well. Their hearts are certainly in the right place; it's their misunderstanding of the situation that leads them to make the comments they do.

Some background is probably necessary. My eldest daughter was killed in a car accident in May of 2008. Several months after that, I began the process of becoming certified for adoption. In February of 2010, I formally adopted my second daughter, Tina who is now ten and a great joy to me. I documented what I called my "journey" in my column in The Wickenburg Sun *newspaper discussing the difficulties of the adoption certification procedure, the rocky terrain of grief, my daughter's organ donation, and other difficult and inter-related topics.*

One thing that surprised me was the sheer number of people—some I knew, some I'd never met–who approached me to let me know that they, too, had lost a child. Always, hugs are exchanged in those circumstances. We belong to a horrible "club" of sorts–the club of bereaved parents. We understand a pain that nobody else can even imagine; a pain that never goes away. We simply learn to live with it.

The pain of losing a child has been likened to a major amputation. This is the best description I have ever found to explain it to people who haven't suffered similarly. The difference is this amputation is invisible; however it is just as painful—the missing piece is just as glaringly gone and just as desperately missed. And, is just as permanent.

As time passes, and the date of my loss gets further away, well-meaning people who don't understand make certain assumptions. And these assumptions make for awkward conversation stoppers. A couple of examples...

"And this is your new little daughter," a smiling man said when I picked Tina up from an activity.

"Yes," I responded, smiling in turn.

"It was a tragedy when you lost your other daughter," he said with a sympathetic frown. "That was, what, two... maybe three years ago?"

"Yes," I said again, feeling a little bit tense. What was coming next?

"Well, and now you have this cute little thing as a replacement, don't you!" he beamed.

I don't know if my face showed the shock and dismay I felt. "No," I replied. "Not at all. No one could replace Ava." I turned away quickly before I said more.

Later, after calming down and considering things, I spoke to my youngest.

"Tina, when that man suggested that you were a replacement, it really upset me."

"Yeah?" she said, looking a little hopeful, I thought.

"Yeah. You aren't anybody's replacement, honey... any more than I could replace you with someone else. Ava was special. You are special. I could never replace either of you!"

Tina smiled and gave me a hug.

In another instance, a friend of a friend shook my hand and said, "You're my hero!" I was baffled and asked why.

"Oh, the way you've gotten over things. The death of your daughter. You've just plowed on through and done really well. It didn't get to you; you didn't dwell in it..." And he went on.

There was nothing I could say to make him understand that he couldn't have been more wrong.

So, let me speak for those of us in this tragic club–and there are a great many of us, surprisingly. We go on, to be sure. But we do not go on unchanged. And we never "get over" the loss–this loss remains with the bereft parent for the remainder of his or her life. We live with our "amputation" as best we can, since the world doesn't stop for us. We aren't heroes; we are survivors.

And there are no replacements.

Out of the Dark, Into the Light

Mitch Carmody knows too much about loss and grief. Having suffered many losses himself, he has found his way back into the world as a healer and advocate for those in grief. He lectures on the grief process, is a keynote speaker, and gives workshops on how to survive the loss of a loved one, some in conjunction with Compassionate Friends and Bereaved Parents USA. Mitch is the author of *Letters to My Son: Turning Loss to Legacy*.

Only recently have I heard the term replacement child as a possible additional pathology in grief for an already disenfranchised group of grievers known as the sibling. When a child dies in a family, it hits like an earthquake and the landscape of life is changed forever... then the tsunami hits and the family can be torn apart and damaged for life.

Being the youngest of seven children, in my quiet thoughts growing up, I often thought I was a replacement child. I had three older sisters and a twin sister and two older brothers. One older brother, John died at birth. I never knew him, no photos, or his name ever mentioned; like some dark secret that John had died with the cord wrapped around his neck. Brother David was born a few years later; it was a late delivery and he was born severely mentally challenged with cerebral palsy and was institutionalized until his death in 1977.

I was born in 1955. My mom and dad finally had a viable, healthy boy, with the bonus of another girl, my twin sister.

I did not have to fight for attention; I only had to choose who adored me. Mom wanted me as her only son, Dad wanted me as his only son, and Grandma now had her only grandson (she never had a son). I felt bad for my twin sister who was left in the shadow of a celebrity twin and the only boy. We never spoke of it, but I felt it up to the day she died in an accident in 1984 at age twenty-eight, with her two young sons.

Early on, I felt guilty for my twin sister's lack of parental attention as well as the pressure on me to be the boy in the family and fill some nebulous shoes that were never worn. John was a mystery and David a prisoner of his own body. I could not replace them but felt the pressure of Dad wanting a man's son and Mom wanting a momma's boy. Mom won. Dad was a war hero, football hero, a typical 1950's male, a truck driver and a cop; in my eyes he had struck out. He died at forty-nine when I was fifteen years old and never really having had that relationship he wanted so badly. My mom's first words after Dad died were, "You are the man of the family now." I secreted away my grief and stood tall; big boys don't cry.

Fast forward to 1987, when my nine-year-old son Kelly dies of a brain tumor after a two year battle with the disease, leaving behind two worn out and shell-shocked parents with a surviving sibling Meagan, only six years old. If it were not for Meagan, my wife and I had discussed doing a "Thelma and Louise" off of a cliff. We did not, so we discussed getting pregnant again.

My wife Barb had a tubal ligation after our daughter was born and we soon found out it was not reversible—she was crushed. We discussed adoption, but soon fell into deep despair and in the apathy of broken dreams, we resigned to the fact we could barely take care of our surviving daughter much less another child in our lives. We accepted defeat on many levels and we functioned at a base level of survival sans joy.

When a child is terminally ill, they become the center of the universe and the healthy sibling is always on the bench. When Kelly died I believe Meagan felt it was "her turn" finally to be the center of our universe and found that her parents could not let go and her brother became deified; it's impossible to compete with a God. She lost her parents and her brother in the deal.

In an odd way, I believe she wanted to be that "replacement child" who was showered with gifts, attention, and travel. Instead, she found herself living with two broken parents who worshipped a dead brother she was soon forgetting; again getting the short straw in life.

When Meagan became pregnant eight years ago, my wife was ecstatic that she could have a boy and she could start all over again loving a little boy and watching him grow up as he should—beyond the age of nine years old. Meg had a girl and although excited, I know my wife was disappointed it was not a boy.

That year, Meg came to a bereaved parent conference to hear me speak and became involved with the sibling program. Now as a mother, she said, "Dad, now I get it." She understood why her parents were screwed up for so long and, as a new mother, she could not comprehend that kind of pain and forgave me. It was huge for both of us. She grieved as an adult for the loss of her brother she experienced at age six.

Four years ago, out of the blue, I received a call from a psychic with a news flash she had apparently received with her gift and had to let me know. She went on to say that Kelly was coming back into our family as a new grandbaby. Low and behold, my daughter was indeed pregnant (although did not know it at the time). She eventually gave birth to our second granddaughter who was born on Kelly's 23rd angel-versary date. They named her Olivia Kelly.

In our minds, my wife and I were already replacing Kelly with this new child coming into our lives. It is probably a good thing she was not a boy, as we would have treated him with so many expectations. I even thought about taking Kelly's old Predator bicycle out of the back shed, cleaning it up and getting some new tires. We are still bereaved parents and we would accept any miracle that would bring our son back into our lives.

We are still, almost thirty years later, processing the death of our son. We have learned much in that time and we have reached the most blessed realization that dead is not gone. We do not have to bury our child with their body; we can maintain a new relationship on a non-physical level.

You do not have to replace what is not gone. Both of my granddaughters talk of Uncle Kelly in the present tense as we keep him present in conversation and they see his image often on the cover of my book and on the wall of their own home. When our granddaughter's cat died, she drew a picture of Kelly holding her cat on the rainbow bridge.

As my daughter was growing up, was she jealous of our continued bond with Kelly? Was she pressured to compete with her dead brother? Was she scarred for life by our actions or lack of action? Did we treat her as a replacement child for Kelly? By her response here to that question, I think not."

Meagan: *"At age six and a half on the night Kelly died, I remember feeling confused and sad, not only for myself but for seeing the pain on my parents' face. I remember locking myself in the bathroom and sitting in the bathtub where I started to cry. I had this overwhelming feeling that I had to be strong and did not want to appear sad as there was enough sadness surrounding me.*

"Those first few months after Kelly died I can remember being surrounded by a blanket of love from family and friends; the same friends who loved me during those long years of Kelly's illness. I always felt loved.

"I didn't want my parents to be sad anymore, but there were always dark clouds appearing and hovering over my family since the cancer came into our lives. Now that the cancer was gone, maybe the clouds could finally start to break away and my parents could once again feel the sun on their face.

"We never forgot about Kelly; we always did something special on the anniversary day of his death. We would do something as a family together. Sometimes we would make "I miss you" cards and throw them in the fireplace where the ashes would ascend into the sky with hopes that our love would reach him. Over the years, my dad made a video of Kelly and my parents would watch and share with others. We had a trunk of all of his things; we would make a yearly ritual to watch this video and look through his trunk of things. As my dad likes to say, we would swim in the grief. I think as a child that this was a way for me to keep his memory alive and felt that it was okay to cry for him; this was a very healing time for me.

"The hardest part of my journey, I believe, was to watch my brother slowly dying, and being a young child, to not totally grasp what was happening to him, other than that he was really sick. In a weird way, I felt a huge sense of relief after he died, like the storm was over and he did not have to suffer anymore. I felt like Dorothy in the Wizard of Oz when the house abruptly landed and all was quiet... and then she opened the door slowly to a new colorful world and heard soft singing in the background, "Step out of the dark, step into the light, step into the sun," and my new life began from pieces of the old.

"I will never forget about my brother and the memories we had together. Both of my children know of their Uncle Kelly. We have a huge picture of him in our house hanging on the wall. Kelly lives on and so do we. I have no regrets."

Mitch: *"There is life after death on both sides of the equation after a significant loss; not only can we survive, we can thrive. We need not replace our loved one who died in our family, but we can embrace their spirit by living with the loss as a part of our daily life. This is what I call "Proactive Grieving®" my philosophy for surviving loss. We can and will find joy again—it is our birthright."*

XII. Final Thoughts

The intellect has little to do on the road to discovery. There comes a leap in consciousness, call it Intuition or what you will, the solution comes to you and you don't know how or why.

—Albert Einstein

◆ The Moment of Recognition

Whether it comes to you as an "aha," an epiphany, or a revelation, the moment of recognition that the reality you've always known has suddenly shifted is truly a monumental one. You have now entered into a totally different space and consciousness and nothing will ever be the same. Many of us experience this on our journeys through life. But this moment of recognition is a very unique one for the replacement child, who has been compelled for a very long period of time to observe and live life in a certain way due to the dictates and expectations of parents and often the extended family as well.

Some adult replacement children have responded to this moment of recognition in this way, "I can't believe I'm in the middle of my life and I'm just becoming aware that I'm a replacement child." So many questions about their life may come flooding in. Confusion and uncertainty may follow once the replacement child begins to wrap his brain around the full impact of this realization on the psyche, sense of self, and self-esteem. Perhaps they had blamed other factors for their issues and conflicts. For some, a pervasive feeling of "not really being all here" is suddenly challenged.

Many individuals respond with a great sense of relief once they learn that there is a term and a phenomenon that describes them, something they have known on some level, have sensed and felt, without validation or confirmation. For some, this feeling of relief is one of a heavy burden suddenly being lifted off their shoulders. Finally, there is a reason that explains why they are the way they are.

Now that there is awareness, there still is the issue of what to do with all of the new information and insights, and how to heal.

In writing this book, our goal is to present a comprehensive overview of the replacement child to mainstream readers. We have made a concerted effort to bring together the best of the existing thought about the replacement child phenomenon including clinical articles and books, as well as first hand accounts that describe what it means to be a replacement child.

Clearly, there is a great need for this gathering of information and sharing of views. Many people who have heard about the book have contacted us wanting to tell their stories and feeling gratified that each one, as an adult replacement child, is finally being recognized.

◆ Therapeutic Questions

Our own research while writing this book, plus numerous interviews with adult replacement children, mirror what has just been expressed. For adults who recognize themselves as replacement children, finding a therapist familiar with the replacement child syndrome can be a real challenge. Many otherwise excellent therapists are completely unaware of the subject. As a result, the core issue may never be addressed in therapy. But this should come as no surprise since there seems to be a real lack of consciousness within the mainstream about the replacement child syndrome and its huge impact on the lives of so many affected by it. Part of our goal for writing this book is to bring this topic to the attention of the therapeutic community so that the unique circumstances, conflicts, and issues can be more fully addressed and understood.

To complicate matters, many individuals who come to therapy hoping for clarification and resolution of long-standing issues, may not even be consciously aware that they present somewhere along the spectrum of the replacement child, or even that the syndrome exists. For many, just learning that there is a name that describes how they have felt for much of their life is a great relief. And that they are not alone.

People seek therapy to better understand themselves and their life circumstances. The goal ultimately is to feel better; perhaps to relieve anxiety, to ease depression, to gather some insight into those areas of their lives where they are overwhelmed or stuck. This might be the way a replacement child initially presents in therapy as well. So how does a therapist read beyond the presenting symptoms and issues and find their way into the story, heart, and soul of the replacement child?

The therapeutic interview covers a lot of territory, but it's essential that the therapist go well beyond the basic questions and topics. It is necessary to probe into the significant circumstances surrounding the family when the replacement child was born or adopted, or later in life, when the role of “replacement” was pushed on a child after a sibling’s life was radically shifted due to accident or illness.

These are some questions and topics that may help illuminate issues specific to the replacement child.

- Was there a death of a sibling prior to a replacement child’s birth?
- Was there a history of abortion or miscarriage prior to another child’s birth?
- Were these events openly spoken about within the family, or were these “family secrets” kept hidden from outsiders, including subsequent children within the family?
- Does any sibling have a physical or emotional disability?
- Did a sibling suffer an accident or illness that rendered them incapacitated?
- What is the birth order of living and deceased siblings and what place does the replacement child occupy within the birth order?
- How did the death or disability of a sibling affect the family as a unit?
- How did parents cope with loss and grief?
- Were unrealistic limitations, or pressures placed upon any child to compensate for the loss of another child?
- What were the differences, if any, in the parent-child relationship with other siblings compared to the replacement child?
- What was the pervading emotional/ psychological atmosphere surrounding the family?

- Was there any pre-existing pathology of one or both parents that complicated family relationships, for example, mental impairment of any kind, and/or a history of drug or alcohol abuse?

Unresolved parental grief should be a huge red flag. Without even being aware of specific events and details, children can often recall the emotional and psychological life of their parents and the home atmosphere in general. The child whose role it is to take away the parents' grief is placed in an untenable position. It's simply an impossible no-win situation since one child can never replace another. There are potentially lifelong consequences for a person who carries the burden for a lost sibling. Often the very high price they pay is giving up pieces of who they are in their own right in favor of assuming an identity that belongs to another.

What is important to note is that parents are often never the same parent with each of their children. A parent may feel very self-assured with one child, yet after the devastating loss of a child may be emotionally depleted and incapable of being available in the same way for a child that follows that loss. The frozen emotions of unresolved grief may make it much more difficult, or even impossible, to have the same healthy connection that was able to be forged with other children in the family.

The adult replacement child will inevitably have many questions they simply don't have answers for. Family events that have challenged the parents and the family in general, may never have been spoken about, and there may even have been an agreement that certain matters should never be discussed. The therapist who understands the replacement child syndrome is an invaluable partner for their patients who are struggling to uncover some of the missing pieces of their lives.

For the replacement child, the task is about finding their way back to who they are and letting go of who they are not. By identifying and creating healthy boundaries that had been otherwise blurred, the replacement child can successfully separate from a shared identity and life, and fully reclaim themselves, as they were meant to be in their own right.

◆ Key Points

◆A subsequent child is not necessarily a replacement child. The main factor in determining if a subsequent child will be treated as a "replacement" for a deceased sibling is unresolved parental grief—about the parent's inability to cope with their loss over time.

◆The classic definition of a "replacement child" is one who replaces a deceased sibling born prior to this child. But the definition has been expanded to include a child who is expected to "fill in" for a sibling who dies later in life, adopted children, if they replace an idealized child that the parents may have wanted but were unable to conceive, and in some instances, a sibling(s) of a mentally, emotionally, or physically handicapped or challenged child in the family.

◆The replacement child phenomenon exists along a continuum, from the most extreme to those with little consequences for the child, to those finding themselves in a "middle of the road" position.

◆Psychological dynamics inherent in the replacement child syndrome are idealization of the deceased, perfectionism, survivor guilt, confusion about one's own identity, and the assignment of specific roles within the family as a result of the loss of another child. Parents who cannot accept the death of a child may carry over their expectations, fears, and guilt to another child. These children are more like substitute children rather than subsequent children.

◆Open communication about the deceased sibling is healthy and essential. The death of a child should not be kept a secret. Children often intuitively understand that something has happened in the family even without a word being spoken. Withholding this information places an extra burden on the family and is anxiety-producing for all.

On the other hand, constant talk of a deceased child in idealized terms often creates unrealistic, impossible expectations that are placed upon another child and which they might be unequipped to understand or cope with.

◆A special place should be made in the family for the deceased child. That child existed and should be acknowledged as an integral part of the family. Remembrances, anniversaries, and memorials honor them.

◆A person's name establishes their unique identity. A child may feel undue pressure if given the same name of the deceased sibling.

◆Up until recently, there has been a lack of consciousness about this issue and its huge impact—even among many therapists. It is imperative that the replacement child's unanswered questions be explored from this perspective, since they may then discover the missing pieces that will help explain years of questions and uncertainty. For the replacement child, becoming whole is developing the consciousness that they can be in a relationship with all of who they are—not who they are expected to be in some else's eyes.

◆With a new awareness and understanding of the dynamics of the "replacement child," parents can work on coming to terms with their grief for their lost child and work to bring about a healing for themselves and their relationship with their other children.

Awareness helps us reframe our perceptions. Children are often victims of circumstance. We don't just outgrow and heal from negative inner feelings but learn to function in spite of them. We must consciously take an active role to heal from the negative inner feelings of childhood. When we recognize that there are reasons why we react/respond in certain ways, we can start to understand what feelings and motivations are behind our thoughts and actions.

◆It's essential for the adult replacement child to gain a full, in-depth understanding of how the events of their life, especially those surrounding a sibling death, have impacted them, profoundly influencing their perceptions and the way they've lived their life. Many replacement children have searched on their own for clues about their situation and experience. Many are very well versed on the literature out there but it is limited, at best.

◆From the perspective of many adult replacement children, there is a place along a continuum that describes them. Adult replacement children invariably feel that a more balanced perspective needs to be explored and included in the discussion. We have touched upon many of the negatives, the potential for pathology and psychological and emotional repercussions. But are there "positives" about being a replacement child? What factors explain the resilience and strength of many who have endured an assault on their identity and yet have emerged more sure of who they are as a result of the conflict?

◆From all perspectives, the constellation of symptoms presented by the replacement child deserves more intensive focus and examination in mainstream therapeutic thought, especially for its implications for intervention in individual treatment. The patient's history, specific clinical issues and symptoms, and unique coping skills *must be considered as a totality,* in order to avoid missing the proper diagnosis and intervention. For example, specific symptoms may easily fall within the broader spectrum of more general symptoms such as anxiety and depression, but in the case of many replacement children, these are often just the tip of the iceberg.

◆By increasing awareness of the phenomenon of the replacement child, we hope to help those individuals who are searching for answers and to further educate mental health professionals so that this population can be more fully served.

Each child holds their own special place in the family. Each child needs to feel appreciated for the unique person they happen to be. Each child is a creation unlike any other. No one can ever replace who you are.

◆

Bibliography

Anisfeld, Leon and Arnold D. Richards. The Replacement Child: Variations on a Theme in History and Psychoanalysis. *Psychoanalytic Study of the Child*, 55, 301-318, 2000.

Balk, David, and Charles A. Corr (editors). *Children's Encounters with Death, Bereavement, and Coping.* New York: Springer Publishing Company, 2010.

Baxter, Angus. *In Search of Your British and Irish Roots.* Genealogical Publishing Company, 2000.

Bergmann, Thesi, and Sidney Wolfe. Observations of the Reactions of Healthy Children to Their Chronically-Ill Siblings. *Bulletin of* the *Philadelphia Association of Psychoanalysis,* 21:145-61, 1971.

Blum, Harold P. Van Gogh's Fantasies of Replacement: Being a Double and a Twin. *Journal of the American Psychoanalytic Association*, Vol. 57, No. 6, 1311-1326, December 2009.

Bolton, Lesley. *The Complete Book of Baby Names.* Naperville, Illinois: Sourcebooks, Inc., 2006/2009.

Brodzinsky, David M., Marshall D. Schechter, and Robin Marantz Henig. *Being Adopted: The Lifelong Search for* Self. Anchor Press (reprinted edition), 1993.

Cain, Albert C., and Barbara S. Cain. On Replacing a Child. *Journal of the American Academy of Child Psychiatry 3*, 443-456, 1964.

Carmody, Mitch. *Letters to My Son: Turning loss to Legacy.* Beaver's Pond Press, 2002.

Dali, Salvador. *The Secret Life of Salvador Dali*. Dover Publications, 1993.

Epstein, Helen. *Children of the Holocaust: Conversations with Sons and Daughters of Survivors.* Penguin Books (reprint edition), 1988.

Fraiberg, Selma, Edna Adelson, and Vivian Shapiro. Ghosts in the Nursery: A Psychoanalytic Approach to the Problems of Impaired Infant-Mother Relationships. *Journal of the American Academy of Child and Adolescent Psychiatry*, 14(3), 387-421, 1975.

Glenn, Jules. Twinship Themes and Fantasies in the Work of Thornton Wilder. *The Psychoanalytic Study of the Child*, Vol. 41, 627-651, 1986.

Green, Morris, and Solnit, Albert J. Reactions to the Threatened Loss of a Child: The Vulnerable Child Syndrome, *Pediatric Management of the Dying Child*, Part III, *Pediatrics*, Vol. 34, No.1, 58-66, 1964.

Hance, Jackie, with Kaplan, Janice. *I'll See You Again*. Gallery Books, 2013.

Hawn, Patti. *Good Girls Don't*. CreateSpace Independent Publishing Platform, 2010.

Horney, Karen. *Our Inner Conflicts: A Constructive Theory of Neurosis*. New York: W.W. Norton & Co., Inc., 1972.

Horney, Karen. *Neurosis and Human Growth*. New York: W.W. Norton & Co., Inc., 1950.

James, John W., and Russell Friedman. *The Grief Recovery Handbook: The Action Program for Moving beyond Death, Divorce and Other Losses*. New York: Harper Perennial, 1998.

King, Alicia. *Sorry for Your Loss: What People Who Are Grieving Wish You Knew*. Nashville, Tennessee: Turner Publishing Co., 2010.

Kolatch, Alfred J. *The Comprehensive Dictionary of English and Hebrew First Names*. Middle Village, N.Y.: Jonathan David Publishers, 2005.

Lamb, Elizabeth H. The Impact of Previous Perinatal Loss on Subsequent Pregnancy and Parenting. *J. Perinat Educ.*, 11(2): 33-40, 2002.

Larson, Emily. *The Best Baby Names Treasury: Your Ultimate Naming Resource*. Naperville: Illinois, Sourcebooks Inc., 2011.

Lauer, Bertrand. John Coltrane and the "Replacement Child" Syndrome, *Jazz Research Journal*, Vol.3, No.1, 2009.

Mandel, Judy, *Replacement Child: A Memoir*. Seal Press, 2013.

O'Leary, Joann. Grief and Its Impact on Prenatal Attachment in the Subsequent Pregnancy, *Archives of Women's Mental Health*. Springer-Verlag (published online), 2004.

Pilato, Herbie J. *Twitch upon a Star: The Bewitched Life and Career of Elizabeth Montgomery*. Taylor Trade Publishing, 2012.

Porot, Maurice, *L'Enfant de Remplacement*. Editions Frison-Roche, 1996.

Poznanski, E. O., The Replacement Child: A Saga of Unresolved Parental Grief, *Journal of Pediatrics,* Vol.81, Issue 6, 1972.

Sabbadini, Andrea, The Replacement Child: The Instance of Being Someone Else. *Contemporary Psychoanalysis*, Vol. 24, No. 4, 528-547, 1988.

Schellinski, Kristina, Life after Death: The Replacement Child's Search for Self. *International Association for Analytical Psychology*, 2009.

Schwab, Gabriele, *Haunting Legacies: Violent Histories and Trans-generational Trauma*. New York: Columbia University Press, 2010.

Silverman, Linda Kreger. Perfectionism: The Crucible of Giftedness. *Advanced Development*, 8, 47-61, 1999.

Solomon, Andrew, *Far from the Tree: Parents, Children and the Search for Identity*. Scribner, 2012.

Stevens, Anthony, *On Jung*. Princeton, N.J.: Princeton University Press, 1990/1999.

Storr, Anthony (editor). *The Essential Jung*. Barnes and Noble Books MJF Books (Fine Communications), 1983.

Virag, Terez, Children of the Holocaust and Their Children's Children: Working through Current Trauma in Psychotherapeutic Process. *Dynamic Psychotherapy* 2, 47-60,1984.

Volkan, Vamik, and William Greer, Jr. Trans-generational Transmission and Deposited Representations: Psychological Burdens Visited by One Generation upon Another. Oa Publishing Co., 2007.

Volkan, Vamik. The Next Chapter: Consequences of Societal Trauma. Oa Publishing Co., 2007.

Volkan, Vamik, and Ozler Aykan. Chosen Trauma and Its Trans-generational Transmission. Oa Publishing, 2007.

Weiner, Marcella Bakur, Paul C. Cooper, and Claude Barbre, (editors). *Psychotherapy and Religion: Many Paths, One Journey*. Lanham, Maryland: Jason Aronson, an imprint of Rowman and Littlefield Publishers, Inc., 2005.

Wesolowska, Monica, *Holding Silvan: A Brief Life*, Portland, Oregon: Hawthorne Books & Literary Arts, 2013.

White, Pleasant Gill. Excerpt from *Sibling Grief: Healing after the Death of a Sister or Brother*. kotapress.com.

Whitmer, Peter O., "Leading to the "Elvis Story,"" twinlesstwins.org.

Withrow, Rebecca, and Schwiebert, Valerie L. Twin Loss: Implications for Counselors Working with Surviving Twins (Practice and Theory), *Journal of Counseling and Development*, Vol.83, Issue 1, 21-28, 2005.

Worden, J.William. *Grief Counseling and Grief Therapy, Fourth Edition: A Handbook for the Mental Health Practitioner*, London: Springer Publishing Co., 2008.

Youngberg, Kjirstin. *Sacred Baby* Names. Cedar Fort, Inc., 2012.

Acknowledgments

Our heartfelt appreciation to the extraordinary people who so generously contributed to this project with stories, insights, and enthusiasm. Some stories are told within the pages of this book. Others enlightened and informed us as we wrote. We are deeply touched by your willingness to share your feelings and experiences with us, inspired by your honesty, and grateful to have learned from you. Without your wonderful contributions this book would not be what it is. We thank you from the bottom of our heart...

Aryn Smith-Avendano, Stephen Brice, Mitch Carmody, Nino Centineo, Liam Coonan, Lorri Cramer, Mitch Cramer, Amalia Crawford, Patricia Decarpentries, Rita Catherine DiRenzo, Diana Doyle, Sharon Eisman, Paul Escamilla, Ethan Frost, Beth Greenfield, Nancy Grossman, Jackie Hance, Katharine Hansen, Patti Hawn, Barbara Ann Jaffe, Ed.D., Carol Joyce, Karla Kaudel, Elizabeth Kilpatrick. Maria Lawson, Andrea Lieber, Judy Mandel, John Massarda, Noelle Massarda, Alicia Moore, Sarah Moore, Lisa Olson, Grace Pearcey, Gladys Roij, Carolyn Shane, Tamara Thomas, AnnMarie Touchette, Mark Wasserman, Melissa Wasserman, and Monica Wesolowska.

An equally big thank you to those contributors whose beautiful stories and insights grace these pages but who wish to remain anonymous.

Katie Couric… Advocate and beacon of compassion, we are honored to have your interest and time with this project. Your conviction to educate and tackle meaningful issues is an inspiration. We thank you for your heartfelt foreword.

Regina Kulik Scully… Through your Herculean efforts to bring awareness to important issues, you inspire change and global consciousness. From the beginning you understood the importance of this project and embraced it heart and soul.

Tory Hartmann… To our wonderful editor and publisher who recognized that this book fills a crucial gap and gave it wings. Your calm discernment and support kept us steady.

Gladys Roij... As an integral part of our team, we are grateful for your therapeutic expertise, sharp perception, thought provoking insights and methodical help with research. Those years of conversations were a major catalyst in the transformation of this book from thoughts to a completed manuscript.

Heather Girardi... The "go-to girl," doing anything and everything whenever we needed it. There are not enough "thank yous" for the multitude of ways you have contributed, for your sharp insights, contagious enthusiasm and constant encouragement.

Judy Mandel... You paved the way with your own candid and beautifully crafted memoir, *Replacement Child,* which brings a much needed awareness to this subject and helped to create a forum for discussion.

Elaine Shocas... We greatly appreciate your friendship, guidance, expertise and personal interest in this project.

Ann Foster... We are grateful to you for enthusiastically embracing our project, for your helpful comments and suggestions, and for shepherding it to its proper publishing home.

Ben Slatkin...A heartfelt "thank you" for taking time to support this project with your thoughtful and invaluable editorial input.

Rita and Abigail

Personal Acknowledgments from Rita

Writing this book has been an incredible journey. The purpose of this journey was the quest for something sacred – truth, wisdom, and wholeness. The journey itself rewarded this traveler with intangible riches: The acquaintance of amazing individuals, growth and self discovery. I am very appreciative for my family and friends, and a life rich in opportunities and experiences. I will be forever grateful to every individual who encouraged, supported and inspired me – and there were many.

Steve: husband, soul mate, and best friend. So appreciative of your constant support and mind-boggling grasp of technology. Thank you for always being there. You have been my compass through smooth roads and challenging terrain.

Kevin and Arielle: You are my dreams come true and have always been the sun, moon, and stars in my universe. I am grateful for your enthusiasm and encouragement about this book. I am most grateful to be your mother.

Jennifer Johnson: Truly the very best and most creative daughter-in-law ever. Your innovative insights, and constructive suggestions for this book, as with so many other things in life, have made such a positive impact.

Abigail Brenner: Enormous appreciation to my good friend and co-author for sharing my vision and grasping the importance and necessity for this project. Your eloquence, intelligence, patience, and most importantly your friendship, has been invaluable in making this book a reality.

Sharon Kleinberg: You make magic as you combine information with knowledge, wisdom and intuition, transforming them into a razor sharp insights.

To my cousins who are not only my great friends but also the best human beings ever: Joan Galanti, Ellen Jacob, Pat Knight, Joyce Nawy, Beth Sosin, & Rita Brody. Thank you for your comments, suggestions, and constant encouragement with this book. Joani - A very special thank you for always being available to help me find the best way to express myself. Your creativity enhances everything you touch.

Nancy Grossman and Candice Grieff for your time, enthusiasm and friendship regarding this project.

Ted Poretz: Immense gratitude for always being so very generous with your friendship, support, time, and professional expertise.

A special "High Five" to Diamond, a true gem of a four legged companion who sat by me during the three years of writing and interviewing. Even though she cannot read, Diamond will be getting a special treat from Pet Central when this book comes out.

Rita Battat Silverman

Personal Acknowledgments from Abigail

This book is dedicated to my children and grandchildren—and to children everywhere.

This project is dedicated to the memory of Kevin Brook Battat Silverman whose great humanity and kindness touched so many people wherever he went.

As a psychiatrist of many years, I am humbled by the outpouring of stories from replacement children everywhere and am grateful that I can play a small part in the lives of those finding their way through to healing and wholeness. Thank you all so much and may you find resolution and peace in your lives. It is the birthright of every child to be nurtured and supported as they grow into their own full potential—into the best that they are. Children are civilization's most precious commodity.

Rita Battat Silverman had a vision. This book is in large part the result of her own journey toward self-recognition and realization. Rita, thank you for your friendship of many years, your dogged determination to get the word out, and for your passionate desire to acknowledge all of those individuals who have struggled to find answers to questions they did not know even existed.

Louise Gikow is a gem of a person—intelligent, clever, funny, imaginative, creative, and so much more. She's also a gifted writer who I called upon countless times for her insight and expertise.

Monique Guffey is an educator and counselor of optimal positive change. She has always supported me unconditionally and "raises me up." Thank you, Mo for your interest in this project and anything I do. I am so grateful for your time and effort out of a very busy life to read the manuscript and provide, thoughtful and thought-provoking insights, comments, and suggestions.

And always to the "usual suspects" who listened to my thoughts, feelings, musings, wanderings, and imaginings...Ray Brenner, David Brenner, Lisa Wall Brenner, Robbie Brenner, Aaron Sanor, Alice Finley, Helen Blair, Nancy Foreman Pollek, Erika Landau, M.D—thank you for being there.

Abigail Brenner, MD

Author Bios

Rita Battat Silverman has a BA in psychology from Texas Wesleyan University and resides with her husband in New York City. She has been a life coach for over 30 years. Ms. Silverman knows firsthand what it is like to grow up as a "replacement child," having been born 18 months after the death of her 14-year-old brother. Upon exploring the subject for many years, she realized understanding this phenomenon holds the key to a new level of awareness and began writing *Replacement Children, The Unconscious Script.*

Abigail Brenner, M.D. attended New York Medical College, becoming a physician in 1977. She completed her internship and residency in psychiatry at New York University-Bellevue Medical Center in 1981, is board certified, and a Fellow of the American Psychiatric Association.

Dr. Brenner is the author of four books—*Transitions: How Women Embrace Change and Celebrate Life, SHIFT: How to Deal When Life Changes, Life Matters: Stories of Transition, Healing, and Hope*, and co-author of *The Essential Guide to Baby's First Year.* In addition, she has written several articles, is a guest on radio and television, and writes a monthly blog for Psychology Today.

Endnotes

[1] Andrea Sabbadini, "The Replacement Child: The Instance of Being Someone Else" (Contemporary Psychoanalysis, Vol. 24, No.4, 1988), 530.

[2] Albert C. Cain, and Barbara S. Cain, "On Replacing a Child" (Journal of Amer.Acad. of Child Psychiatry, Vol.3, 1964), p. 447.

[3] Ibid, 449.

[4] Leon Anisfeld and Arnold D. Richards, "The Replacement Child: Variations on a Theme in History and Psychoanalysis" (The Psychoanalytic Study of the Child, Vol.55, 2000), 303

[5] David M. Brodzinsky, Marshall D. Schecter, and Robin Marantz Henig, *Being Adopted: The Lifelong Search for Self* (Anchor Press, reprinted edition, 1993), 9.

[6] Marcella Bakur Weiner, Paul C. Cooper, and Claude Barbre (editors), *Psychotherapy and Religion: Many Paths, One Journey* (Lanham, Maryland: Jason Aronson, 2005), 235.

[7] Elizabeth H. Lamb, "The Impact of Previous Perinatal Loss on Subsequent Pregnancy and Parenting" (J. Perinatal Education, 11(2), 2002), p.33.

[8] Ibid, 35.

[9] Joann O'Leary, "Grief and Its Impact on Prenatal Attachment in the Subsequent Pregnancy" (Archives of Women's Mental Health, 00:1-12, published online by Springer-Verlag, 2004), 2.

[10] Kristina Schellinski, "Life after Death: The Replacement Child's Search for Self" (International Association for Analytical Psychology, 2009), p.4.

[11] Kate Stone Lombardi, "Exploring Artistic Creativity and Its Link to Madness," The New York Times, April 27, 1997.

[12] Kristina Schellinski, "Life after Death: The Replacement Child's Search for Self" (International Association for Analytical

Psychology, 2009), 5.

[13] James Barrie, *Margaret Ogilvy* (Echo Library, 2007), 12-13.

[14] Anthony Storr, *The Essential Jung* (New York: Barnes and Noble Books, 1983), 76.

[15] Bertrand Lauer, "John Coltrane and the Replacement Child" (Jazz Research Journal, Vol.3, No.1, 2009), 2.

[16] Ibid, 3.

[17] Barbara Walters, *Audition: A Memoir*, New York, Vintage Books, 2009, page 4.

[18] Karen Horney, *Our Inner Conflicts* (New York: W.W. Norton & Co.,1972), 98.

[19] Leon Anisfeld and Arnold D.Richards, "The Replacement Child: Variations on a Theme in History and Psychoanalysis" (Psychoanalytic Study of the Child, 55:301-318, 2000), 313.

[20] Gabriele Schwab, *Haunting Legacies: Violent Histories and Trans-generational Trauma* (New York: Columbia University Press, 2010), 143.

[21] Donald W. Winnicott, "Ego Distortion in Terms of True and False Self, in The Maturational Process and the Facilitating Environment: Studies in the Theory of Emotional Development" (New York: International UP Inc., 1965), 143.

[22] David E. Balk, and Charles A. Corr (editors), *Children's Encounters with Death, Bereavement, and Coping* (New York: Springer Publishing Company, 2010), 207.

[23] Ibid, 207.

[24] Nancy Verrier, "The Primal Wound: Legacy of the Adopted Child" (American Adoption Congress International Convention, 1991), 3.

[25] Karen Horney, *Neurosis and Human Growth* (New York: W.W. Norton & Company, Inc., 1950), 24.

[26] Ibid, 65.

[27] David E. Balk and Charles A. Corr (editors), *Children's Encounter with Death, Bereavement, and Coping* (New York: Springer Publishing Company, 2010), 204.

[28] Kristina Schellinski, "Life after Death: The Replacement Child's Search for Self" (Association for Graduate Analytical Psychologists, 2009), 4.

[29] Gabriele Schwab, *Haunting Legacies: Violent Histories and Trans-generational Trauma* (New York: Columbia University Press, 2010), 125.

[30] Vamik Volkan, and William F.Greer, "Trans-generational Transmission and Deposited Representations: Psychological Burdens Visited by One Generation upon Another" (Oa Publishing Company, 2007), 4-5.

[31] Vamik Volkan, "The Next Chapter: Consequences of Societal Trauma" (Oa Publishing Company, 2007)

[32] Gabriele Schwab, *Haunting Legacies: Violent Histories and Trans-generational Trauma* (New York: Columbia University Press, 2010), 125.

[33] Natan Kellermann, "Psychopathology in Children of Holocaust Survivors: A Review of the Research Literature" (Israel Journal of Psychiatry and Related Sciences, Vol.38, No.1, 2001), 1.

[34] Ibid, 9.

[35] Pleasant Gill White, *Sibling Grief: Healing after the Death of a Sister or Brother* (iUniverse, 2008), excerpted on kotapress.com

CPSIA information can be obtained
at www.ICGtesting.com
Printed in the USA
LVOW04s2006220516
489467LV00045B/2123/P